Lifestyle of

The Vedic People

Reconstructing Indian History & Culture
(ISSN 0971-3824)

1. Society in Ancient India; by Sures Chandra Banerji (ISBN 81-246-0000-7)
2. Political Thought in Ancient India; by G.P. Singh (ISBN 81-246-0001-5)
3. Early Indian Historical Tradition and Archaeology; by G.P. Singh (ISBN 81-246-0005-8)
4. Vasantotsava: The Spring Festivals of India; by Leona M. Anderson (ISBN 81-246-0011-2)
5. Ecological Readings in the Veda; by M. Vannucci (ISBN 81-246-0009-0)
6. Vṛndāvana in Vaiṣṇava Literature; by Maura Corcoran (ISBN 81-246-0024-4)
7. Social History of the Tamils (1707-1947); by P. Subramanian (ISBN 81-246-0045-7)
8. Ancient Indian Coinage; by Rekha Jain (ISBN 81-246-0051-1)
9. Buddhism and Socio-Economic Life of Eastern India; by Bimal Chandra Mohapatra (ISBN 81-246-0055-4)
10. Chandragupta Maurya; by P.L. Bhargava (ISBN 81-246-0056-2)
11. Mṛtyu: Concept of Death in Indian Traditions; by Gian Giuseppe Filippi (ISBN 81-246-0072-4)
12. Yama: The Glorious Lord of the Other World; by Kusum P. Merh (ISBN 81-246-0066-X)
13. Sacred Complex of Ujjain; by D.K. Samanta (ISBN 81-246-0078-3)
14. Vedic View of the Earth; by S.R.N. Murthy (ISBN 81-246-0091-0)
15. Society in the Atharvaveda; by B.S. Kharade (ISBN 81-246-0093-7)
16. Orissan History, Culture and Archaeology; by S. Pradhan (ISBN 81-246-0117-8)
17. Education in Ancient India; by Mitali Chatterjee (ISBN 81-246-0113-5)
18. Surā: The Liquor and the Vedic Sacrifice; by M.B. Kolhatkar (ISBN 81-246-0114-3)
19. Human Ecology in the Vedas; by Marta Vannucci (ISBN 81-246-0115-1)
20. Governance in Ancient India; by Anupa Chandra Pandey (ISBN 81-246-0135-6)
21. The Cultural Glory of Ancient India: A Literary Overview; by Sures Chandra Banerji (ISBN 81-246-0137-2)
22. Kauṭilya's Arthaśāstra in the light of Modern Science & Technology; by Sunil Sen Sarma (ISBN 81-246-0187-9)
23. History of Jainism — With Special Reference to Mathurā; by V.K. Sharma (ISBN 81-246-0195-X)
24. Cultural Tourism in India: Museums, Monuments & Arts — Theory and Practice; by S.P. Gupta; Krishna Lal; Mahua Bhattacharya (ISBN 81-246-0215-8)
25. Ancient Indian Historiography — Sources and Interpretations; by G.P. Singh (ISBN 81-246-0228-X)
26. Republics, Kingdoms, Towns and Cities in Ancient India; by G.P. Singh (ISBN 81-246-0237-9)
27. Facets of Ancient Indian History and Culture — New Perception; by G.P. Singh (ISBN 81-246-0238-7)
28. Kamakhya — A Socio-cultural Study; by Nihar Ranjan Mishra (ISBN 81-246-0251-4)
29. History and Culture of Tamil Nadu as Gleaned from the Sanskrit Inscriptions Vol. 1 (up to c. AD 1310); by Chithra Madhavan (ISBN 81-246-0308-1).
30. Life Style of the Vedic People; by Pranati Ghosal (ISBN 81-246-0344-8)

Reconstructing Indian History & Culture, no. 30

Lifestyle of
The Vedic People

by

Pranati Ghosal

D.K. Printworld (P) Ltd.
New Delhi

Cataloging in Publication Data — DK
[Courtesy: D.K. Agencies (P) Ltd. <docinfo@dkagencies.com>]

Ghosal, Pranati, 1956-
The lifestyle of Vedic people / by Pranati Ghosal.
(Reconstructing Indian history & culture, no. 30)
p. 23 cm.
Includes bibliographical references (p.)
Includes index.
ISBN 8124603448

1. Civilization, Hindu. 2. India — Social life and customs — To 1200. I. Title. II. Series: Reconstructing Indian history & culture, no. 30.

DDC 934 21

ISBN 81-246-0344-8
First Published in India in 2006

Published and printed by:
D.K. Printworld (P) Ltd.
Regd. office : *"Sri Kunj,"* F-52, Bali Nagar
New Delhi - 110 015
Phones : (011) 2545-3975; 2546-6019; *Fax* : (011) 2546-5926
E-mail: dkprintworld@vsnl.net
Web: www.dkprintworld.com

Dedicated
To

The Loving Memory of
My Affectionate Father
Late Dr. Sachindra Nath Ghosal

&

To a Noble Soul
Smt. Bimla Poddar
Devoted to the Service of
Indian Culture and Vedic Studies

Foreword

To peep into a society, of which no material remains are traceable, is a Herculean task but a fascinating theme. Dr. Pranati Ghosal accepted this challenge and met with big success in her brilliant work *Lifestyle of the Vedic People*. It is a strange juxtaposition that the Vedic people lived, had splendid vision, philosophy and views about creation, cosmos and life on earth, which have been handed down to us since time immemorial. But except for the earliest scriptures of the world, the four Vedas and particularly the *Ṛgveda*, no other account is seen. We cannot deny the fact that the Vedic culture exists in all reality despite the total absence of antiquarian remains. A remarkable phenomenon is that the castle of Indian culture stands on the solid foundation of Vedic heritage. For example, the architecture is in direct succession of the Vedic forestry workmanship and it continued till the Mauryan-Śuṅga age when stone was preferred for monuments. At the same time, timber was sought for residential purposes till late medieval period and it has a firm footing even now in the countryside.

The *ṛṣis* endeavoured to unfold the mystery of creation (*sṛṣṭi-vidyā*) and to find its quintessence, i.e., the Supreme (*brahma-vidyā*). This did not require materialistic attainments. Their daily life depended on perishable items, like straw, bamboo, reeds, timber, mud, etc., which were easily available in the forests. It was the *āraṇyaka* or *āśrama* culture in true sense. When the material was destroyed or decomposed, it was replaced by fresh items, which also lasted for some decades. Under such circumstances, the permanent material remains, which make the base for cultural reconstruction, are wanting.

We, therefore, have to depend on the introspection (*antaḥ sākṣya*) of the Vedic literature. Traditional *puṇḍits* who accept the Vedic hymns as the "divine speech" have been reluctant in tracing any historical or cultural chronology in the Vedas, but those who long for deeper probe have to find their ways and try to get a glimpse of the Vedic society. The author Dr. Pranati Ghosal is a rare combination of faith and research and she has faithfully but critically analysed the Vedic literature to paint an excellent picture of the life of the Vedic people.

The work authentically informs about food and drinks, cosmetics and fashion, architecture, particularly the dwellings, professions and manufacturing, recreation, learning and teachings and other allied aspects related to the daily life of the Vedic period.

The author is silent about the use of writing in the Vedic period because of the fact that the Vedic Saṁhitās are known as Śrutis, i.e., oral. The system of learning in the form of *padapāṭha* and *kramapāṭha* or *kramaka* and the figures from one to billion do suggest that the system of writing had evolved with expansion of Vedic texts.

Dr. Ghosal has cited a large number of the Vedic references to support her findings. At the same time, she has occasionally sought shelter of the early Upaniṣads and Sūtra literature also, where the Vedic references are wanting. After all, the Vedic traditions were followed for long. The book bears the stamp of brilliant rendering, in-depth study of the subject and maturity of scholarship. I hope this will be warmly received by scholars and researchers. Let me wish all the best with this hymn:

'उच्छ्रयस्व महते सौभगाय'

ucchrayasva mahate saubhagāya — *Ṛ̥V* 3.8.2

Prof. R.C. Sharma
Former Director General/V.C.
National Museum/Institute
New Delhi

Preface

IT gives me pleasure to place before readers the *Lifestyle of the Vedic People*, which was originally entitled *Everyday Life in the Vedic India* and was submitted as a PhD dissertation at the Rabindrabharati University, Kolkata in the year 1997. After a long interval I hope the same will be able to draw the kind attention of the scholarly world especially interested in the study of Vedic Culture.

Though religious and philosophical ideas occupy the major part of the vast Vedic literature, information on people's lifestyle also found scattered in them have been collected and processed in order to have a complete picture of the daily life in the Vedic age because details of people's lifestyle is reflected in their daily activities. Original Vedic texts are the primary sources used for the present investigation. Apart from it, all the related works and secondary literature dealing with daily life of ancient people have been consulted as far as possible. I am afraid, a few such may have been missed, most probably because of their non-availability. I regret my inability.

The result of the investigation is presented in the form of eight chapters dealing with:

1. Food Habits
2. Dress Arrangements
3. Housing Systems
4. Modes of Production and Other Occupations
5. Entertainment

6. Education
7. Social Life
8. View of Life

They are preceded by an Introduction and followed by a Bibliography.

Ceremonial thanksgiving is not befitting the Indian tradition. But I must express my sense of gratitude to the forerunners, whose works I have utilized to my benefit. I shall remain ever grateful to my revered teacher Dr. S.C. Chakrabarti, Professor and Director, School of Vedic Studies, Rabindrabharati University, whose kind supervision and precious instruction helped me to reach the goal. I am indebted to all the teachers of the Sanskrit Department, Rabindrabharati University, for their valuable suggestions at every stage of my work. Many thanks are credited to IGNCA authorities, who provided me leave facilities generously. Cordial thanks are due to my friends for their generous help rendered to me. I remain obliged to the School of Vedic Studies, Rabindrabharati University, for providing me the Library facilities. I am thankful to Prof. Bishwanath Bhattacharya for rendering valuable instructions at the stage of revising this dissertation before publication. My sincere regards are credited to Prof. R.C. Sharma without whose active initiation the work would have never seen the light of the day. He has been kind enough to write a Foreword to the present work. I am equally thankful to Sri Ṣusheel Kumar Mittal of D.K. Printworld, New Delhi, who has taken a keen interest in publishing the work.

I would be blessed if my effort serves any purpose in the scholarly world.

Pranati Ghosal

Contents

Key to Transliteration

VOWELS

अ *a*	आ *ā*	इ *i*	ई *ī*	उ *u*	ऊ *ū*
(but)	(palm)	(it)	(beet)	(put)	(pool)
ऋ *ṛ*	ए *e*	ऐ *ai*	ओ *o*	औ *au*	
(rhythm)	(play)	(air)	(toe)	(loud)	

CONSONANTS

Guttural	क *ka*	ख* *kha*	ग *ga*	घ *gha*	ङ *ṅa*
	(skate)	(blockhead)	(gate)	(ghost)	(sing)
Palatal	च *ca*	छ* *cha*	ज *ja*	झ *jha*	ञ *ña*
	(chunk)	(catch him)	(john)	(hedgehog)	(bunch)
Cerebral	ट *ṭa*	ठ* *ṭha*	ड *ḍa*	ढ* *ḍha*	ण* *ṇa*
	(start)	(anthill)	(dart)	(godhead)	(under)
Dental	त *ta*	थ *tha*	द *da*	ध* *dha*	न *na*
	(path)	(thunder)	(that)	(breathe)	(numb)
Labial	प *pa*	फ* *pha*	ब *ba*	भ *bha*	म *ma*
	(spin)	(philosophy)	(bin)	(abhor)	(much)
Semi-vowel	य *ya*	र *ra*	ल *la*	व *va*	
	(young)	(drama)	(luck)	(vile)	
Sibilants	श *śa*	ष *ṣa*	स *sa*	ह *ha*	
	(shove)	(bushel)	(so)	(hum)	
Others	क्ष *kṣa*	त्र *tra*	ज्ञ *jña*	ळ* ḷ	ॠ* *ṝ*
	(*kṣatriya*)	(*triśūla*)	(*jñānī*)	(*play*)	

अं (ं) *ṁ anusvāra* (nasalisation of preceding vowel) like *saṁskṛti*

अः *visarga* = *ḥ* (aspiration of preceding vowel) like (*prātaḥ*)

ऽ *Avagraha* consonant #'consonant (like:- *ime 'vasthitā*)

Anusvāra at the end of a line is presented by m (म्) and not ṁ

HINDI LETTERS (extras)

ँ = *ñ*	ं = ṅ	ड़ = *ṛa*	ढ़ = *ṛha*
(*candrabindu*)	(*anusvāra*)		

* No exact English equivalents for these letters.

In the present thesis, *candrabindu* (ँ) is a modification or replacement of last ***n*** of the words. Acoding to *nuścānunāsikam* (IV.14) and *svara aupśaviḥ* (III.132) of *Vājasaneyi Prātiśākhya*, the words ending with ***n***, when followed by sibilants (*śa, ṣa, sa, ha*) or semi-vowels (*ya, ra, la, va*) or vowels, will become nasalised and be replaced by *candrabindu* (ँ), which will be added to the prior vowel. Hence, *svargān* has become *svargā̐*, *asmin loke* has become *asmi̐loke*, etc.

Abbreviations

AĀ	:	*Aitareya Āraṇyaka*
AB	:	*Aitareya Brāhmaṇa*
ĀGS	:	*Āśvalāyana Gṛhya-Sūtra*
ĀpDS	:	*Āpastamba Dharma-Sūtra*
AU	:	*Aitareyopaniṣad*
AV	:	*Atharvaveda Saṁhitā*
AV (P)	:	*Atharvaveda Saṁhitā* (Paippalāda)
AV tr. Bloomfield	:	*Hymns of the Atharvaveda*
AV tr. Griffith	:	*Hymns of the Atharvaveda*
AV tr. Whitney	:	*Atharvaveda Saṁhitā*
AIE	:	*Ancient Indian Education*
Ār	:	*Āraṇyaka*
BDS	:	*Baudhāyana Dharma-Sūtra*
BGS	:	*Baudhāyana Gṛhya-Sūtra*
BhS	:	*Bhāṣika Sūtra of Kātyāyana*
Brs	:	Brāhmaṇas
BS	:	*Brahma-Sūtra*
BŚS	:	*Baudhāyana Śrauta-Sūtra*
BU	:	*Bṛhadāraṇyakopaniṣad*

CIDLA	:	*Classical Indian Dance in Literature and Arts*
CU	:	*Chāndogyopaniṣad*
DLAI	:	*Daily Life in Ancient India*
DPSL	:	*Dice Play in Sanskrit Literature*
EFAI	:	*Economy and Food in Ancient India*
GB	:	*Gopatha Brāhmaṇa*
GDS	:	*Gautama Dharma-Sūtra*
GGS	:	*Gobhila Gṛhya-Sūtra*
GSH	:	*Gṛhya-Sūtra of Hiraṇyakeśin*
HDS	:	*History of Dharma-śāstra*
HIL	:	*History of Indian Literature*
HSL	:	*History of Sanskrit Literature*
IAB	:	*India of the Age of the Brāhmaṇas*
IVKS	:	*India of the Vedic Kalpa-Sūtras*
Īśa	:	*Īśavāsyopaniṣad*
JB	:	*Jaiminīya Brāhmaṇa*
JUB	:	*Jaiminīyopaniṣad Brāhmaṇa*
KapKS	:	*Kapisthala Kaṭha Saṁhitā*
KS	:	*Kāṭhaka Saṁhitā*
Kaṭha	:	*Kaṭhopaniṣad*
KŚS	:	*Kātyāyana Śrauta-Sūtra*
KauŚS	:	*Kauśika Śrauta-Sūtra*
Kauṣ	:	*Kauṣītakyupaniṣad*
KB = SāB	:	*Kauṣītaki Brāhmaṇa (Sāṅkhyāyana*

		Brāhmaṇa)
Kena	:	*Kenopaniṣad*
LŚS	:	*Lāṭyāyana Śrauta-Sūtra*
LauGS	:	*Laugākṣi Gṛhya Sūtra*
Mahī	:	Mahīdhara
MS	:	*Maitrāyaṇī Saṁhitā*
Maitri	:	*Maitrāyaṇyupaniṣad*
MLBD	:	Motilal Banarsidass
Manu	:	*Manu-Smṛti*
Muṇḍ	:	*Muṇḍakopaniṣad*
M-W	:	Monier-Williams
NŚ	:	*Nāradiyā Śikṣā*
Nir	:	*The Nighaṇṭu and Nirukta*
PB = TMB	:	*Pañcaviṁśa Brāhmaṇa*
PGS	:	*Pāraskara Gṛhya-Sūtra*
Praśna	:	*Praśnopaniṣad*
PS	:	*Puṣpasūtram*
ṚB	:	*Rigveda Brāhmaṇas*
ṚP	:	*Ṛgveda Prātiśākhya*
ṚV	:	*Ṛgveda Saṁhitā*
ṚV tr. Griffith	:	*Hymns of the Rigveda*
ṚV tr. Wilson	:	*Rigveda Saṁhitā*
Ś	:	Śaṅkarācārya
Sā	:	Sāyaṇācārya
SĀ	:	*Sāṅkhyāyana Āraṇyaka*

Sā tr. Keith	:	*The Sāṅkhyāyana Āraṇyaka*
ṢaḍB	:	*Ṣaḍviṁśa Brāhmaṇa*
ŚB	:	*Śatapatha Brāhmaṇa*
ŚB tr. Eggeling	:	*The Śatapatha Brāhmaṇa*
SBE	:	Sacred Book of the East
SGS	:	*Sāṅkhyāyana Gṛhya-Sūtra*
SRV	:	*Ṛgveda* (Śākala **Recensioṇ**)
SuS	:	*Suśruta Saṁhitā*
SV	:	*Sāmaveda*
Śvet	:	*Śvetāśvataropaniṣad*
TĀ	:	*Taittirīya Āraṇyaka*
TB	:	*Taittirīya Brāhmaṇa*
TMB	:	*Tāṇḍya Mahā Brāhmaṇa*
Taitt	:	*Taittirīyopaniṣad*
TS	:	*Taittirīya Saṁhitā*
TS tr. Keith	:	The Veda of Black Yajus School entitled *Taittirīya Saṁhitā*
UP	:	Upaniṣads
VI	:	*Vedic Index of Names and Subjects*
VDS	:	*Vaikhānasa Dharma Sūtra*
VS	:	*Vājasaneyi Saṁhitā*
YV = *VS* tr. Griffith	:	*The Texts of White Yajurveda*

Introduction

THE present work aims at a study of the *Lifestyle of Vedic People,* as it has been depicted in the Vedic Literature. Though the Vedas are usually regarded as the ultimate source book of Hindu religion, yet they contain information on the life of people and the material aspects of their culture. Hence, it is an investigation into their way of life, viz., food, clothing, etc. Though the pursuits of Vedic people like those in other countries in various ages started with the minimum requirements of life, it will be discussed how the sphere of attention of people broadened into the refinement of things, which ultimately led them to the height of Supreme Bliss.

From the survey of previous works, we find that daily life or life-pattern of common people appears as an interesting topic to the scholars. They have selected this as the subject of their research covering different periods of different civilizations. The works, which handled every day life, may be classified into three groups:

1. To the first group belong the works, which have been entirely devoted to the discussion of every day life.

At first, we should mention *Daily Life in Ancient India* by Jeanine Auboyer. Jeanine, the curator of Muśee Guimet in Paris had contributed a lot on this subject. In the daily life series she had at least 7/8 works, viz.:

(i) *Daily life of Aztec on the eve of Spanish Conquest,*

(ii) *Daily life in the Vienna of Mozart and Schubert,*

(iii) *Daily life in Palestine at the time of Christ,*

(iv) *Daily life in Rembrandt's Holland,*

(v) *Daily life of the Etruscans,*

(vi) *Daily life in the French Revolution,* and

(vii) *Daily life in Greece at the time of Pericles.*

The subject matter and time of the said works are quite clear from their titles. *Daily Life in Ancient India* is an addition to this series. In this book, Auboyer has covered nine centuries ending with political upheavals of the seventh century AD. Throughout the work, the authoress has evoked fascinating complexities of India's ancient epoch with its caste-system, its endless ritual and the ceremonial nature of human relations even in the matters of love. In order to reconstruct daily life of this period, she mainly depended on the *Rāmāyaṇa*, the *Mahābhārata*, the *Arthaśāstra*, the *Kāmasūtra*, Smṛti texts, Purāṇas, *Raghuvaṁśa*, *Kādambarī*, Buddhist texts (e.g., *Dhammapada*, *Mahāvagga*, *Mahāvastu*, *Aṭṭhasālinī*, etc.). In her work, Auboyer has described the daily routine of a fashionable young man (Part III, Ch.1), a king's daily life, lifestyle of the members of royal harem (Part III, Ch.2), that of the monks at monasteries (Part II, Ch.4), etc.

Everyday Life in Early India by Michael Edwards is another work on the same topic. Edwards, in his work, has tried to focus on everyday life of early India covering a period of roughly thousand years from the third century BC up to the eighth century AD. Edwards himself considered this work to be an introduction only to a complex and fascinating subject. He tried to give a description of everyday life of this period mainly from the Epics, the *Kāmasūtra*, the *Arthaśāstra* and *Jātaka* tales. The work also contains a chapter named "The Daily Round." In this chapter, the author has described the construction of village and city life (including food, dress, housing and amusement). V.S. Agrawala in his *India as known to Pāṇini* has given a pen-picture of daily life of the Pāṇinian age. In this book, Prof. Agrawala has discussed on geography, social life, education, economic, political and religious condition of the said period. *Life in Ancient India* by Bandana Mukhopadhyay is another work in this daily life series. Her work is based on *Dhammapada: Aṭṭhakathā*. B.C. Law in his work *India as described in the Early Texts of Buddhism and Jainism* has covered a specific age to describe daily life. J.C. Jain in *India as depicted in Jaina Canons* has dealt with the subject based on Jaina texts.

2. To the second group, we find the works where everyday life has been discussed as a part of the main work. As for example, we may mention here the name of Prof. Ram Gopal's *India of the Vedic Kalpa Sūtras*. In this work, an entire Chapter (VIII) has been devoted to describe the everyday life of the Sūtra period.

In this group, we find another work, i.e., *Wonder that was India* by A.L. Basham. In this book, Basham has discussed Indian History from the pre-historic age up to the medieval age (Vijayanagara Empire, i.e., roughly sixteenth century AD). In this book, everyday life has been discussed as a part of the main work. As because this book has covered an unusually long period, Basham has discussed the topic in a nutshell. In this chapter, he has tried to give a rough idea about daily life in the city and villages. In doing so, he has touched upon only some of its various aspects, e.g., agriculture and stock-breeding, amusement, food and drink, guild, technical achievements, trade and finance, etc. But a notable point here is that as regards information on the Vedic period, there are a few remarks only. Discussions are mostly based on the Epics, Jātaka literature and in some cases on the travellers' accounts.

3. In the third category, we find some work, which has not discussed everyday life directly, but some aspects, which are very much concerned with people's everyday life. *The*

Common Life in the Ṛgveda and Atharvaveda by Chhanda Chakraborty belongs to this group. The subject and period of the work has been clear from the title. The authoress has dealt with different aspects of common life as they have been reflected in these two Saṁhitās. Popular beliefs and superstitions, food and drink, manners and customs, amusements, etc., have been stressed in this work. Jogiraj Basu in his *India of the Age of Brāhmaṇas* has given a description of Indian society of Brahmanic age, including its political and religious aspects. In doing so, he has discussed caste system, women and marriage, education, music and dance, games and sports, dress and decoration, food and drink, utensils and tools, agriculture and pasturage, trade and commerce, house building, transport, various sacraments, different forms of sacrifice, members of royal family and their position, etc.

Apart from this, many articles have appeared covering different aspects of everyday life, e.g., G.P. Majumdar contributed a series of articles under the title "Man's Indebtedness to the Plants" dealing with food, dress and other personal requisites in ancient India. All these topics are closely related with people's everyday life. These articles have been published in different volumes of the journal *Indian Culture* in 1934-37.

But in none of these works the everyday life of the Vedic people has been treated as the main thrust area; only some matters concerning people's life have been discussed in every case. Therefore, a systematic study of the said topic (mentioned above), is still demanded. Accordingly, the present work was undertaken.

The scope of the present work is limited to a study of the life-pattern of the Vedic people based on their everyday life. The primary sources used for the investigation comprise the entire Vedic literature, i.e., from the *Ṛgveda* up to the

Upaniṣads. Now, as regards the daily life of the Vedic people, at first we must confess that, as because the Vedic texts are not daily chronicles of that period, it is difficult to get a complete picture therefrom.

Everyday life has been portrayed in some later texts more distinctly. Detailed routine of a king's daily life has been recorded in the *Manu Saṁhitā* (7.145-225). Similarly, daily life of a fashionable young man (belonging to the Gupta period) has been traced in the *Kāmasūtra* of Vātsyāyana (1.4.8) and the *Suśruta Saṁhitā* (*Cikitsāsthāna*, 24th Ch.). But no such attempt was made in the Vedic texts. Nor is it expected either; for the Vedic literature was principally religious in content and their culture was mainly concerned with religion and philosophy of the Vedic people. That is why, in their literature also, discussion on sacrificial matters has been emphasized. Whatever they told, be it about their food preparation or style of dress/ornaments or hair-fashioning or building of house, they have discussed everything in a ritual context. Therefore, in all aspects of human life, information has been culled from the ritual contexts. Because all the religious and ritual practices are but man's own lifestyle.

As a general principle, in all the ages man offers food to gods according to his own likings. The remnants of sacrificial oblations are partaken of by the sacrificer and his priests. Therefore, an idea of the food habit of Vedic people may be formed from the nature of oblations, offered at Vedic sacrifices. In a few cases, however, Vedic texts indicate differences in god's food from the human food (e.g., *surā* — *TB*, 1.3.3.3; *puroḍāśa* — *ŚB*, 1.2.2.9).

In some cases, in order to discuss various sacrifices and their preparations Vedic texts (especially the Brāhmaṇa texts) occasionally recorded some observations on human practices too, just to show their difference from the divine ones. In the context of sacrificer's initiation in the Agniṣṭoma sacrifice, the *ŚB* refers to human practices with regard to various activities. In the human practice, the activities like trimming of nails, combing hair, shaving, anointing eyes, everything starts from the left side, i.e., just in the reverse order of divine/ritual fashion. Similarly, while describing the preparation of Somayāga, the *ŚB*, has discussed construction of cart-shed (*havirdhāna*), tent (*sadas*), hearths (*dhiṣṇyā*), etc. With reference to this context, occasional remarks on the human practice of constructing hut, hall, etc., have been traced in the *ŚB* (3.1.1.7, 3.6.1.23).

From the study of Vedic texts, we find that mostly seers and elite have been represented. Description of common people's (vaiśya and śūdra community) lifestyle was not their primary concern. So, these people are not well represented in the Vedas; and the picture of their everyday life is not clearly reflected here either. An attempt will be made in the subsequent chapters to portray the lifestyle of common people on the basis of materials gleaned from Vedic literature.

As already mentioned references have been taken mainly from the Saṁhitā, Brāhmaṇa, Āraṇyaka and Upaniṣads. But whenever it is felt necessary for fuller details of the topic, materials have been collected from the Sūtra texts as well.

The study starts with the food habits of Vedic people since in everyday life, everyone's matters of primary concern are food along with clothing and shelter. Different types of food and drinks (used by people), their preparation, required utensils and implements, etc., have been discussed in detail. The subject matter of the second chapter is dress arrangement. It covers people's clothing, ornaments, hair fashioning and cosmetics (of both men and women). Varieties of dress and ornaments, their various materials, different people's dress (e.g., *vrātyas*' dress, students' dress, royal dress, bridal dress, etc.) have been described in this chapter. After food and clothing, man's next requirement is a safe shelter. Housing system has been handled in the third chapter. Different names of houses, houses built for various purposes (e.g., hut, palace, gambling house, castle, guest house, etc.), different parts of the houses, building plan, construction of the building and the required materials, have been spoken of in this chapter.

In the fourth chapter, various modes of production and occupations have been discussed, which people had to pursue in order to meet their basic requirements. But they could not remain satisfied with these bare necessities of life; they needed some recreation and that is why they devised different modes of entertainment, viz., dicing, racing, sports/games, music, dance, etc. The fifth chapter discusses these points.

Apart from these basic requirements and entertainments, people felt the necessity of cultivation of education for their intellectual development. Moreover, study of different subjects (esp. *kalpa, jyotiṣa*) was necessary for the proper performance of religious rites. Hence, learning was practised as a part of religion. R.K. Mookerji was right to remark on this purpose of education: "learning in India through the ages had been prized and pursued, not for its own sake, if we may so put it, but for the sake of and as a part of religion . . . ." (*AIE*, Prologue, p. xxi). Further, in the Upaniṣads, we have seen that learning has been sought as a means to reach the final goal, i.e., Self-Realization/Emancipation, nothing other than *Brahman* (*prajñānaṁ brahma* — *AU* 3.1.3). The subject matter of the sixth chapter is education. In this chapter, students, teachers, their relationship, subjects of study, time and place of study, holidays, etc., have been discussed. Discussion on women's education and that of the common people also has been included in the chapter.

As regards people's social life, we find that one's course of life was mainly controlled by one's social status, which has been already determined by the four castes (*varṇa*s) and further four orders of life (*āśrama*s). Origin of these four *varṇa*s, their characteristic features, occupation and status, as reflected through their regular activities, have been discussed. But details about social status of these four classes and their inter-relationship have already been discussed by the authors like J. Basu (*IAB*, I, Ch. 2, pp. 9-32) and Ram Gopal (*IVKS* VI, pp. 114-28). In order to avoid redundancy, the discussion of the same has been avoided. Further, people's daily activities vary according to the particular stage of life, which they belong to, e.g., daily duties of a student, householder and monks should obviously be different. In the seventh chapter "Social Life," people's everyday activities according to their stage of life have been described.

The last chapter focuses on the Vedic people's view of life, as it has been reflected in their thought and activities. From the study of Vedic literature, we find that a well-balanced attitude towards the fourfold aims of life has been adopted by people, which may be called pragmatic but not hedonistic. In course of time, a change has been noticed in their practices, which gradually led them to the height of Supreme Bliss. Finally, it has been found that knowledge was sought as a means to reach this Highest Goal. In order to show this gradual heightening, people's practice of *trivarga*, popular beliefs and superstition, attitude towards death, desire for heaven and ultimately quest for Supreme Knowledge/*Brahman*, etc., have been discussed.

1

Food Habit

IN all the ages and countries human pursuits start with the basic requirements of life, viz., food, clothing and shelter. The case was the same with Vedic Indians. Therefore it may not be wrong to start our discussion with these aspects which are very much concerned with people's everyday life. Thereby we will try to imagine a picture of everyday life of Vedic people as it has been reflected in their food habit, style of dress and ornaments, housing system and other practices.

If we glance at their food habit we find that there is a long list of food articles which can be divided under some groups, viz.:

(i) Various forms of grains and their products, e.g., cakes, mess, porridge, etc.

(ii) Milk and milk products like curd, butter, etc.

(iii) Fruits and vegetables.

(iv) Meat and fish.

From this list it appears that people were habituated to taking various forms of grains and foods prepared from grains, milk, butter, curd, fruits, and vegetables as their regular food. It is interesting to note that meat and fish items also were included in their menu. At first we will discuss on grains and their products.

Grains

References to varieties of grains scattered throughout Vedic literature, have made it clear that people depended mainly on grains for their food. They were accustomed to take varieties of items, which were either some form of grains or dishes prepared with grains. In order to prepare items like *apūpa, odana, puroḍāśa, karambha, yavāgu,* etc., people used various grains both the domesticated and wild types. The *TS*[1] refers to the cultivation of seven types of domesticated and seven wild grains. In course of time people learnt to cultivate more and more species. We come across a list of ten domesticated grains (has been traced) in the *BU* (6.4.13) : *daśa grāmyāṇi dhānyāni bhavanti vrīhi yavāstilamāṣā aṇu priyaṅgavo godhūmāśca khalvāśca khalakulāśca.* From this it appears that people were habituated to use both types of grains as their food component. Some of them were not fit for offerings.[2] But use of some wild grains has been mentioned in the *YS*[3] and the *Br-s* for preparing mess to be offered to the deities. These indicate that use of both species of grains were common to the people.

According to nature, these grains may be classified into several classes, e.g., cereals, rice-grains, pulse-seeds, oil-seeds, shoots, etc.

In the cereal group there are three varieties, barley, rice, and wheat. Besides these *āmba/nāmba,*[4] *aṇu*[5] (millet), *śyāmāka*[6]

---

1. *sapta grāmyā oṣadhayaḥ saptā 'raṇyāḥ . . .* — *TS* 5.2.2.5.
2. (i) *anāhutir vai jartilā gavīdhukāśca . . .* — *MS* 1.4.10; *KS* 32.7; *TS* 5.4.3.2.
   (ii) *ayajñīyā vai māṣāḥ* — *MS* 1.4.10.
3. *TS* 1.8.9.2, 1.8.10.1; *ŚB* 5.2.4.11, 5.2.4.13, 5.3.1.10.
4. *āmba* — *TS* 1.8.10.1; *nāmba* — *ŚB* 5.3.3.8.
5. *aṇu* — *MS* 2.11.4; *KS* 18.9; *TS* 4.7.4.2; *VS* 18.12; *BU* 6.4.12.
6. *śyāmāka* — *MS* 2.11.4; *KS* 10.2; *TS* 1.8.1.2; *ŚB* 10.6.3.2.

(millet), *priyaṅgu*[7] (panic seed), *upavāka*[8] also belong to the cereal group. Mainly these grains were used for preparing sacrificial foods.

BARLEY

In this cereal group barley was in the most important position. Sometimes parched barley itself was used as a popular item though at that time it was called by a different name, i.e., *dhānā*.[9] Occasionally, its flour meal was used to prepare items like *apūpa, puroḍāśa, karambha*,[10] etc. Sometimes the same one was used as the taste maker of drinks (mainly *soma*); then its name was *yavāśir*.[11] Popular drink *yavāgū*[12] was prepared with it. In course of time people learnt to cultivate different species of rice grains and gradually there was a tendency among people to replace *yava* by various sorts of rice grains, though use of *yava* was not out of practice.

WHEAT

That wheat was used mainly as a substitute for barley, has been indicated through the references to *godhūma*,[13] which has been differentiated very clearly from *vrīhi* (rice) and *yava* (barley). Sometimes parched grains of wheat were mixed with *surā* (*TB* 2.6.11.1).

RICE

Rice occupies an important position in the late Vedic period. Its total absence in the *ṚV* indicates that cultivation of rice

7. *priyaṅgu* — *MS* 2.1.8; *KS* 10.11; *TS* 2.2.11.4; *VS* 18.12; *AB* 8.16; *TB* 3.8.4.6; *BU* 6.4.13.
8. *upavāka* — *VS* 19.22, 19.30, 21.30; *ŚB* 12.7.1.3, 12.7.2.9, etc.
9. *bhṛṣṭayavāḥ dhānāḥ* — Sā on *ṚV* 8.91.2.
10. *imaṁ jambhasutaṁpiba dhānāvantaṁ karambhiṇaṁ apūpavantam ukthinam* — *ṚV* 8.91.2.
11. *ṚV* 1.187.9, 2.22.1, 3.42.7, 8.92.4, etc.
12. *KS* 11.2; *TS* 6.2.5.2; *KB* 4.13; *TĀ* 2.8.8.
13. *MS* 1.2.8; *VS* 18.12, 19.22, 19.89, 21.29; *ŚB* 5.2.1.16; *BU* 6.4.13.

was unknown to the early Vedic Indians. However, its specific varieties have been mentioned in the Yajurvedic Saṁhitā and Brāhmaṇas.

(1)	Rice (in general)	-	(i) *taṇḍula* - (a) *karṇā* and *akarṇā* (*TS* 1.8.9.3)
			(ii) *vrīhi* - (a) *kṛṣṇā* and *śuklā* (*TS* 1.8.10.1)
(2)	Large rice	-	*mahāvrīhi* (*TS* 1.8.10.1; *AB* 8.16)
(3)	Wild-rice	-	*nīvāra* (*MS* 3.4.10; *KS* 12.4; *ŚB* 1.4.1.14; *TB* 1.3.6.7)
(4)	Red-rice	-	*hāyana* (*KS* 16.5; *ŚB* 5.3.3.6)
(5)	Fast grown rice	-	*āśu* (*TS* 1.8.10.1) and *plāśuka* (*ŚB* 5.3.3.2)
(6)		-	*masūsya** (*TB* 3.8.14.6)

Now, its absence in the early Vedic literature and frequent occurrence in the later age makes us suppose that gradually use of rice became popular and the use of rice as a staple food was comparatively a late one. So far as records are concerned its earliest use has been traced in the *AV*. In various passages of the *AV*[14] preparation of rice has been described stage by stage (i.e., winnowing of rice grains, washing, placing the vessel on oven, etc.).

The cakes and puddings were prepared with different types of rice meal.[15] Parched rice could be taken alone in the

---

* It is a sort of wild-rice, grown in the northern country. But its name (Eng. equivalent) has not been specified in any text book.

14. *AV* 11.1.9-19, 12.3.28-30.

15. *agnaye gṛhapataye puroḍāśam aṣṭākapālṁ nirvapati kṛṣṇānāṁ vrīhiṇāṁ . . . savitre satyaprasavāya puroḍāśam dvādaśakapālam āśūnāṁ vrīhiṇāṁ . . . indrāya jyeṣṭhāya puroḍāśam ekādaśakapālaṁ mahāvrīhiṇām*
— *TS* 1.8.10.1.

form of *parivāpa*[16] or *lāja*.[17] Sometimes it was prepared into a drink, i.e., *lājamaṇḍa*, after boiling it in water (*AV* 6.5.1). From the *ŚĀ* (12.8) and the *BU* (6.4.13-18) we have been informed that varieties of mess were prepared with rice. The names *kṣīraudana, māṁsaudana, dadhyodana, tilaudana, udaudana, ghṛtaudana, mudgaudana* (recorded in the *BU*) indicate the use of rice in combination with various things like milk, meat, curd, sesame, ghee, beans, etc.

Beside these, *dhānā, parivāpa, lāja, pṛthuka*[18] suggest that people liked to taste various forms of parched grains. They had a little difference among themselves. According to the commentators, *lājā vrīhiprabhavāḥ puṣpavad vikaśitāḥ* (Sā on *TB* 1.8.15), while *pṛthukāścipiṭakāḥ* (*ibid.* 3.8.14). *Dhānā*[19] parched with ghee, was very popular. Devī Bhāratī had a special liking for *parivāpa*.[20]

Sometimes fried grains were used to prepare a famous drink *māsara*.[21] Pounded grains were used to prepare porridges like *karambha*.[22] Sometimes it was prepared with pounded grains and curdled with milk/ghee.[23] Indra enjoyed very much the praises, accompanied with *karambha*.[24] According to the *ŚB*,[25] the same was prepared with unhusked, kneaded and

---

16. *TS* 3.1.10.1, 6.5.11.4; *KS* 34.11; *VS* 19.21-22; *AB* 2.24; *TB* 1.5.11.2.
17. *MS* 3.11.2; *VS* 19.13; 21.42; *ŚB* 12.8.2.7; *TB* 2.6.4.
18. Sā on *TB* 1.8.15, 3.18.14, etc.
19. *imā dhānā ghṛtasnuvo harī ihopavakṣataḥ* ।
 indraṁ sukhata me rathe ॥ — *ṚV* 4.24.7.
20. *dhānābhir aśvināvabhiṣajyatāṁ devī bhāratī parivāpeṇa* — *TB* 1.5.11.2.
21. *MS* 3.11.2, 3.11.9; *VS* 19.14; *TB* 2.6.11.4.
22. *ṚV* 3.52.7, 6.56.1, etc.
23. *TS* 3.1.10.2, 6.5.11.4, etc.
24. *imaṁ jambhasutaṁ piba dhānāvantaṁ karambhiṇam apūpavantam ukthinam* — *ṚV* 8.91.2.
25. *ŚB* 2.5.2.14, 4.2.4.18, etc.

parched barley. A sort of *karambha* prepared with seasame has been mentioned in the *AV*.[26]

Besides these cereals and rice-grains people knew use of pulse-seeds[27] and beans,[28] specially for cooking varieties of mess and porridges. Use of oil-seeds[29] also has been indicated.

Apart from various grains (themselves), people prepared varieties of items from the pounded meal of these grains, e.g., cakes, mess, gruel, etc. *Pakti, apūpa, puroḍāśa*, etc., appearing frequently suggest that people had a liking for different types of cakes and sweet-meats. Among them *pakti* is rather a general name for any food. In some places it denotes a sort of cake[30] (though not in the modern sense). Its exact nature has not been mentioned anywhere. That *apūpa* was equally popular, has been proved from its frequent occurrence from the *ṚV*[31] up to the Upaniṣads.[32] Probably it was prepared with the flour meal of rice or barley and baked with butter on slow-fire.[33] Sometimes honey was added to sweeten it.[34] The term *puroḍāśa* denotes sacrificial cake. As regards its ingredients, late Vedic literature informs us that both *yava* and *vrīhi* were used for this purpose; still the use of various species of *vrīhi*[35] was more prevalent. Occasionally, meats were used to prepare it. In the Sāmavedic Brāhmaṇas, one Gaurīvīthi has been mentioned,

---

26. *karambhaṁ kṛtvā tiryam pībaspākam udārathim* I — *AV* 4.7.3.
27. *KS* 10.11; *TS* 2.4.4.1-2; *VS* 18.12; *CU* 1.10.2, 1.10.7; *BU* 6.3.13.
28. *AV* 6.140.2, 12.2.53; *MS* 1.4.10, 4.3.2; *KS* 12.7; *TS* 5.1.8.1; *ŚB* 1.1.1.10; *BU* 6.3.13.
29. *AV* 2.8.3, 6.140.2, 18.3.69, 18.4.32; *VS* 18.12; *CU* 5.10.6; *BU* 6.3.13.
30. *ṚV* 4.24.5, 4.24.7.
31. *ṚV* 3.52.7, 8.91.2, 10.45.9.
32. *CU* 3.1.1.
33. *yaste adya kṛṇavad bhadraśoce apūpaṁ deva ghṛtavantam agne* I — *ṚV* 10.45.9.
34. *apūpavān madhumām̐ś carur eha sīdatu* — *AV* 17.4.22.
35. *TS* 1.8.9, 1.8.10, etc.

who used meat as *puroḍāśa*.[36] But whether meat itself was used as *puroḍāśa* or used as ingredient to prepare it — is still a question. In the *ŚB*[37] the proper shape and size of *puroḍāśa* (used as oblation) has been stated in a distinct language. The sentence *taṁ na satrā pṛthu kuryāt, mānuṣaṁ ha kuryāt yat pṛthu kuryāt* (*ŚB* 1.2.2.9) makes it clear that apart from ritual purpose people prepared *puroḍāśa* as regular food item also.

Milk

In the Vedic literature milk has been called by different names, viz., *go, kṣīra, payas, pratiduḥ,* etc. Wide use of milk for both domestic and ritual purposes can be easily assumed from these different names and their frequent occurrences (from the *ṚV* onwards).

Warm milk (*pakvaṁ payaḥ*) was a favourite drink. The name *kṣīrapākam odanam* (*ṚV* 8.77.10) informs us that from the Ṛgvedic period people knew to prepare delicious items with milk. Necessity and benefits of drinking milk have been described in the *TS*[38]: " . . . . milk is the brilliance, verily by brilliance he endows himself with brilliance and milk. Again by milk foetuses grow. The man who is consecrated as it were a foetus, in that milk is his drink. Verily thus he causes himself to grow."

In the Brāhmaṇa[39] literature, we find the name of a vow '*payo-vrata*,' in which the sacrificer was enjoined to subsist on

---

36. (i) *etena vai gaurīvītiḥ śāktyas tarasa puroḍāśo . . .*
— *PB* 25.7.2.

(ii) *śāktyās tarasapuroḍāśās satram āsata* — *JB* 3.18.

37. *taṁ na satrā pṛthu kuryāt . . . aśvaśaphamātraṁ kuryād ityuhaika āhuḥ*
— *ŚB* 1.2.2.9-10.

38. *tejaḥ payas tejasaiva tejaḥ paya ātman dhatte'tho payasā vai garbhā vardhante garbha iva khalu vā eṣa yaddīkṣito yad asya payo vrataṁ bhavaty ātmānam eva tad vardhayati . . .* — *TS* 6.2.5.3.

39. *KB* 8.9; *ŚB* 2.5.3.4, 9.5.1.1, etc.

milk only. Actually during the sacrifice, the initiated sacrificer was allowed to take milk (the remaining portion of oblation) only. It was known as *payo-vrata*.

In the Agnihotra[40] milk was used as a regular offering. Usually boiled milk was offered.

Use of goat's milk for both ritual and domestic purposes has been met with in the late Vedic Saṁhitās.[41]

In the coronation ceremony milk was used with the consecration water.[42]

MILK PRODUCTS

Apart from milk, milk-products also had a great and important role in the everyday life of Vedic Indians.

The names *ghṛta, navanīta, phāṇṭa, pṛṣātaka, payasyā, dadhi, āmikṣā, vājina*, etc., scattered in various passages of the Vedic Saṁhitā[43] and Brāhmaṇas, inform us that they were accustomed to use varieties of butter and curds for both domestic and ritual purposes.

Butter : Clarified butter *ghṛta* has been called by various names, e.g., *ājya, sarpis, āyuta, navanīta, phāṇṭa, mastu, niṣpakva*, etc. Actually all these are more or less of the same category having slight difference in their nature. Sāyaṇācārya[44] in his commentary on the *AB* has clarified their nature that *ghṛta* is hardened butter while *ājya* is the molten one. These different forms served the purpose of gods, men, the manes and the

---

40. *AB* 5.26, 5.27, etc.
41. *MS* 3.1.8, 3.3.4; *KS* 19.7, 21.6; *TS* 2.2.4.4-5, 5.4.3.1-2.
42. *AV* 4.8.5-6; *AB* 8.8; *ŚB* 5.3.4.19.
43. *ṚV* 1.134.6, 2.10.4; *AV* 3.13.5; *VS* 2.22; *AB* 1.3; *ŚB* 1.8.1.7, 9.2.1.1, etc.
44. *ājyaghṛtayor bhedāḥ pūrvācāryair udāhṛtāḥ sarpir vilīnam ājyaṁ syāt ghanībhūtaṁ ghṛtaṁ viduḥ* — Sā on *AB* 1.3

embryo respectively.[45] The *TS*[46] shows a little difference in their names, i.e., butter for gods is *ghṛta*, that for manes is *mastu* and that for men is *niṣpakva*. According to Sāyaṇa[47] *mastu* is same as *āyuta*, the slightly molten variety and *niṣpakva* is same as *ājya*, molten entirely.

As regards varieties of butter, we find here some new names, viz., fresh butter (*navanīta*), creamy butter (*phāṇṭa*), sprinkled butter (*pṛṣadājya*), mixed butter (*pṛṣātaka*), etc. Actually by nature they were butter, the names varied only due to their form, e.g., *navanītabhāvāt prāgavasthāpannaṁ dravyaṁ phāṇṭam* (Sā on *ŚB* 3.1.3.8). It proves that *phāṇṭa* is the first particle of butter, the prior stage of *navanīta*. *Pṛṣadājya* has been rendered as clotted butter (SBE, tr. Eggeling 12, p. 418), whereas *pṛṣātaka* (*AV* 20.135.8) has been explained as mixed butter prepared with curds, honey and *ājya*.

Curds : The *TS*[48] has declared curds as a popular village food. *Dadhi* and *payasyā*, both these names have been used to mean curds; though *dadhi* in some cases meant sour milk[49] also. It was used as an admixture (*dadhyāśir*[50]) of Soma.

Payasyā has been described as curds made of sour milk and hot or cold fresh milk (Eggelling, SBE (tr.) 12.381). The *TB*[51] has described it as favourite item of Mitra and Varuṇa.

---

45. *ājyaṁ vai devānāṁ surabhighṛtaṁ manuṣyāṇām āyutaṁ pitṝṇāṁ navanītaṁ garbhāṇam* — Sā on *AB* 1.3.
46. *ghṛtaṁ devānāṁ mastu pitṝṇāṁ niṣpakvaṁ manuṣyāṇām* — *TS* 6.1.1.4.
47. *īṣad vilinaṁ mastu, niḥśeṣeṇa vilīnaṁ niṣpakvam* — Sā on *AB* 1.3.
48. *grāmyaṁ vā etadannam yad dadhyāraṇyaṁ madhu* — *TS* 5.2.8.6.
49. *ṚV* 8.2.9, 9.87.1; *AV* 3.12.7, 4.34.6; *TS* 2.5.3.4.
50. *ṚV* 1.5.5, 1.137.2, 5.51.7, 7.32.4, etc.
51. *dhānābhir aśvināvabhiṣajyatām devī bhārati parivāpeṇa mitṝāvaruṇau payasyayā* — *TB* 1.5.11.2.

A sour curd *mastu* has been mentioned in the *ŚB*.[52] According to Eggeling it is actually whey.

Clotted Curds : *Āmikṣā*,[53] also was a type of curd, though of a somewhat different nature. Actually the solid extract coming out of the mixture of hot fresh milk and sour milk has been named as *āmikṣā* and the remainder, sour liquid has been named as *vājina*. In the Sūtra texts its nature has been explained: *tapte payasi dadhni kṣipte ghanabhāgā āmikṣā śiṣṭaṁ vājinam* (*BŚS* 5.1.4).

Fruits and Vegetables

In the list of people's daily diet there were fruits also. The *ṚV*[54] informs us of the forest containing delicious fruits. Method of plucking fruits also has been instructed there.[55] *Sugandhi puṣṭivardhana ūrvāruka* has been mentioned repeatedly from the *ṚV*[56] onwards. With reference to different ritual contexts we came across names of various fruits, e.g., date (*kharjūra* — *TS* 2.4.9; *MS* 1.10.12; *KS* 36.7), varieties of jujubes (i) *badara* — *MS* 2.4.1; *KS* 12.10; *TS* 6.6.7; (ii) *kuvala* — *KS* 12.10; *MS* 2.3.9; (iii) *karkandhu* — *VS* 21.32.24.2; *ŚB* 12.9.1.5; *JB* 2.152; wood-apple (*bilva* — *ŚB* 13.4.4.8), sugarcane, myrobalan fruit (*āmalaka* — *CU* 7.3.1), mango (*āmra* — *BU* 4.3.36), etc.

Pounded meal of dried *kuvala*, *karkandhu* and *badara* were used as taste maker of drinks and offered to deities like Aśvins, which they liked very much. Beside these, *karkandhu*

---

52. *ŚB* 1.8.1.7, 3.3.3.2, etc.

53. *AV* 10.9.13; *MS* 2.1.9; *VS* 19.21, 19.23; *TS* 2.5.5.4, 3.3.9.2; *TĀ* 2.8.8, etc.

54. *na vā araṇyānir hantiyanyaścennābhigacchati* ।
svādoḥ phalasya jagdhvāya yathākāmaṁ nipadyate ॥
— *ṚV* 10.146.5

55. *vṛkṣaṁ pakvaṁ phalam aṅkīva dhūnuhīndra sampāraṇaṁ basu*
— *ṚV* 3.45.4.

56. *ṚV* 7.59.10; *AV* 14.1.17; *MS* 1.10.4; *TS* 1.8.6.2; *VS* 3.60.

was used to prepare porridges like *karambha*.[57] Ripe mango and its sweet flavour has been mentioned in the late Vedic literature.[58]

On the basis of this use of dried fruits and their popularity, a modern scholar opined that fruits formed a common part of people's regular diet (Om Prakash, *EFAI*, I, p. 78).

As regards vegetables the *R̥V*[59] presents before us the names of cucumber, lotus-stalk, etc. Besides these, names of numerous edible plants and roots have been recorded in the *AV* (though in a different context). They are as follows: bottle-gourd (*AV* 8.10.29-30), lotus-root (*AV* 4.34.5), *trabispinoja* (*AV* 4.34.5), *śaphaka* (*AV* 4.34.5), *mūlālī* (*AV* 4.34.5), *āṇḍīka* (*AV* 4.34.5), *avakā* (*AV* 4.37.8) and *madhuka* (read as *madugha* or *madhūka* also).

It is remarkable that our texts supply only some names of vegetables. But as regards vegetables consumption or their cooking process, they keep total silence. Therefore, on the basis of such information it is difficult to suppose that people used these as food articles.

Meat

That meat formed a regular part of people's diet, has been suggested from the references to meat consumption scattered throughout Vedic Literature. "Meat has been declared as the best food"[60] — this sentence proves that meat was widely used at that time.

Men offered meat of various animals to the gods (*R̥V* 1.162.10, 10.91.14; *AV* 6.71.1; *VS* 20.76) on various occasions and distributed the remnants to the priests (*AB* 7.1),

---

57. *TS* 1.8.21; *MS* 2.3.9; *KS* 12.10; *ŚB* 12.9.1.5. — Sa on *TB* 1.8.5.
58. *BU* 4.3.36; *ĀpDS* 1.7.20.3.
59. (*Urvāruka*) *R̥V* 7.59.10; (*Visa*) *R̥V* 6.61.2.
60. *etad u ha vai paramamannaṁ yanmāṁsam* — *ŚB* 7.5.2.42.

sometimes the offered-meat was distributed to common people in a feast[61] (Griffith, tr. *AV* II, p.34). From this it may not be wrong to suppose that people at that period had a strong liking for meat-items and they were habituated to take the flesh of various animals. The offering of bull belonged to Indra, sheep to Sarasvatī and goat to Aśvins;[62] though goat has been mentioned already as the favourite item of Pūṣan.[63] Cows were slaughtered on a large scale for the purpose of food.[64] Slaughter of great ox or great goat was a regular practice for guest entertainment[65] as well as on the marriage ceremony.[66]

ye vājinaṁ paripaśyanti pakvaṁ ya imāhuḥ surabhirnihareti I
ye cārvato māsambhikṣāmupāsata teṣām abhigūrtir na invatu II
— *Ṛ̥V* 1.162.12

This description of cooking horse meat and people's reaction at its relishing smell makes us assume that people had a special liking for horse meat but its use was not common, rather occasional. From the reference to Vāmadeva's cooking dog's entrail *avartyā śuna āntrāṇi pece* (*Ṛ̥V* 4.18.13), it appears that when people were distressed and in utmost need they had to use even dog's flesh also as food.

Fish

It is very much interesting to note that there is hardly any reference to the use of fish as a food item in the early Vedic

---

61. *ye te devi śamitāraḥ paktāro ye ca te janāḥ* I
te tvā sarve gopsyanti . . . — *AV* 10.9.7.

62. *aśvibhyāṁ chāgaṁ sarasvatyai meṣam indrāya ṛṣabham* — *VS* 21.59.

63. *eṣa chāgaḥ puro aśvena vajinā pūṣṇo bhāgo nīyate viśvadevyaḥ* I
abhipriyam yat puroḍāśam arvatā tvaṣṭedenaṁ sauśravasāya jinvati II
— *Ṛ̥V* 1.162.3.

64. *Ṛ̥V* 5.29.8, 6.16.47, 6.17.11, 10.86.13-14; *TS* 1.3.14.7, etc.

65. *atha yasmād ātithyaṁ nāma . . . rājñe brāhmaṇāya vā mahokṣam mahājaṁ vā pacet* — *ŚB* 3.4.1.2.

66. *aghāsu hanyante gāvo arjunyoḥ pary upāhyate* — *Ṛ̥V* 10.85.13.

age. Still references to the fish and its being caught in nets[67] (*Ṛ̥V* 7.18.6, 10.68.8) makes us infer that catching of fish was in practice. In that case its use as a food article may not be impossible at least within a group of people.

In the later ages the *YS*[68] and *Br-s* refer to a swarm of people who were explained as fishermen by the commentators.[69] Now, existence of these people makes us suppose that gradually people (at least a sect of people) became accustomed to take fish during the late Vedic age.

According to the *Pāraskara Gṛhya-Sūtra* (1.19.8), use of fish was conventional in the *annaprāśana* rite by the close of Vedic period.

Preparation of Food

From the beginning of Vedic literature, it has been noticed that people were habituated to use cooked food for both sacrificial purpose and their own use. The names like *pakva* (*Ṛ̥V* 1.180.3), *pacata* (*Ṛ̥V* 1.61.7), *pakti* (*Ṛ̥V* 6.29.4), *pitu* (*Ṛ̥V* 1.61.8) (meaning any cooked food) prove the validity of this statement. Boiled milk was offered to gods (*Ṛ̥V* 1.62.9). The *AV* (11.1.12-21) has described vividly the preparation of rice

---

67. *puroḷā intur vaśo yakṣur āsīdrāye matsyāso niśitā apīva* ।
sruṣṭir cakrur bhṛgavo druhyavaśca sakhā sakhāyamatarad viṣūcoḥ ॥
— *Ṛ̥V* 7.18.6.

68. *sarobhyo dhaivaraṁ upasthāvareābhyo dāśaṁ vaiśantābhyo baindaṁ naḍvalābhyaḥ śauṣkalaṁ pārāya mārgāram avārāya kaivartaṁ tīrthebhya āṇḍaṁ viṣamebhyo mainālaṁ svanebhyaḥ parṇakam*
— *VS* 30.16; *TB* 3.4.12.1.

69. *dhaivaram ubhayato jālaṁ baddhvā titaunā matsyagrāhiṇam, . . . dāśaṁ baḍiśena matsyagrāhiṇam, nāvā 'ntaḥ praviśya matsyagrāhiṇam eke . . . baindaṁ bindaṁ jālaṁ tena jīvatiti, uḍuvavidale taran yo matsyaṁ gṛhṇātīty anye, śauṣkalaṁ baḍiśajīvanaṁ mahāmatsyānutthāpya grahītāram eke, kaivartaṁ kule matsyānāṁ puñjīkṛtya hantāram . . . mārgāram antarjale hastābhyāṁ mārgaṇaśīlam . . . āndaṁ tīrthe sāmiṣayantra bandhanena . . . mainālam jālajīvinam . . . saviṣam parṇam jālasyopari sthāpayitvā matsyagrāhiṇam . . .* — Bhaṭṭabhāskara on *TB* 3.4.12.1.

stage by stage (i.e., husking and winnowing of grains, washing, putting the vessel on the oven, etc.). Further, names of varieties of *odana* (recorded in the *BU* 6.4.13-18) are clear proofs that rice was prepared in varieties (esp. *kṣīraudana, māṁsaudana,* etc.). Again, *sukṛtā tacchamitāraḥ kṛṇvantu ta medhaṁ śṛtapākaṁ pacatu* (*ṚV* 1.162.10) makes it evident that meat was offered to gods only after it was processed and cooked. This processing and cooking have been mentioned in a clear language. As regards its cooking recipe, we find that either it was roasted (*ṚV* 1.162.11) or boiled in the cauldron (*ṚV* 1.162.13).

Moreover preparation of *apūpa*, by baking it with butter on the slow fire (*yas te adya kṛṇavad bhadraśoce apūpaṁ deva ghṛtavantam agne* — *ṚV* 10.45.9) proves that people knew to prepare sweetmeats also. "It is probably the earliest sweet preparation known to us" (Omprakash, *EFAI* II, p. 76). Names of varieties of *apūpas*, viz., *tailāpūpa, traiyambaka apūpa,* etc., have been recorded in the Sūtra[70] texts. Its shape and size also have been mentioned there.

Use of Cooking Spices

Names of mustard,[71] long turmeric,[72] long pepper,[73] citron,[74] sesamum[75] oil, salt,[76] etc., have been recorded in the late Vedic texts (from the *AV* onwards). On the basis of these names and description of cooking (esp. meat), Omprakash in his work has suggested that though these names have been mentioned with reference to a different context, still these were actually

70. *Kāṭhaka Gṛhya-Sūtra* 70.1; *GGS* 3.10.9-12.
71. *AV* 8.6.3, 8.6.6-7; *ṢaḍB* 6.2.1; *CU* 3.14.3.
72. *ŚB* 13.8.1.16; *BU* 2.3.6.
73. *AV* 6.109.1-2; *ŚB* 14.7.1.41; (*BU* 4.3.36).
74. *MS* 3.15.3; *KS* 5.21; *VS* 15.3.
75. *AV* 1.7.2, 20.136.16; *ŚĀ* 11.4.
76. *AV* 7.76.1; *ŚB* 5.2.1.16-17; *BU* 2.4.12; *CU* 6.13.1-3.

cooking spices and probably use of these components as cooking mediums was known to the people of that age (Omprakash, *EFAI* II, p. 76). But it is true that the same articles were used to serve some other purpose also.

In the *Kauśika Sūtra*[77] (31.17) red salt has been mentioned, which has been explained by the commentator as rock salt.[78] Use of this salt has been prohibited during sacrificial occasions.[79] From this prohibition on the use of salt we may easily guess that people knew the use of salt as a taste maker. Prof. Ram Gopal in his work has remarked about the Sūtra period, "salt and sugar were, of course, added to impart special flavour to dishes . . . *Śarkarā* (candied sugar) was also consumed" (Ram Gopal, *IVKS* VII, p. 163). Both the black pepper and red pepper have been mentioned in the *ĀpDS*[80] (1.7.20.12) which were used as condiments. In the category of prohibited foods, onion, garlic, red garlic, etc., have been listed.[81]

Utensils/Implements

In order to prepare food and to meet some other requirements of everyday life people used some utensils and implements. From the study of Vedic texts we find that utensils/implements of daily use were mainly of three types: (1) metal, (2) earthenware and (3) wooden.

The Aśvasūkta of *R̥V* presents before us:

yannīkaṣaṇaṁ māṁspacanyā ukhāyā yā pātrāṇi yūṣṇa āsecanāni ।
uṣmaṇyāpidhānā carūṇāmaṅkāḥ sūnāḥ paribhūṣantyaśvam ॥
— *R̥V* 1.162.13

---

77. *lohita lavaṇaṁ saṁkṣudyābhiniṣṭhīvati* — *KauS* 31.17.
78. *saindhava lavaṇam cūrṇīkr̥tyāpacitikr̥tvā* . . . Dārlia on *KauS loc.cit.*
79. *KauS* 1.31-32; Śā on *ŚS* 4.1.3.
80. *pippalī marīce dhānyaṁ māṁsam āyudham* . . . — *ĀpDS* 1.7.20.12.
81. *karañjapalāṇḍu parārīkāḥ* — *ĀpDS* 1.5.17.26.

These are the names of a set of utensils, e.g., *nīkaṣaṇa, māṁspacanī ukhā, caru, āsecana, sūnā*, etc., which the people required for cooking meat. Among them *nīkaṣaṇa* was probably used as a trial stick to examine whether the cooking was effected or not. A thing to be noted here is that the utensils or implements which people used for cooking or other domestic purpose were mainly metal. Earthenware pots also were used, e.g., *kumbha*,[82] *kalaśa*[83] were used as water jars or any other liquid container. It is interesting to observe that they were habituated to use leather bags (*dṛti*,[84] *bhastrā*[85]) also specially for containing liquids (like *surā* or milk) and sometimes grains also.

The utensils/implements used for ritual or sacrificial purpose were mainly wooden or earthenware, e.g.:

(1) varieties of wooden ladles or spoons, viz., *camasa, sruk, sruva, jūhu, upabhṛt, dhruvā, upayamanī, darvī*, etc.

(2) Soma container like *droṇa, dru, sadhastha, kośa.*

(3) tongs, e.g., *dhṛṣṭi, śapha* were used.

Sacrificial milk was boiled in an earthenware pot called *gharma*.[86] *Sthālī*[87] was the name of a cooking pot. Its four varieties *āditya sthālī, ukthyasthālī, dhruvāsthālī* and *āgrayaṇa sthālī* have been mentioned in the *TB*[88] (1.4.1.6). Beside these, a strainer made of sheep's wool/cow hide called *pavitra*[89] was

---

82. *ṚV* 1.116.7, 1.117.6, 10.89.7; *AV* 3.12.7.
83. *ṚV* 1.117.12, 3.12.15, 4.27.5; *AV* 9.1.6, 9.4.15, etc.
84. *ṚV* 1.191.10, 4.51.1, 5.83.7; *AV* 7.18.1; *TB* 1.8.3.4; *PB* 14.11.26.
85. *ŚB* 1.1.2.7, 1.6.3.16, etc.
86. *ṚV* 3.53.14, 5.30.15, 5.43.7; *AV* 7.73.6; *VS* 8.61, etc.
87. *AV* 8.6.17; *TS* 6.5.10.5; *VS* 19.27; *AB* 1.11.8; *TB* 1.4.1.6.
88. *kāścatasra sthālī . . . iyaṁ vai pṛśni tām āditya ādityasthālyā . . . tām indra ukthyasthālyendriyam . . . tāṁ viśvedevā āgrayaṇa sthālyorjam . . . tāṁ manuṣyā dhruvasthālyāyur aduhran* I — *TB* 1.4.1.6.
89. *ṚV* 9.16.2, 9.65.25, 9.70.7, 9.86.47.

used for purifying Soma. Grains were pounded at first in mortar and pestles[90] (*adri-grāvā* or *ulūkhala-musala*) and then were winnowed in a wicker-work basket called *śūrpa*.[91]

Use of metal pots (for ritual purposes) was not common but it was not out of practice. The use of metal wine-goblet (*surākaṁsa*[92] — to be used in the coronation ceremony) or iron bowl (*ayasmaya*[93] *caru* — used for offering *sviṣṭakṛt* oblations) have been mentioned in the Brāhmaṇa texts. Again fire-extinguishers[94]/coal-shovel (*aṅgārā-vakṣayaṇa* — *BU* 3.9.18; or *ulumukāvakṣayaṇa* — *ŚB* 4.6.8.7, 11.6.3.3) also bear the proof of using metal pots.

Drinks

Beside these food-articles normally people required some drinks also to quench their thirst. Normally water, honey and milk were consumed. Water was the main drink for both men and animals.[95] People used it as an offering to the manes.[96] Even during vows and rites water was permissible.[97] Water was considered as the essence of life[98] and food as well.[99]

---

90. *ṚV* 1.83.6, 1.130.2, 1.135.5, 1.137.1.
91. *AV* 9.6.16, 10.9.26; *TS* 1.6.8.3; *TB* 1.6.5.4.
92. *atha surākaṁsaṁ hasta ādadhāti* — *AB* 8.8.
93. *ayasmayena caruṇā dvitīyāmāhutiñjuhoti* । — *ŚB* 13.3.4.5.
94. *tvaṁ svic chākalya brāhmaṇā ulmukāvakṣayaṇā akratā* ।
— *ŚB* 11.6.3.3; cf. *BU* 3.9.18.
95. *ṚV* 1.23.18, 1.63.8, 1.116.9, 1.125.5, 1.153.4, 1.161.8, 2.36.1, 3.35.8, 5.34.9, 10.9.4, etc.; *AV* 1.6.1, 1.6.4, 2.29.5, 3.13.5, 4.8.5, 6.61.1, 7.19.2; *VS* 36.12; *TB* 1.2.1.1, 2.5.8.5, etc.
96. (i) *apūpavānapavām̐ścarur eha sīdatu* । — *AV* 18.4.16.
(ii) *ūrjaṁ bahantīr amṛtaṁ ghṛtaṁ payaḥ kīlālaṁ parisrutam* । *svadhā tarpayata me pitṝn* ॥ — *VS* 2.34.
97. *etāpo 'śnāti tannevāśitaṁ naivānaśitam* . . . — *TS* 1.6.7.4.
98. *kāmam apaḥ piba, āpomayaḥ prāṇo, na pibato vicchetsyata iti* ।
— *CU* 6.7.1.
99. *annaṁ vā'āpaḥ* । — *ŚB* 8.2.3.6.

In the section on milk we have already discussed milk and its products as food. Now comes honey, which has appeared frequently in the Vedas but used to denote various meanings, e.g., any sweet food or drink,[100] milk,[101] *soma*[102] or its epithet and honey[103] as well. It is very much interesting to note here that all these meanings are running parallel from the *ṚV* onwards. It was used as the taste maker of *soma* and *surā* as well.

Apart from these, people were accumstomed to use different intoxicating/invigorating drinks, viz., *soma, kīlāla, māsara, parisrut, surā, madya,* etc. In the late Vedic literature a flat name for drinks has been traced, i.e., *pāna.*[104]

In the list of drinks *soma* occupied an important position. Mainly it was a divine drink,[105] and people consumed it on sacrificial occasions, as a part of a ritual.[106] The ninth book of *ṚV*[107] has given us a detailed description of *soma* processing and preparation. Sometimes *soma* was steeped into water to increase the juice.[108] Before preparation it was pounded with two stones, viz., *adri* and *grāvā.*[109] Sometimes mortar and pestle were used for the same purpose.[110] After pressing it was

---

100. *ṚV* 1.187.2, 3.1.7-8, 4.42.3, 4.34.6, 4.43.4; *VS* 6.2, 38.10; *TB* 3.1.2.2, 3.1.2.4-5, etc.
101. *ṚV* 1.169.4, 1.177.3; *VS* 6.2.
102. *ṚV* 1.19.9, 2.19.2, 2.34.5, 2.36.4, 3.43.3, 4.18.2.
103. *ṚV* 3.8.1, 4.45.4-5, 7.24.2, 7.32.2, 8.4.8; *AV* 9.1.17, 9.1.19, 9.1.22; *MS* 4.9.7; *TS* 7.5.10.1; *AB* 7.15, 8.5; *ŚB* 11.5.4.18; *CU* 6.7.1, etc.
104. *yathā rājānam āyāntamugrāḥ . . . annaiḥ pānair āvasathaiḥ pratikalpante . . .* — *BU* 4.3.37.
105. *etad vai devānāṁ paramam annaṁ yat somaḥ* I — *TB* 1.3.3.2.
106. *TB* 1.3.3.2-1.3.3.6; *ŚB* 12.7.3.5-14.
107. *ṚV* 9.66.7-12, 9.69.8-10, 9.74.8, etc.
108. *ṚV* 9.74.9; *MS* 4.5.5, etc.
109. *ṚV* 1.83.6, 1.130.2, 1.135.5, 1.137.1, etc.
110. *ṚV* 1.28.6; *AV* 9.6.15, 10.9.26, 11.3.3; *ŚB* 1.1.1.22.

purified through an woollen sieve[111] or that of skin/cow-hide.[112] *Soma* was normally used unmixed. Later on this practice was dropped and some admixtures were used to make the drink pungent. The expression *tryāśir* (*R̥V* 5.27.5) proves that at least three types of admixtures were used, viz., *yavāśir* (*R̥V* 1.187.9, 2.29.1, 3.42.7); *gavāśir* (*R̥V* 1.137.1, 2.41.3) and *dadhyāśir* (*R̥V* 1.5.5, 5.57.2). Besides these two other names *rasāśir* (*R̥V* 3.48.1) and *sūda* (*R̥V* 7.36.3) have been traced in the same context. Probably they were some form of milk. Sometimes honey was used as taste-maker of *soma*.[113] On some special occasion *surā*[114] was mingled to it.

Owing to the difficulty of obtaining actual *soma* plant several substitutes were used.[115] By nature *soma* was opposed to *surā*. This difference has been mentioned in a clear language, in the *ŚB*.[116] Drinking of *soma* was almost compulsory for brāhmaṇas (*TS* 2.1.5.5; *AB* 7.29). Interruption of drinking *soma* for three generations continuously was considered a serious offence for brāhmaṇas. In that case an expiatory rite has been prescribed.[117]

In contrast to *soma*, a ritual drink, there was *surā*, use of which was a common practice of people since the time of *R̥V*;[118] though references are there on both sides to the approval[119] of, and denouncement[120] against, its use.

111. *R̥V* 2.26.1, 9.16.2, 9.86.11, etc.

112. *R̥V* 9.65.25, 9.66.29, 10.24.9, 10.116.4, etc.

113. *adha dhārayā madhvā pr̥cānastiro soma pavate adridugdhaḥ* ।
— *R̥V* 9.97.11.

114. *R̥V* 10.131.4-5; *ŚB* 12.7.3.8.

115. *ŚB* 5.10.1.1-6.

116. *satyaṁ śrīr jyotiḥ somo 'nr̥taṁ pāpmā tamaḥ surā* ।
— *ŚB* 5.1.2.10; cf. *MS* 2.4.2; *KS* 14.6.

117. *TS* 2.1.5.5-6.

118. *Passim* in the *R̥V* and the *AV*; *TS* 1.3.3.2; *ŚB* 12.7.3.8, etc.

119. *AB* 8.5; 8.8; *ŚB* 12.7.3.8, 12.7.3.12, 12.8.1.4.

120. *R̥V* 7.86.6, 8.2.12, 8.21.14; *MS* 1.11.6, 2.4.2, 2.4.1, etc.

Surā was a common name to mean intoxicating liquor. Different types of *surā* were prepared either from fermented grains[121] or from pounded meals of plants.[122] The *KŚS*[123] has given a detailed description of its preparation. Being opposed to *soma* it has been declared as the drink of ordinary people,[124] especially that of *sabhā*[125] and gave rise to the broils.[126] The kṣatriyas had no right to enjoy *soma*[127] but *surā* was allowed for them. In the Brāhmaṇa[128] texts *surā* has been declared as the essence of food and power, most probably that's because wine-drinking became a part of ritual in the king's coronation ceremony.[129] Its use in other sacrifices like Vājapeya[130] and Sautrāmaṇī[131] proves its popularity. But use of *surā* was strictly forbidden for brāhmaṇas.[132] Very often it has been associated with meat and dice and considered as an evil.[133] Now it is a remarkable point that the *madya*, the most common term for wine, appears frequently but denotes wine once only (*CU* 5.11.5).

---

121. Mahīdhara on *VS* 19.1.
122. Mahī on *VS* 19.14.
123. *KŚS* 19.1.20-27.
124. *etan manuṣyāṇāṁ yat surā* I — *TB* 1.3.3.3.
125. *ṚV* 7.86.6; *AV* 14.1.35-36, 15.9.1-2, etc.
126. *na sa svo dakṣo varuṇadhrutiḥ sā surā manyur vibhīdako acittiḥ* I — *ṚV* 7.86.6.
127. *indrasya aṇu vṛyddhiṁ kṣatraṁ somapīthena vyardhatāpīndraḥ somapītho-'bhavat . . . tad vṛyddhamevādyāpi kṣatraṁ somapīthena* — *AB* 7.2.
128. (i) *atha yat surā bhavati kṣatrarūpaṁ tadatho annasya rasaḥ* I — *AB* 8.8.

     (ii) *sā surā 'bhavadannasya rasaḥ* — *ŚB* 12.7.3.8.
129. *atha surākaṁsaṁ hasta ādadhāti* I — *AB* 8.8.
130. *ŚB* 5.5.4.12-22.
131. *ŚB* 12.7.1.1, 12.7.3.5, 12.8.1.16.
132. *tasmād brāhmaṇaḥ surāṁ na pibet* — *MS* 2.4.2.
133. *yathā māṁsaṁ yathāsurā yathā 'kṣā adhidevane* I — *AV* 6.70.1; cf. *AV* 14.1.35-36, 15.9.1-2.

Besides these *soma* and *surā*, use of some other drinks including spirituous ones, e.g., *kīlāla, māsara, parisrut* were known to the people. These were various forms of beverages. Among them *kīlāla* was prepared from fermented rice[134] or some other grains. The expression *kīlālāya surākāraḥ* (*VS* 30.11; *TB* 3.4.9.1) the distiller to be staked to *kīlāla* indicates it must have been a form of liquor. Probably *kīlāla* was offered to the manes.

Māsara[135] was an article used for the guest-entertainment. Mahīdhara[136] in his commentary on the *VS* explained it as "a mixture prepared from pounded meal of rice, *śyāmāka* grain with grass and parched barley." Bhaṭṭabhāskara[137] suggested another recipe for the same purpose. Description of its preparation in various ways proves its popularity.

Parisrut[138] was the name of a household beverage. According to Mahīdhara it was prepared from the essence of flowers.[139] According to the *ŚB* (5.1.2.14) it had a contrast to both the *soma* and *surā*.

Naiṣa somo na surā yat parisrut (*ŚB* 5.1.2.14). Sāyaṇācārya[140] has tried to clarify this difference — *surā* was prepared from matured shoots of rice, etc., whereas *parisrut* from those which were not ripe. Western scholars consider it as a kind of liquor (*SBE* tr. Eggeling 41, p. 9).

---

134. *kīlālaḥ annasambandhi rasaḥ* I — Mahī on *VS* 3.43.

135. *ātithyarūpaṁ māsaram* . . . — *VS* 19.14.

136. *śaṣpa-tokma-lāja-nagnahucūrṇaiḥ saṁsargo māsaram* I
— Mahī on *VS* 19.1, 19.14, etc.

137. *māsaraṁ takramiśritaṁ sūkṣma yavacūrṇam* I — Bhaṭṭa on *TB* 2.6.11.3.

138. *AV* 3.12.7, 20.127.9; *MS* 3.11.2; *VS* 19.15, 20.15, 20.63.

139. *pariśrutaṁ bahantīḥ puṣpebhyo niḥsṛtam sāram* I — Mahī on *VS* 2.34.

140. *loke hi surā tatsādhanabhūtaiḥ paripakvadravyaiḥ kriyate, atra tu surāsādhanāya paryāptapākaiḥ śaṣpairniṣpanno rasaḥ parisrudityucyate* I
— Sā on *ŚB* 5.1.2.14.

Food Prescribed on Sacrificial Occasions

Now arises a question, which would be considered as food-items during sacrifice? Should the sacrificer fast totally during sacrifice or he would be allowed to take something ?

According to the *KŚS* (2.1.13) this question arises regarding the evening-meal of the sacrificer (just before the day of new-moon rite) which he was allowed to take after the completion of his regular fire-rite. Generally total fasting was preferred. Both the *TS* (1.6.7.3) and the *ŚB* (1.1.1.9) have stated, "if he can fast totally Manes would be his divinity."[141] But if that is not possible he may take something so that even after eating, it would be considered as not eaten.[142] The *TS*[143] has allowed him to drink water. With special reference to Manu men are permitted to drink thrice in the morning, midday and in the evening.[144] The article would vary according to the caste of the sacrificer; milk would be proper for brāhmaṇas, barley gruel for kṣatriyas and clotted curds for the vaiśyas.[145] The *PB*[146] has prescribed to take clarified butter on sacrificial occasion. The *ŚB*[147] has permitted eating of forest plants of which no offering is made.

In the context of Agnihotra the *AB* has instructed,

sāyaṁ prātar juhvati, sāyaṁ prātar vrataṁ prayacchanti
— *AB* 3.40

---

141. *yad anāśvānupavaset pitṛdevatyaḥ syāt* — *TS* 1.6.7.3.; cf. *ŚB* 1.1.1.9.
142. *sa yadevāśitamanaśitaṁ tadaśnīyāt* — *ŚB loc. cit.*
143. *āpo'śnāti tannaivāśitaṁ naivānaśitam* — *TS loc. cit.*
144. *trivrato vai manur āsīt . . . prātarmadhyandine sāyam tan manor vratam āsīt* — *TS* 6.2.5.3-4.
145. *yavāgu rājanyasya vratam . . . āmikṣā vaiśyasya . . . payo brāhmaṇasya. . .* — *TS* 6.2.5.3-4.
146. *ghṛtavrato bhavati* — *PB* 18.2.5.
147. *yasya vai havir na gṛhṇanti tad aśitam anaśitam* — *ŚB loc. cit.*

The sacrificer should offer the rite in the evening and in the morning, and he should partake the remnants of oblation after the completion of rite. On the occasion of coronation ceremony a different sacrificial drink has been prescribed for the sacrificer according to his caste, i.e., *soma* for brāhmaṇas, curds for vaiśyas, water for śūdras, while for the kṣatriya sacrificer juice of the fruits and roots of *nyagrodha, udumbara, plakṣa* and *aśvattha* has been prescribed.[148]

First Food to the Child

As regards the first food of the child Sūtra literature has furnished some information.

According to the *ŚGS* (1.24.13), 'in the *jātakarman* rite a father should give his male baby the mixture of butter, milk, curds, honey and water or that of flour of rice and barley thrice from a golden vessel.

The *ĀGS* (1.15.1) has prescribed that first feeding of the child should be with butter and honey from a golden spoon obviously by the father.

In the context of *annaprāśana* rite, the *AV*[149] has prescribed for the baby to use *vrīhi, yava, tila* and *māṣa*. In the later ages Sūtra literature has sanctioned the use of some more things for the same purpose. With a desire to have baby's nourishment the father made him (the son) to eat goat's flesh, mixed with curds, honey and ghee. If the baby's splendour was intended, in that case flesh of partridge and boiled rice were given (*ĀGS* 1.16.1-5). Pāraskara, Hiraṇyakeśin, etc., have prescribed the use of fish, flesh of Bhāradvājī bird, Partridge, Kṛkasa, Āṭi, etc., curds, honey, ghee and boiled rice for the same purpose (*PGS* 1.19.7-13; *GSH* 1.5.2-3).

---

148. *AB* 7.29-32.

149. *vrīhimattaṁ yavamattamatho māṣamathotilam* — *AV* 6.140.2.

Manners Concerning Food

It is interesting to observe that even in that ancient age people maintained several manners concerning food at the time of serving and dining as well, e.g., the *AB* has instructed one to offer the first drink to the king — *rājño vai pūrva peyam* — (*AB* 3.37).

In the context of *ātithyeṣṭi* cooking of bull or goat has been mentioned in the Brāhmaṇa texts in honour of esteemed guest like king or a brāhmaṇa.[150]

The Yajurvedic Saṁhitā[151] and Brāhmaṇas have advised to serve the food from right side and to take it also with the right hand. The *ŚB* has mentioned some special practices, e.g., a person willing to get a vigorous son, should not eat in his wife's presence[152] or women should eat apart from men,[153] etc.

Restrictions and Prohibitions on the Use of Food

With reference to the context of manners concerning food, Vedic literature has put forth some restrictions and prohibitions also. We may divide these prohibitions into two/three groups, e.g.:

(i) prohibitions regarding food items,

(ii) that, regarding persons, whose food is not permitted, and

(iii) places, where one must not take any food.

---

150. *atha yasmād ātithyaṁ nāma . . . rājñe brāhmaṇāya vā mahokṣaṁ mahājaṁ vā pacet* I — *ŚB* 3.4.1.2; *AB* 1.15.

151. (i) *dakṣiṇato vā'nnasyaopacāraḥ* I — *ŚB* 9.3.4.11.
(ii) *dakṣiṇenannam adyate . . .*
— *TS* 5.3.3.2-3; cf. *MS* 3.2.10; *KS* 20.12-13, etc.

152. *tajjāyāyā ante nāśnīyāt, vīryavān hā'smājjāyate* I
viryavantam u ha, sa janayati yasya ante nāśnāti II — *ŚB* 10.5.2.9.

153. *tasmād imā mānuṣyaḥ striyas tira'ivaiva puṁso jighatsanti*
— *ŚB* 1.9.2.12.

The *AV* (9.6.39) has prohibited the use of any delicious item like milk or meat in the presence of a *śrotriya* guest. Cow-slaughter was permissible for the purpose of food, but a brāhmaṇa's cow should never be slaughtered even for the sake of food.[154] According to the *TS*, enjoyment of meat was prohibited during sacrifice. In the context of Darśapūrṇamāsa rite the *ŚB* has stated :

aparāhṇe dīkṣeta, purā . . . yat kāmayeta tadaśnīyāt
— *ŚB* 3.1.2.1

From this sentence it appears that before initiation the sacrificer could enjoy any food. But after the rite of initiation restrictions were imposed on his food. Again with reference to the piling of fire the *ŚB*[155] has specifically prohibited the *agnicit* (sacrificer who has arranged sacrificial fire) to enjoy the flesh of any bird. The use of animals like *kiṁpuruṣa, gauramṛga, gavaya* and *uṣṭra* (which owe their origin due to the loss of sacrificial part of a higher species of the same class) as food, has been prohibited in the *AB*.[156*] In the context of Vājapeya sacrifice, the *ŚB*[157] has put forth a prohibition on the use of foodstuffs offered at the sacrifice for the sacrificer so long as he lives.

Normally use of improper and impure food makes a man polluted. Similarly foodstuffs given by a śūdra or any other low caste was considered forbidden. But reference to Bāmadeva's cooking of dog's entrails indicates that in the time of distress when people's main concern was to survive

154. *AV* 5.18.1-4, 5.18.7, etc.

155. *na bayaso 'gnicid aśnīyāt* . . . — *ŚB* 10.1.4.13.

156. *ta eta utkrāntamedhā amedhyā paśavastasmād eteṣāṁ nāśnīyāt* . . .
— *AB* 2.8.

* According to the *ĀpDS* (1.1.2.23) students were not entitled to consume meat.

157. *saptadaśānnāni sambharanti, saptadaśa prajāpatiriti badantas tad u tathā na kuryāt . . . tasya nā 'śnīyāt yāvajjīvaṁ* . . . — *ŚB* 5.2.2.3-4.

somehow, then consumption of any food material, even dog's flesh, was permissible.[158] Not only that, the story of Uṣasti Cākrāyaṇa (narrated in the *CU*) proves that any censurable act like ort-eating of a low caste was not condemnable.[159] But it should be noted here, even at that time those should not be taken in a great quantity, but only so much as to sustain one's life. That's because Uṣasti Cākrāyaṇa ate up orts of an elephant-owner but could not drink his left-off water because of its easy availability.[160]

As regards prohibition on the drinks we find that wine drinking was strictly prohibited for brāhmaṇas.[161] The *AB*[162] informed us that during the sacrifice drinks were prescribed to the people according to their caste, violation of which caused suffering and misery.

As regards the prohibition on the use of food materials (which people had to follow) the Sūtra texts have given a clear list of forbidden flesh, milk and other food materials. According to this prohibition people could not use the flesh of dog, village pigs and cocks, carnivorous animals and birds, one hoofed animals, camels, gayals, herons of *plava* or *śakaṭavila* species, cranes, swans, Brāhmaṇī ducks and falcons.[163] Mushroom also was considered improper as food article.[164] Among fishes, *ceṭa*, snake-headed fish, misshaped ones, alligators were not to be taken.[165] Cow milk and that (milk) of

158. *avartyā śuna āntrāṇi pece* — *ṚV* 4.18.13.

159. *CU* 1.10.1-4.

160. *hantānupānamiti* । *ucchiṣṭam vai me pītam syāditi hovāca* । *na svidete-'pyucchiṣṭā iti* । *na vā ajīviṣyam imam akhādanniti hovāca, kāmo me udapānam iti* । — *CU* 1.10.3-4.

161. *tasmād brāhmaṇo surāṁ na pibet* — *MS* 2.4.2.

162. *AB* 7.29-30.

163. *ĀpDS* 1.5.17.28-29, 32-39; *GDS* 17.27-31; *BDS* 1.5.12.1-7.

164. *ĀpDS* 1.5.17.28; *GDS* 17.32-33.

165. *ĀpDS* 1.5.17.38-39; *GDS* 17.36; *BDS* 1.5.12.18.

other animals (e.g., sheep, goat, etc.) during first ten days after their calving was considered improper and forbidden.[166] Apart from that people could not use milk of that cow whose calf died, or that of the animal from whose udders milk always flows spontaneously.[167] According to *ĀpDS* use of butter, butter milk, oil cake, honey was to be avoided especially during vows.[168] Meat also (even lawful) was not to be taken during sacrificial performances.

Besides the forbidden food articles the Sūtra has provided a list of forbidden persons whose food people should not accept (normally). The food given by a śūdra or eunuchs was not acceptable.[169] The persons living on trades, acting, obeying a śūdra, theft, practice of medicine, cattle-rearing, were declared forbidden persons. Again artisans, bards, servants, usurers, artists (singer/dancer) were declared denounced.[170] The brāhmaṇas were forbidden to follow these professions and to take the food of these persons, violation of which caused loss of status and caste.[171]

---

166. *ĀpDS* 1.5.17.22-24; *GDS* 17.22-24; *BDS* 1.5.12.9.
167. *GDS* 17.25-26; *BDS* 1.5.12-10.
168. *ĀpDS* 1.5.17.14-20.
169. *ĀpDS* 1.5.17.22, 1.6.19.27.
170. *ĀpDS* 1.6.19.1ff, 1.6.19.10, 14-15, 1.6.18.19-33.
171. *yassamarghamr̥ṇaṁ gr̥hya mahārghaṁyaḥ prayojayet* ।
sa vai vārdhuṣiko nāma sarvadharmeṣu garhitaḥ ॥
vr̥ddhiṁ ca bhrūṇahatyāṁ ca tulayā samatolayat ।
atiṣṭhat bhrūṇahā koṭyāṁ vārdhuṣissamakampateti ॥
gorakṣakān vāṇijakān tathā kārukuṣīlakān ।
preṣyāṇ vārdhuṣikāṁścaiva viprāh śūdravad ācaret ॥
— *BDS* 1.5.10.24-25.

2

Dress Arrangement

THE second basic requirement of everyday life is clothing for one's protection against cold and maintenance of decency in outward appearance. References to various types of dress,[1] their parts,[2] materials,[3] and use of different dresses on different occasions[4] throughout Vedic literature indicate that even in that remote past people were fond of splendid garments and decorations and they knew that proper dress makes a man perfect outwardly.[5]

Stitching of coats[6] and sewn garments[7] have been mentioned in several places, which make us suppose that use

---

1. (*vāsas*) *ṚV* 1.95.7, 1.140.2, 3.39.2, etc.; *AV* 5.1.3, *TS* 1.5.2.4.
   (*adhīvāsa*) *ṚV* 1.140.9, 8.26.16; *AB* 1.3; *ŚB* 5.4.3.3, etc.
   (*paridhāna*) *AV* 8.2.16; *ŚA* 11.4; *BU* 6.1.10.
   (*nīvi*) *AV* 8.2.16; *TS* 6.1.1.3.
   (*drāpi*) *ṚV* 1.25.13, 9.100.9; *AV* 5.7.10, etc.
   (*varma*) *AV* 19.58.4.
2. *ṚV* 3.53.2, 10.18.11; *AV* 14.2.61; *TS* 6.1.1.3; *PB* 17.1.15, etc.
3. (cotton — *tantu*) *AV* 2.1.5; *ŚB* 3.1.2.18; (Linen): *AV* 18.4.37; *TS* 6.1.1.3-4; *KS* 23.1, etc.
   (Silk): *TS* 2.4.11.6; *ŚB* 5.2.1.21; (Wool): *ṚV* 10.26.6, 10.85.29; *JUB* 1.38.4, etc.
4. *ṚV* 10.85.6, 10.85.34; *AV* 2.13.5; *ŚB* 3.1.2.13, 5.2.1.18, etc.
5. *rūpaṁ vā etat puruṣasya yat vāsaḥ* — *ŚB* 13.4.1.15.
6. *brajaṁ kṛṇudhvaṁ sa hi vo nṛpāṇo varmasīvyadhvaṁ bahulā pṛthūni . . .* — *AV* 19.58.4.
7. *. . . punarniṣkṛto ratho dakṣiṇā punar utsyūtaṁ vāsaḥ* — *TS* 1.5.2.4.

of sewn garments was known. Home-woven[8] garments also were in use.

Dress: As a General Term

In the range of Vedic literature, so many names of garments have been recorded, viz., *vastra, vasana, vāsas, adhivastra/ adhīvāsa, nīvi, paridhāna, atka, drāpi, varma, peśas, vādhūya, kavaca,* etc. Among them the terms *vastra, vasana* and *vāsas* were used to mean dress in general[9] though somewhere *vāsas* has been used in its narrower sense, i.e., an undergarment.[10]

Varieties of Dress

From the references to the above-cited names, it appears that people used to put on a pair of garments, i.e., a lower[11] (*nīvi*) and an upper one[12] (*adhīvāsa*). *Paridhāna*[13] occurring in the *AV* for the first time, appears to be another dress name. From the textual context, its nature has not been clarified. However, according to the commentator Sāyaṇācārya, *paridhāna* has been explained as *upari ācchādanīyaṁ vastra,*[14] i.e., an outer garment. The *kausumbhaparidhāna* "saffron dyed garment" (*ŚĀ* 11.4) helps us to infer that at that time technique of dying clothes was known to the people. The *AB,*[15] in the context of sacrificer's

8. *amotaṁ vāso dadyād hiraṇyam api dakṣiṇām* — *AV* 9.5.14.
9. *Ṛ̥V* 1.95.7, 1.140.1, 7.77.2; *AV* 7.37.1, etc.
10. *AV* 8.2.16, 14.2.50; *AB* 1.3.
11. (i) *yat te vāsaḥ paridhānaṁ yā nīviṁ kṛṇuṣe tvam* — *AV* 8.2.16.
    (ii) *tasyāgre vanaspate nīviṁ kṛṇuṣva mā vayaṁ riṣāma* — *AV* 14.2.50.
12. *Ṛ̥V* 1.140.9, 8.26.13, 10.5.4; *AB* 1.3; *ŚB* 13.2.8.1, 13.5.2.1.
13. *AV* 8.2.16; *ŚĀ* 11.4; *BU* 6.1.10.
14. *he bālaka! te tava paridhānam upari ācchādanīyaṁ vāso 'sti . . .* — Sā on *AV* 8.2.16.
15. *vāsasā prorṇuvanti, ulbaṁ vā etad dīkṣitasya yad vāsaḥ . . . kṛṣṇājinam uttaraṁ bhavati . . .* — *AB* 1.3.

initiation refers to the use of black antelope-skin as the upper garment on ritual occasion.

The names like *vātapāna*,[16] *pravara/prāvāra*[17] referred to in late Vedic literature suggest that at that period people were habituated to use additional garment as a scarf for protection against wind.

Further, *yajñopavīta* formed a regular part of garment, to be worn by the male candidates of three upper castes.[18] From the late Vedic Saṁhitā[19] and Brāhmaṇas we have been informed that the wearing style of sacrificial thread varied according to Gods, Fathers and men: *nivītaṁ manuṣyāṇāṁ prācīnāvītaṁ pitṝṇām upavītaṁ devānāṁ* (*TS* 2.5.11.1). *Nivīta*, to wear the thread round the neck was human style, *prācīnāvita* to wear it over the right shoulder was meant for *pitṛ*s and *upavīta* to wear over the left shoulder was meant for gods. It is interesting to note that B.G. Tilak[20] in his work explained *nivīta*, *upavīta* and *prācīnāvīta* as names of garments and not as wearing style of sacrificial thread. In the context of *dīkṣaṇīyeṣṭi* the *TS*[21] prescribes the use of girdle made of *śara* grass for the sacrificer and yoke for his wife. The *ŚB*[22] informs that girdle of the consecrated sacrificer should be made of hemp. It should

16. *vāsasā dīkṣayati saumyaṁ vai kṣaumaṁ . . . vāyor vātapānam . . .* — *TS* 6.1.1.6.
17. *vijñāyate hāsti hiraṇyasyāpāttaṁ go aśvānāṁ dāsīnāṁ prāvārāṇāṁ paridhānasya . . .* — *BU* 6.2.7.
18. *TS* 2.5.11.1; *VS* 16.17; *ŚB* 2.4.2.2, 2.4.2.9, 12.5.1.6.
19. *MS* 2.9.3; *KS* 17.12; *KapKS* 27.3; *TS* 2.5.11.1; *VS* 16.17-20; *ŚB* 2.4.2.2, 2.4.2.9; *TB* 2.4.6.6; *TĀ* 2.1.
20. B.G. Tilak, *Orion*, p. 146.
21. *mekhalayā yajamānaṁ dīkṣayati yoktreṇa patnīm . . .* — *TS* 6.1.3.5; cf. *AV* 6.133.1; *MS* 3.6.7; *KS* 23.4, etc.
22. *atha mekhalāṁ pariharate . . . sā vai śāṇī bhavati . . . sā vai trivṛt bhavati . . . muñjavalśenānvastā bhavati . . . virakṣatāyai stukāsargaṁ sṛṣṭā bhavati* । *sā yat pralasa visṛṣṭā syāt . . . mānuṣī syāt* । *yadvapalasavisṛṣṭā syāt pitṛdevatyaṁ syāt* — *ŚB* 3.2.1.10-13.

be a triple cord, intertwined with a reed of *muñja*-grass and plaited after the manner of a braid of hair. If it were twisted sun-wise it would be human and if it were twisted contrary to the course of sun, it would be sacred to the Fathers. According to the Sūtra literature[23] material of this girdle varied from caste to caste. From the *TĀ*,[24] we came to know antelope-skin also was used as sacred cord.

Apart from this, several other names have been met with, e.g., *atka*,[25] *drāpi*,[26] *varma*,[27] etc., from which use of several types of coats of mail/mantle and corselets, has been indicated. But the exact material, from which it was made, is uncertain. However, reference to the sewing of the same[28] may be reckoned in favour of cloth-made corselets. But the description of corselets made of *ayas, loha, rajata* and *hiraṇya* (*JUB* 4.1.3-6) creates a puzzle for us, regarding its material. The terms like *kavaca, kavaca-pāśa* (strap of corselet) mentioned in the *AV*[29]

---

23. *teṣāṁ mekhalā mauñjī brāhmaṇasya dhanurjyā kṣatriyasyābī vaiśyasya* —*ĀGS* 1.19.12; *BhGS* 1.2.

24. *ajinaṁ vāso vā dakṣiṇata upavīya dakṣiṇaṁ bāhum uddharate 'vadhatte savyam iti yajñopavītam — etad eva viparītaṁ prācināvītaṁ saṁvītaṁ mānuṣāṇām* — *TĀ* 2.1.

25. (*atka*): *ṚV* 1.95.7, 1.122.2, 2.35.14, 4.18.5, 5.55.6, 5.74.5, 6.29.3, 8.41.7, 9.101.14, 9.107.3, 10.123.7, etc.

26. (*drāpi*) *ṚV* 1.25.13, 1.116.10, 4.53.2, 9.86.14, 9.100.9; *AV* 5.7.10, 13.3.1, etc.

27. (*varma*) *ṚV* 1.31.15, 10.101.8; *AV* 19.58.4; *JUB* 4.1.3-6, etc.

28. (i) *tvam agne prayata dakṣiṇaṁ naraṁ*
varmeva syūtaṁ paripāsi viśvataḥ
— *ṚV* 1.31.15.

(ii) *brajaṁ kṛṇudhvaṁ sa hi vo nṛpāṇo*
varma sīvyadhvaṁ bahulā pṛthūni
— *ṚV* 10.101.8; cf. *AV* 19.58.4.

29. *yaśca kavacī yaścākavaco 'mitro yaścāśmani* ।
jyāpāśaiḥ kavacapāśaiḥ rajmanābhihataḥ śayām ॥
— *AV* 11.10.22; *AB* 7.29.2.

may be regarded as an indication of using another sort of mantle, which at the same time may mean armour also.

In the late Vedic literature some other dress names have been found, e.g., *dūrśa*[30] and *barāsī*, exact nature of which is questionable. However, some western scholars interpret the term *dūrśa* as the garment of aborigins.[31] In the context of Daśapeya kratu the *PB*[32] mentions the name of *barāsī* to be given to the Neṣṭṛ. The commentator Sāyaṇācārya[33] has taken *barāsī* for a sort of coarse cloth.

Variety of Materials Used for Dress

At the time of discussing varieties of garments we find people knew the use of garments made of various materials, e.g., cotton, linen, silk, wool, etc. Even grass, feather and skin did not escape their notice as dress materials.

It is a remarkable point that there is hardly any direct reference to cotton-made dress. Still the word *tantu*[34] has been mentioned frequently, from which it may be conjectured that cotton-made dresses were used. References to the use of silken[35] and linen[36] garments have been traced in the Brāhmaṇas,

---

30. (i) *paratairastvā paryakrīṇan dūrśebhir ajinairuta* ।
prakrīrasi tvam oṣadhe 'bhri khāte na svarūpaḥ ॥
— *AV* 4.7.6.

(ii) *ye kukundhā kukurābhāḥ kṛtīr dūrśāni vibhrati* ।
— *AV* 8.6.11.

31. Weber, *Indische Studien* 18.29 referred by Macdonell & Keith, VI, I, p. 372.

32. *barāsī neṣṭuranulambeva hyeṣā hotrā* — *PB* 18.9.16; cf. *KS* 15.4.

33. *kārpāsāpekṣayā hīnavṛkṣatvacā nirmitā seyaṁ barāsī*
— Sā on *PB* 18.9.16.

34. *AV* 2.1.5, 14.2.1, 15.3.6.

35. *TS* 2.4.11.6; *ŚB* 5.2.1.21.

36. *AV* 18.4.37; *TS* 6.1.1.4-4; *KS* 23.1.

especially in the context of the coronation ceremony. Woollen garments also were known to the people from the early Vedic period.[37]

The *TS*[38] in the context of horse-sacrifice refers to the feather garments, which makes us suppose that use of feather garments was not unknown, though its use was very rare. Garment made of grass was used by the sacrificer's wife on ritual occasion only.[39]

From the description of gods, clad in animal-skin[40] and existence of *ajina-sandha*[41] — a hide-dresser, as a separate professional, we are to guess that the use of skin as garment was prevalent. Generally deer skin was used for this purpose.[42] But sheep skin also has been mentioned for the same purpose. According to the *ŚB*,[43] on a special ritual occasion the sacrificer should give everything (even his own dress) to the priest and should clad himself in sheep skin.

Use of Different Dresses on Different Occasions

Women dancers used to wear beautifully embroidered

---

37. *Ṛ̥V* 10.26.6, 10.85.29; *JUB* 1.38.4.
38. *suparṇaṁ vaste mṛgo 'syādanto gīrbhiḥ sannaddhā patati prasūtā* — *TS* 4.6.6.4.
39. *atha neṣṭā patnīm udāneṣyan kauśaṁ vāśaḥ paridhāpayati ।*
    kauśaṁ vā caṇḍātakam antaraṁ dīkṣitavasanāt . . . — *ŚB* 5.2.1.8.
40. *Ṛ̥V* 1.166.10, 8.90.6; *AV* 5.21.7; *TS* 1.8.6.2, 4.5.10.4; *VS* 3.61, etc.
41. *ṛbhubhyo 'jinasandham* — *VS* 30.15; *TB* 3.4.13.1.
42. *Ṛ̥V* 1.166.10; *AV* 5.21.7.
43. *purāhitā hāsya bhavanti । mukha āhitāḥ । tasmād u tat sarvaṁ dattvā ajinavāsī bhavati* — *ŚB* 3.9.1.12.
    — *tasmād u tasmādeva kāraṇāt sarvaṁ brāhmaṇebhyo dattvā ajinavāsī ajinam ācchādya sañcarati* — Sā on *ŚB* 3.9.1.12.

garments.[44] According to the information of the *AB*,[45] it appears that embroidered clothes were in use. Use of *vādhūya*, a special bridal costume was known from the Ṛgvedic[46] age. In the context of the Vājapeya and the Rājasūya sacrifices, the *ŚB*[47] refers to a set of ritual-dress, viz., *tārpya* "a silken undergarment," *adhīvāsa* "an overgarment," *uṣṇīṣa* "turban" and *pāṇḍva* "an uncoloured woollen garment" to be used by the king.

Vrātya's special dress has been mentioned explicitly in the *PB*.[48] Some of them wore black cloth, bordered with black and white goat-skin, while others used red-bordered cloth, a turban on head, silver necklace round their neck and shoes in feet. They used black and white leather belt and carried whip and bow also in their hand.

The uniform of a student has been discussed with all the minute specifications in the Sūtra[49] texts. That uniform consisted of an animal skin (*ajina*), a piece of cloth (*vāsas*), a girdle (*mekhalā*) and a staff (*daṇḍa*). This uniform varied according to the caste of the student. Normally the brāhmaṇa

---

44. *ṚV* 1.92.4-5, 2.3.6, 4.36.7, 7.34.11, 7.42.1, 10.1.6; *VS* 19.62, 19-89, 20.40, 28.29, 30.9, etc.

45. *peśā vā utkhānāṁ yannividaḥ* । *tad yad purastādukthānām prātaḥ savane dhīyante yathaiva pravayaṇataḥ peśaḥ kuryāt tādṛk tat yanmadhyato madhyandine dhīyante yathaiva madhyataḥ peśaḥ kuryāt tādṛk tat* । *tadyadantato stṛtīyasavane dhīyante yathaivāva prajjanato peśaḥ kuryāt tādṛk tat* — *AB* 3.10.

46. *sūryāṁ yo brahmā vidyāt sa idvādhūyam arhati* — *ṚV* 10.85.34.

47. *athainaṁ vāsāṁsi paridhāpayati* । *tattārpyam iti vāso bhavati . . . athainaṁ pāṇḍvam paridhāpayati . . . athadhīvāsaṁ pratimuñcati . . . athoṣṇīṣaṁ saṁhṛtya . . .* — *ŚB* 5.3.5.20-23.

48. *uṣṇīṣañca pratodaśca jyāhroḍaśca vipathaśca phalakāstīrṇaḥ kṛṣṇaśaṁ vāsaḥ kṛṣṇavalakṣe ajine rajato niṣkastad gṛhapateḥ, valūkāntāni dāmatūṣāṇītareṣāṁ dve dve dāmanī dve dve upānahau dvisaṁhi-tānyajināni,* —*PB*17.1.14-15.

49. *ĀGS* 1.19.8-13; *ŚGS* 2.1.2, 2.1.4-5; *PGS* 2.5.17-27; *GGS* 2.10.7-11, etc.

boy wore black antelope skin (*aiṇeyam ajinam*), kṣatriya wore that of a spotted deer (*rauravam*) and vaiśya used the skin of goat or cow (*ājaṁ gavyaṁ vā*[50]). The *Kāṭhaka Gṛhya-Sūtra* (41.13) has prescribed tiger skin for the kṣatriya, while the *PGS*[51] opined that, on the non-availability of prescribed particular skin, students of all castes could use cow-hide as their uniform.

The colour of their cloth has been mentioned in the *ĀGS*.[52] Reddish yellow garment (*kāṣāyaṁ*) was meant for the brāhmaṇa boys, kṣatriyas' garment was dyed with madder (*māñjiṣṭha*), vaiśyas' dress was yellow (*pīta*). In the *PGS*[53] the material of their garment has been recorded; e.g., hemp (*śaṇa*), linen (*kṣauma*) and woollen clothes were used by brāhmaṇa, kṣatriya and vaiśya *brahmacārins* respectively.

Girdles (*mekhalā*) also varied according to the caste of the candidate. Brāhmaṇa boys used girdle made of *muñja*-grass, kṣatriyas used that of bow-string (*jyā*) and vaiśyas wore that of wool.[54]

Staffs used by students of three castes were made of *palāśa*, *udumbara* and *bilva* woods respectively. Its size also varied from caste to caste. Brāhmaṇa's staff was as long as his hair, that for kṣatriya's was up to his forehead and vaiśya's staff was up to his breast.[55]

---

50. *BhGS* 1.1; *ĀGS* 1.19.8; *ŚGS* 2.1.2; *PGS* 2.5.17-19; *BGS* 2.5.16; *GSH* 1.1.5; *GGS* 2.10.8, etc.

51. *sarveṣāṁ vā gavyam asati pradhānatvāt* — *PGS* 2.5.20.

52. *yadi vāsāṁsi vasīran raktāni vasīran* ı *kāṣāyaṁ brāhmaṇo* ı *māñjisṭhaṁ kṣātriyo hāridraṁ vaiśyaḥ* ı — *ĀGS* 1.19.9.

53. *vāsāṁsi śāṇa kṣaumāvikāni* — PGS 2.5.16.

54. *teṣāṁ mekhalāḥ* ı *mauñjī brāhmaṇasya dhanurjyāṁ kṣatriyasya āvī vaiśyasya* — *ĀGS* 1.19.10-11.

55. *teṣaṁ daṇḍāḥ* ı *pālāśaṁ brāhmaṇasya audumbara kṣātriyasya bailvo vaiśyasya* ı *keśasaṁmito brāhmaṇasya, lalāṭasaṁmito kṣatriyasya, prāṇasaṁmito vaiśyasya* — *ĀGS* 1.19.13.

According to the *ŚB*,[56] the sacrificer at the time of his initiation should use a new garment. If, to put on new dress is not possible, a separate pure garment (which has not been washed in some sharp cleansing substance) may be worn. The same one may be used for the purpose of regular worship also, but only after taking a bath.

Turban : Generally turban was used by men.[57] In this connection we may cite here the example of Indrāṇī's variegated turban (*VS* 38.3) which indicates that women also used some sort of head-band (may not be turban exactly), especially on ritual occasions. While glorifying the Lord Ekavrātya the *AV* (15.2.1) has described the day-light as His turban (*ahar uṣṇīṣam*). From the *PB* (17.1.14-15) also we have been informed that turban formed a regular part of Vrātyas' dress. At the coronation ceremony turban was worn by the king, as a token of his royal status.[58]

Shoes : Sandals/shoes made of boar skin were in use.[59] Sandals made of black antelope skin (*MS* 3.3.5; *KS* 21.7; *TS* 5.4.4.4) suggest that people preferred to use the sandals/slippers prepared out of deer skin. According to the *ŚB*[60] shoes were considered an invariable part of royal dress. The expression *daṇḍopānaha* (*KB* 3.3) indicates that use of sandal and staff was common in the Brāhmaṇa period. Shoes and umbrella have been mentioned in the list of things, which were given to the student before his *samāvartana* ceremony which

56. *atha vāsaḥ paridhatte . . . tadvā ahataṁ syāt, ayātayāmatāyai tadvā niṣpeṣṭavai brūyād yadevāsyātrāmedhyamākṛṇatti vā vayati vā tadasya medhyaṁ asaditi yadyadahataṁ syādadbhir abhyukṣen medhyam asadityatho yad idaṁ snātavasyaṁ nihitam apalyūlanakṛtaṁ bhavati tenohāpi dīkṣeta । tat paridhatte ।* — *ŚB* 3.1.2.13, 3.1.2.19.

57. *AB* 6.1; *ŚB* 3.3.2.3, 4.5.2.7.

58. *yat tārpyam ulbaṁ pāṇḍaraṁ nābhir uṣṇīṣaḥ . . .* *MS* 4.4.3; cf. *ŚB* 5.3.5.23.

59. *atha vārāhyā 'upānahā upamuñcate* — *ŚB* 5.4.3.19.

60. *āsandyā upānahā 'upamuñcate । upānadbhyām adhi yadasya yānaṁ bhavati ratho vā . . .* — *ŚB* 5.5.3.7.

clearly indicates that students were not entitled to use shoes and umbrella (especially during the period of studenthood).[61]

Ornaments

After clothings, now it will not be irrelevant to come to the point of ornaments. From the study of Vedic passages it is evident that both men and women were fond of beautification. Fashion of wearing ornaments was common to both of them. In the Vedic literature we find a large variety of ornaments, viz., *hiraṇya, añji, khādi, vṛṣakhādi, karṇaśobhanā, pravarta, niṣka, rukma, sraj, śiprā, nyocanī, prākāśa, manā, phaṇa*, etc. From this list, ornaments of (people's) daily decoration may be classified under some groups according to their placement on the body, e.g. :

(i) Ornaments for fore-arm/upper arm and feet,

(ii) Ear ornament,

(iii) Necklace or chains and breast plates, and

(iv) Head ornaments like tiara, diadem, etc.

In this connection at first we should mention that from the *ṚV* onwards some among the fore-cited names, e.g., *añji*,[62] *hiraṇya*,[63] *ānūka*,[64] appear to mean ornaments as general names, in some cases ornamentation[65] only.

As regards ornaments for hands, we see the only term *khādi* appears frequently in the *ṚV*.[66] It is interesting to note

61. *ŚGS* 3.1.9-11; *ĀGS* 3.8.14; *PGS* 2.6.30; *GGS* 3.4.26, etc.

62. *ṚV* 1.31.2, 1.36.13, 1.64.4, 1.85.1, 1.85.3, 1.166.9-10, 4.58.9, 5.57.5, 10.77.2.

63. *ṚV* 2.33.9, 10.75.8, 10.93.13; *AV* 7.99.1, 18.4.56; *VS* 28.31.

64. *uta tye ma mārutamaśvasya śoṇāḥ kratvām adhāso vidathasya rātau* ।
sahasrā me cyavatāno dadāna ānūkamaryo vapuṣe nārṣat ॥
— *ṚV* 5.33.9.

65. *ṚV* 1.85.1, 4.58.9, 7.56.6; *AV* 5.12.6, 6.22.1; *TS* 2.2.12.7, etc.

66. *ṚV* 1.166.9, 1.168.3, 2.34.2, 5.53.4, 5.58.2, 7.56.13, 10.38.1, etc.

here that the same term has been rendered variously in various places, somewhere as bracelet[67] which is an ornament of fore-arm, again somewhere as armlet,[68] to be worn on the upper arm or on the shoulder; or as anklet,[69] an ornament for feet. Some of the scholars have rendered it as gold ring only.[70] It is really difficult to ascertain its actual placement.

For the ears, *karṇaśobhanā*[71] may be mentioned. Besides this, *vṛṣa-khādi*[72] in the context of Marut's description and *pravarta*[73] in the description of Vrātyas' dress, suggest that several types of ear ornaments were used at that time. But the scholars are not unanimous regarding the exact nature of these items, e.g., *pravarta* has been rendered as circular ornament (*AV* tr. Griffith II, p. 150), whereas *vṛṣakhādi* has been translated as rings for strong men (*ṚV* tr. Griffith, I, p. 89), but they have thrown hardly any light about its nature. However, according to the commentator[74] both of these are ear ornaments.

Throughout Vedic literature *rukma* occurs frequently. As regards the clarification of its exact nature, our textbooks help very little and the same term has been rendered variously by scholars like Griffith, Wilson, etc., in different places, e.g.,

---

67. *ṚV* 5.53.4, 5.58.2; *ṚV* tr. Griffith I, p. 528.
68. *ṚV* 1.166.9, 1.168.3, 2.34.2, 7.56.13, 10.38.1; *ṚV* tr. Griffith I, p. 302.
69. *aṁseṣu vah ṛṣṭyaḥ patsu khādayo vakṣaḥsu rukmā maruto ratheśubhaḥ*
— *ṚV* 5.54.11.
70. (i) Zimmer, *Altindisches Leben*, p. 262, referred by Macdonell & Keith, VI, I, p. 216;
(ii) Muir, *Original Sanskrit Texts*, V, p. 149.
71. *uta naḥ karṇaśobhanā purūṇi dhṛṣṇavā bhara* । — *ṚV* 8.78.3.
72. *viśvavedaso rayibhiḥ samokaso saṁmiślās tavisībhir virapśinaḥ* ।
astāra iṣuṁ dadhire gabhastyor anantaśuṣmā vṛṣakhādayo namaḥ ॥
— *ṚV* 1.64.10.
73. *vijñānaṁ vāso 'haruṣṇīṣaṁ rātri keśāḥ haritau pravartau . . .*
— *AV* 15.2.1
74. *. . . 'tasmin pravartam avadadhāti 'itica* । *pravartaḥ karṇābharaṇaṁ kuṇḍalam* . . . Sā on *TS* 2.3.11.5 — (*TS* Bibl. Ind. Roer ed.)

breast plate,[75] goldchain,[76] pendant (*VS* 12.1), etc. Still, *rukma* in many places on account of its being associated with *vakṣas* appears to be a gold ornament to be worn on the breast.[77]

References to *niṣka*,[78] *sraj*,[79] etc., indicate use of various forms of necklace or gold chains at that time. From the example of *niṣka-kaṇṭhī āḍhya-duhitṛs* (*AB* 8.22) and *niṣkagrīva bṛhaduktha* (*ṚV* 5.19.3), etc., *niṣka* seems to be a gold ornament to be worn round the neck. But its exact form (whether a necklace or chain) is not clear. However, frequent occurrence proves its popularity throughout the ages. Description of Vrātyas wearing *rajata-niṣka* indicates use of silver necklace also was prevalent.[80] The *Kaṭhopaniṣad*[81] presents before us a doubtful name, i.e., *sṛṅkā* which has been interpreted as "multiformed variegated necklace" by the commentator Śaṅkarācārya.[82]

For the beautification of head and hair, there were several ornaments, use of which was prevalent from the Ṛgvedic age. They are namely *śiprā hiraṇyayī*,[83] *nyocanī*,[84] *tirīṭa*,[85] *kurīra*, *kumba*,

75. (*rukma*, as breast plate): *ṚV* 2.34.2, 5.53.4, 5.54.11, 5.55.1; *AV* 6.22.2.
76. (*rukma*, as goldchain): *ṚV* 1.64.4, 1.166.10.
77. *ṚV* 1.166.10, 5.54.11, 7.56.13, 7.57.3, 10.78.2; *AV* 6.22.2.
78. *niṣka*: *ṚV* 2.33.10, 5.19.3, 7.56.11, 8.47.15; *AV* 5.14.3, 5.17.14, 7.99.1, 19.57.5, 20.137.5; *AB* 8.22; *ŚB* 13.4.1.7, 13.4.1.11; *CU* 4.3.1-4; *JUB* 1.35.7-8.
79. *sraj*: *ṚV* 4.38.6, 5.53.4, 8.47.15, 8.56.3, 10.184.3; Śrī Sūkta-1; *AV* 1.14.1, 10.6.4; *TS* 1.8.18.1; *PB* 18.3.2, 18.7.6; *ŚB* 13.5.2.4, etc.
80. *kṛṣṇaśaṁ vāsaḥ kṛṣṇavalakṣe ajine rajato niṣkastad gṛhapateḥ* — *PB* 17.1.14.
81. *tavaiva nāmnā bhavitāyam agni sṛṅkāṁ cemām anekarūpāṁ gṛhāṇa* — *Kaṭha* 1.1.16.
82. *kiñca sṛṅkām śabdavatīṁ ratnamayīṁ mālām imām anekarūpāṁ victirāṁ gṛhāṇa* — Ś on *Kaṭha* 1.1.16.
83. *agnibharājaso vidyuto gabhastyoḥ śiprāḥ śīrṣasu vitatā hiranyayīh* ı — *ṚV* 5.54.11.
84. *raibhyāsīd anudeyī nārāśaṁsī nyocanī* ı — *ṚV* 10.85.6.
85. *rajatānt sahatām itaḥ klīvarūpāstirīṭinaḥ* ı — *AV* 8.6.7.

opaśa, etc. From the textual context it appears that these items were used as tiara/diadem or some form of head-band. Among them *nyocanī* and *kurīra* occurring in the marriage-hymn (*ṚV* 10.85.8) appear to be bridal ornaments. According to Geldner's interpretation the term *opaśa* means horn and when applied to Indra indicates diadem.[86] *Kurīra*,[87] *opaśa*, etc., appearing separately in the same verse applicable to Sinīvāli, seem to be various forms of head ornaments, used by girls for hair-dressing. But description of Maruts wearing golden tiara indicates head ornaments were equally popular among men.[88]

Apart from this, there are several other names, e.g., *manā*,[89] *phaṇa*,[90] *prākāśa*,[91] etc., which appear to be some form of ornament; but their specific nature has not been clear from the textual context. We are to remember here that more or less in case of every ornament there is scope of doubt to some extent.

Variety of Materials Used for Ornaments

From this discussion it is clear that both gold and silver ornaments were in use. Gold[92] ornaments have been mentioned frequently, from which people's preference towards gold ornaments may be assumed. The *ŚB*'s[93] remark "gold is a symbol of noble rank" lends support to this fact.

86. *yajña indram abardhayat yad bhūmiṁ vyāvartayat cakrāṇa opaśaṁ divi* ।
— *ṚV* 8.14.5.

87. *ṚV* 10.85.8; *AV* 6.138.1-3; *VS* 11.56; *ŚB* 6.5.1.10.

88. *ṚV* 2.34.2, 5.54.11, etc.

89. *āno bhara vyañjanaṁ gām aśvam abhyañjanam* ।
sa cā manā hiraṇyayā ॥ —*ṚV* 8.78.2.

90. *tāṁ pañcāśatānyapsarasā pratiyanti . . . śataṁ phaṇahastā* . . . — *Kauṣ* 1.4.

91. . . . *prākāśādhvaryave dadāti* । — *TS* 1.8.18.1.

92. *ṚV* 1.64.4, 1.166.10, 2.33.9-10, 2.34.2-3, 5.57.5-6, 5.58.2, 7.56.13, 7.57.3, 8.20.11, 10.75.8, 10.77.2, 10.78.2; *AV* 5.12.6, 6.22.1, 9.5.24-25; *VS* 12.1, 28.31; *TS* 2.2.12.7, 2.3.2.2; *AB* 8.22; *ŚB* 6.1.1.1-7, 13.4.1.7, etc.

93. *etaddhi kṣatrasya rūpaṁ yaddhiraṇyam* — *ŚB* 13.2-2.17.

Still, description of *suvarṇarajatasrajā lakṣmī* in the Śrī Sūkta (1) and that of Vrātyas wearing silver necklace, has made it clear that silver ornaments also were used.

Again, from references to the people wearing jewelleries,[94] prayer for gems and jewels,[95] presence of *maṇikāra* "the jeweller," as a separate professional (*VS* 30.7; *TB* 3.4.4.1) it can be safely stated that gems and jewelleries also served the purpose of ornaments.

The name *vimuktā (Ṣaḍ B* 5.6.) listed in the enumeration of valuables, *kṛśana* (*ṚV* 1.126.4, 10.68.1) and *kācamaṇi*[96] used for decorating a racing horse and that of the horse-sacrifice help us suppose that use of pearl ornaments was probably known to the people.

Further, it is interesting to note that flowers also did not escape people's notice and they were habituated to use it for ornamentation[97] specially on festive occasions like marriage ceremony.[98] Garlands also were given in the sacrificial ceremony.[99]

Hair-dressing

In spite of having clothes and ornaments a person needs hair dressing and some cosmetics for the completion of his/her dress.

---

94. *ṚV* 10.18.7; *AV* 20.128.6-7.

95. *nidhiṁ vibhratī bahudhāguhā vasu maṇiṁ hiraṇyaṁ pṛthivī dadātu me* ।
— *AV* 12.1.44.

96. *yat kācān āvayanti . . . ekaśatam ekaṁ kācānāvayanti . . .*
— *ŚB* 13.2.6.8.

97. *ṚV* 4.38.6, 5.53.4, 8.47.15, 8.56.3, 10.184.3; *TS* 1.8.18.1; *SV* 13.5.4.2.

98. *uta smāsu prathamaḥ sariṣyan niveveti śreṇibhī rathānāṁ* ।
srajaṁ kṛṇvāno janyo na śubhvā reṇuṁ rerihat kiraṇaṁ dadaśvān ॥
— *ṚV* 4.38.6.

99. *sadyo dīkṣayanti* । *sadyaḥ somaṁ krīnanti puṇḍarisrajāṁ prayacchati*
— *TS* 1.8.18.1.

Hair dressing was practised by men and women[100] alike. That various types of hair styles were practised, has been indicated through the references to various terms, e.g., *kaparda, stuka, stūpa, pṛthuṣṭukā, viṣitastukā, śikhā*, etc.

Normally girls maintained long hair, and wearing various types of braids and plaits on hair, was popular fashion among girls. The *ṚV*[101] refers to a *catuṣkapardā* maiden who arranged her hair in four plaits. On the authenticity of *pṛthuṣṭukā* Sinīvāli's reference mentioned throughout Vedic Saṁhitās,[102] it may not be wrong to guess the fashion of arranging broad styled plaits on hair. Besides this, the expression *svaupaśā*[103] meaning "one preparing braids with her own (i.e., natural) hair" may be considered as an indication that arranging false plaits of hair also, was in practice. Further, to arrange locks on the fore-part of hair in a loosened manner was another style.[104]

For the beautification of hair style people used different ornaments like tiara, diadem, etc. We have discussed it already under "Ornaments" section.

Now comes the practice of men's hair dressing. The epithet *kapardin* meaning "the man wearing his hair braided" applied to Rudra[105] and Pūṣan[106] indicates that wearing braids and plaits

---

100. *ṚV* 1.114.1, 1.114.15, 7.33.1, 9.67.11, 10.102.8, 10.114.13; *AV* 6.60.1, 6.138.1-2; *MS* 2.9.4-5; *KS* 17.13-14; *KapKS* 27.3-4; *TS* 4.5.5.1; *VS* 11.86, 16.9, 18.28-29.

101. *catuṣkapardā yuvatiḥ supeśā ghṛtapratīkā vayunāni vaste* |
— *ṚV* 10.114.3.

102. *sinīvāli pṛthuṣṭukā yā devānām asi svasā* |
— *ṚV* 2.32.6; *AV* 7.48.1; *KS* 13.16; *TS* 3.1.4.3; *VS* 14.10, etc.

103. *sinīvāli sukapardā sukurīrā svaupaśā* |
— *MS* 2.7.5; *RS* 7.1.5.2-3; *VS* 11.56; *ŚB* 6.5.1.10, etc.

104. *ṚV* 1.167; *AV* 6.60.1.

105. *ṚV* 1.114.1, 1.114.5; *TS* 4.5.1.4, 4.5.5.1; *VS* 16.9, 16.43, etc.

106. *ṚV* 6.65.2, 9.67.11.

was a popular fashion among men also. Now, it may not be irrelevant to set the example *dakṣiṇataskapardā* Vasiṣṭhas[107] who wore plaits on their hair in a special manner, i.e., on right side only. Not only that, the name of *Viṣitastuka* Aryamā[108] (with loosened locks in front) may be mentioned here as an instance of boys maintaining locks in the fore-part of hair.

Lastly the terms like *stūpa,*[109] *stuka,*[110] *śikhā*[111] meaning top knot of hair worn on the upper part of head may indicate existence of another type of hair style applicable for men.

As because fashion of wearing varieties of knots and braids on the hair was prevalent, therefore it can be easily presumed that use of comb was known to the people, though its use has not been attested in the Vedic Saṁhitās. Earliest record of using comb has been traced in the *ŚB* (2.6.4.5-7, 3.1.2.5.). In course of discussing sacrificer's toilet procedure, before his initiation, style of combing has been instructed in the *ŚB*.[112] A three-spotted porcupine's quill (*tryenīśalalī*) was used as comb.[113]

From the *ŚGS* (1.12.6-7) we find in the marriage ceremony a mirror and a comb of porcupine's quill were given to the bride by her husband as a part of ritual.

Cosmetics

After clothing, ornaments and hair style, now man needs some

107. *svityañco mā dakṣiṇataskapardā dhiyaṁ jinvāso abhi hi pramanduḥ* ।
uttiṣṭhan voce pari barhiṣo nṝn na me dūrād avitave vasiṣṭhāḥ ॥
— *ṚV* 7.33.1, 7.83.8.

108. *ayam āyātvaryamā purastād viṣitastupaḥ* । — *AV* 6.60.1.

109. *MS* 1.1.2, 1.1.12, 4.1.2; *VS* 2.2, 25.2.

110. *ṚV* 9.97.17; *AV* 7.78.2.

111. *yatra vāṇāḥ sampatanti kumārā viśikhā iva* — *ṚV* 6.35.17; (*śikhā*)
— *TS* 7.4.9.1, 1.3.3.5.

112. *sa dakṣiṇam evāgre godānaṁ vivartayati savyaṁ vā agre mānuṣe*
— *ŚB* 3.1.2.5.

113. *tat tryenī śalalī bhavati, lohaḥ kṣuraḥ . . . tena parivartayate* ।
— *ŚB* 2.6.4.5-7.

cosmetics in order to create a beautiful overall appearance. While studying the passages of Vedic Saṁhitā and Brāhmaṇas, we have seen that people were aware of this fact. The *ŚB*, in the context of using cosmetics has remarked that "these are but human embellishments" *eṣo ha mānuṣo 'laṁkāra* (*ŚB* 13.8.4.7). The *PB*[114] also has expressed the purpose of cosmetics in a distinct language.

Āñjana, occurring frequently from the *R̥V*[115] onwards appears to be a common name for any cosmetics/ointments, though generally the term means collyrium and in some case it (*āñjana*) appears also in this sense.[116] However, whatever may be its exact nature its frequent occurrence proves the popularity of cosmetics among both men and women. In the list of decoration regularly used by people, we find there were mainly (i) collyrium; (ii) ointments (for body,[117] face; (*TB* 23.10.2); and feet (*ŚB* 13.8.4.7); (iii) powder (*Kauṣ* 1.4); and (iv) perfumes (*ŚB* 9.4.1.4).

Though use of cosmetics was prevalent among both men and women, still from the prayer to the sweet scented forest queen[118] and description of well decorated[119] girls, it appears that cosmetics were more popular among girls. Still, we may refer here to the *AV*, which records use of cosmetics by men. While instructing about people's manners, the *AV* (20.128.6-7)

---

114. *yadā cāñjate 'bhicāñjate śubham evātmandadhate* — *PB* 24.13.3.

115. *R̥V* 10.18.7, 10.146.6; *AV* 4.9.1, 4.9.8, 6.102.3, 12.2.31, 18.3.57. *āñjana*: 20.128.6-7; *VS* 23.8; *TS* 6.1.1.5-6; *AB* 1.3-4; *ŚB* 3.1.3.10 ff.

116. (*āñjana*, as collyrium): *AV* 4.9.8, 6.102.3, 7.30.1, 7.36.1; *TS* 6.1.1.5-6; *AB* 1.3.

117. *R̥V* 10.18.7, 10.146.7; *AV* 4.9.8, 6.124.3, 20.128.6-7; *TS* 6.1.1.5; *ŚB* 3.1.3.10 ff.

118. *āñjanagandhiṁ surabhiṁ vahvannāma kr̥ṣīvalām* ।
prāhaṁ mr̥gāṇāṁ mātaram araṇyānim aśaṁsiṣam ॥
— *R̥V* 10.146.6.

119. *R̥V* 10.18.7; cf. 12.2.31, 18.3.57, etc.

has remarked that a man becomes eligible for priesthood only after furnishing himself with proper anointments and ornaments.[120]

In the context of sacrificer's initiation late Vedic Saṁhitā and Brāhmaṇas[121] have prescribed the sacrificer to anoint his body with butter and eyes with collyrium. It is interesting to note that even the manner and time of anointing (*pañcakr̥tvaḥ anakti* — *ŚB* 3.1.3.17) has been mentioned in a specific language. From the *AB*[122] we have been informed that these anointments varied according to the person, e.g., butter was for gods, fragrant butter for men, slightly melted one for Fathers and fresh butter was for embryos. From this it is clear that various forms of butter were used as anointing object.

Apart from this collyrium and other body-ointments, people usually liked to dye their feet with another type of anointment.*

The *ŚB*,[123] in the context of funeral rites has suggested to give anointments for eyes and feet to the mourners, on their return from the crematorium.

The *TB*'s[124] reference to *sthāgara* while describing Sītā's marriage makes us suppose the use of a special facial make-up. Probably girls used this article on special occasions.

---

120. *ya āktākṣaḥ sabhyaktaḥ sumaṇiḥ suhiraṇyavaḥ* ।
subrahmā subrahamaṇaḥputra stotā kalpeṣu saṁmita ॥
— *AV* 20.128.7.

121. *TS* 6.1.1.5-6; *AB* 1.3-4; *ŚB* 3.1.3.10 ff.

122. *ājyaṁ vai devānāṁ surabhighr̥taṁ manuṣyānām āyutaṁ pitr̥̄ṇāṁ navanītaṁ garbhāṇām* — *AB* 1.3.

123. *tadā āgatebhyo śmaśānebhyo 'ñjanam abhyañjanaṁ pradīyate*
— *ŚB* 13.8.4.7.

* Actually it was *alakta-rasa*, a red juice extracted from the resin of a certain tree; though it was not mentioned as such in the Vedic texts.

124. *tasyā ha sthāgaram alaṁkāraṁ mukhe kalpayitvā* . . . — *TB* 2.3.10.2.

Earliest record of using powder can be traced in the *Kauṣītaki*[125] *Upaniṣad* with reference to *cūrṇa hastā* apsarases. The aspirant on his way to the *Brahmaloka* should be greeted by divine ladies with anointments, aromatic powder, garlands, new garments, ornaments, etc. On the basis of this reference it may not be wrong to infer that use of some type of aromatic powder (may be pounded sandal or something else) was prevalent by the late Vedic period.

Puṇya gandhā womens' reference may be mentioned here as the earliest record of using perfumes.[126] Forest, as the source of perfumeries, has been mentioned in the Araṇyāṇī[127] Sūkta. As regards the use of perfumes we find in the Brāhmaṇa literature, people used it to cultivate a beautiful appearance. The *ŚB*'s[128] remark to the general practice of using perfumes by couples indicates that both the form and smell enhance sexual attraction. Origin of these perfumes and cosmetics has been narrated in the *PB*[129] through a myth: when Agni was about to enter the office of Hotṛ for gods, he shook himself: what was his flesh became *bdellium* (*guggulu*), the muscles became fragrant reed-grass and bones formed pine woods. These are the perfumes of gods.

Presence of *āñjanakarī*, a female expert of preparing perfumes and unguents as a separate professional (*VS* 30.14; *TB* 3.4.10.1), makes us guess the existence of perfumery works as a separate cottage industry. Further the *CU*[130] in the narrative

---

125. *pañcaśatāny apsarasā pratiyanti, śataṁ cūrṇahastāḥ* . . . — *Kauṣ* 1.4.

126. *proṣṭheśayā vahyeśayā narīr yā talpaśivarīḥ* ।
striyo yāḥ puṇyagandhāstāḥ sarvāḥ svāpayāmasi ॥ — *ṚV* 7.55.8.

127. *āñjanagandhiṁ surabhiṁ bahvannāma kṛṣībalām* ।
prāham mṛgāṇām mātaram araṇyānim aśaṁsiṣam ॥ — *ṚV* 10.146.6.

128. *gandhena ca vai rūpeṇa gandharvāścaranti* । *tasmādyaḥ kaśca mithunam upa praiti gandhaṁ caiva rūpañca kāmayate* । — *ŚB* 9.4.1.4.

129. *PB* 24.13.5.

130. *ṛgvedaṁ bhagavo 'dhyemi* . . . *sarpadevajanavidyām etad bhagavo 'dhyemi* — *CU* 7.1.2.

of Nārada and Sanatkumāra has recorded *devajanavidyā* as one of the subjects to be studied regularly by students. The commentator Śaṅkarācārya[131] has explained the said term as cultivation of various crafts, viz., music and dance, perfumery works, etc. Hence, we can assume it safely that there were some arrangements for training in these subjects for the betterment of production in the respective faculties.

131. *devajanavidyāṁ gandhayuktinṛtyagītavādyaśilpādi vijñānāni*
— Ś on CU *loc. cit.*

3

Housing System

AFTER food and clothes, man's next requirement is a safe shelter/habitation where he can reside along with his family members and other belongings.

Praise of the house and its chief architect Vāstospati, and glorious description of houses at various places signify that people felt the necessity of building a house not only to protect themselves against cold and rain but from the attack of wild animals also. An entire hymn in the *ṚV* (7.55) is addressed to the chief architect Vāstospati. The *ŚB*[1] has declared house as a firm support because it provides people as well as cattle, rest at night.[2] Moreover in this resting place people perform religious rites[3] as well as other duties.[4]

In search of the housing system of the Vedic people, we see that throughout Vedas there are numerous names for house, viz., *gṛha, gaya, dama, duroṇa, sadana, sadma, sādana, āyatana, āvasatha*, etc., which are common names only for abode or dwelling, though in some cases specific meanings can be

---

1. *gṛhā vai gārhapatyo gṛhā vai pratiṣṭheti* — *ŚB* 1.1.1.19.
2. *AV* 9.3.13-14, 9.3.17, etc.
3. *AV* 3.12.9, 9.3.21, 9.3.25-29; *ŚB* 1.1.1.18-19.
4. (i) *kulāye 'dhi kulāyaṁ kośe kośaḥ samubjitaḥ* ।
   tatra marto vijāyate yasmād viśvaṁ prajāyate ॥ — *AV* 9.3.20.

   (ii) *gṛhā vai gārhapatyastad gṛheṣvevaitanmithunaṁ prajananaṁ kriyate* — *ŚB* 1.1.1.18.

traced from the same. Yāska,[5] in his *Nirukta* has stated that there are twentytwo synonyms for house. Actual list is furnished in the *Nighaṇṭu*.[6]

Now from references to various building names, different portions of the house, building parts and materials, we are to suppose that people at that period knew techniques of constructing various types of buildings, which can be classified under several headings, viz.:

i) house as a general name,

ii) sacrificial hut/chamber,

iii) spacious dwelling,

iv) mansion/palaces,

v) castles/forts and

vi) buildings, meant for some other purposes, e.g.,

(a) guest house,
(b) treasury building,
(c) gambling house, etc.

In the vast range of Vedic literature (starting with the *ṚV* and reaching up to Upaniṣads) so many names have been traced which mean dwelling place or resting place in general[7] (in some cases dwelling for animals[8] also), viz., *dama, gṛha, gaya, duroṇa, sadma, sadana, sādana, agāra, āyatana, āvasatha, śaraṇa,*

---

5. *gṛhanāmānyuttarāṇi dvāviṁśatiḥ* । — *Nir* 3.13.

6. *gayaḥ, kṛdaraḥ, gartaḥ, harmyam, astam, pastyam, duroṇe, nīḍam, duryāḥ, svasarāṇi, amā, dame, kṛttiḥ, yoniḥ, sadman, śaraṇam, varūtham, chardiḥ, chadiḥ, chāyā, śarma, ajmeti gṛhāṇām* । — *Nigh.* 3.4.

7. *ṚV* 1.1.8, 1.28.5, 1.69.2, 1.71.4, 1.73.4, 1.74.4, 1.75.4, 5.10.3, 5.44.7; *AV* 2.6.3, 5.31.5, 6.120.1, 6.121.2, etc.; *TS* 4.3.1.1; *VS* 3.39, 3.53, 19.18, 33.1, 33.3, etc.

8. *prati yatsyā nīthādarśi dasyor oko* ।
nācchā sadanaṁ jānatī gāt ॥ — *ṚV* 1.104.5.

saṁvaraṇa, niveśana, etc. It is interesting to note here that all these terms denote more or less the same meaning though some of them apart from their general meaning include some specific meaning also (some of them occur rarely) e.g.:

i) *gaya* indicates household in total,[9]

ii) *āvasatha* conveys the sense of guest house,[10] and some times palace,[11] and

iii) *sadana* denotes mansion,[12] in some cases seat[13] only.

Apart from the general concept of house, that the idea of mansion and palaces was not unknown to the Vedic people, has been indicated through the terms, viz., *chardi, barti, okas, dhāman, harmya, śālā, śarman, śaraṇa, varūtha, kṣaya*, etc. The above cited list shows us that there are at least eight/nine names for mansion or well-ordered prosperous habitation. But it is very difficult to ascertain their exact nature. Still, from the expressions like *bṛhantaṁ, varūtham* (*ṚV* 4.56.6), *bṛhantaṁ kṣayam* (*ṚV* 10.47.8), *acchidraṁ śaraṇam* (*ṚV* 2.3.8), *ayohataṁ yonim* (*VS* 26.26), *sukṛtañca yonim* (*ṚV* 10.34.11), etc., it can be safely stated that at least the idea of well-ordered building was nothing new to them. Further, people's preference for multistoreyed building has been reflected in the occurrences, e.g., *trivarūtha gṛha*,[14] *tribhuja-śayāna*,[15] *tridhātu*

---

9. *ṚV* 1.74.2, 5.10.3, 5.44.7; *AV* 2.6.3, 6.84.1, 7.84.1.

10. *jānaśrutir ha pautrāyaṇaḥ śraddhādeyo bahudāyī bahupākya āsa* ।
sa ha sarvata āvasathān māpayāñcakre sarvata eva me 'nnamatsyantīti ॥
— *CU* 4.1.1.

11. *tad yathā rājānam āyāntamugrāḥ pratyenasaḥ sūta grāmaṇyo 'nnaiḥ pānairāvasathaiḥ prati kalpante* — *BU* 4.3.37.

12. *aśvatthe vo niṣadanaṁ paṇe vo vasatiṣkṛtā* — *VS* 12.79.

13. *AV* 7.99.1; *TS* 4.3.1.1; *AB* 1.28, etc.

14. *ṚV* 8.20-21, 8.42.2, etc.

15. *yo akrandayat salilaṁ mahitvā yoniṁ kṛtvā tribhujaṁ śayānaḥ*
— *AV* 8.9.2.

śarman,[16] *tridhātuśaraṇa,*[17] etc. According to the commentator[18] terms *trivarūtha gṛha,* etc., suggest the idea of strongly built habitations, which were triply defended from cold, heat and rain.

The term *prāsāda* itself is absent in the early Vedic literature, but the concept of palace was not unknown. From the description of Varuṇa's palace having thousand columns (*sahasrasthūṇā sadas* — *ṚV* 2.41.5) and thousand doors (*sahasradvāraṁ gṛham* — *ṚV* 7.88.5) it may not be wrong to suppose that the technique of fashioning palaces was known to the masons of that period. In this connection we may mention here the *dvipakṣā/catuṣpakṣā/ṣaṭpakṣā/aṣṭapakṣā/daśapakṣā* building described in the *AV* (9.3.21) which bespeaks of the high standard of architectural skill of that period. Expert masons built up not only iron houses but golden ones also. King Varuṇa's golden palace has been mentioned in the *AV.*[19] Another golden palace is referred to in the *ŚB*[20] in the narrative of the King Pururavas and the nymph Urvaśī.

However, according to Macdonell and Keith (VI, I, p. 51) the term *prāsāda* to mean palace has been recorded for the first time in the *Adbhuta Brāhmaṇa.*[21]

Besides these mansions, palaces, etc., terms like *pur, purī, pūḥ* indicate that strongholds/fortresses/ramparts were built for defence. The epithets *pṛthvī,*[22] *ūrvī* associated with *pur* and

---

16. *tridhātunā śarmaṇā pātamasmān vayaṁ syāma* . . . — *ṚV* 8.40.12.
17. *indra tridhātu śaraṇaṁ trivarūthaṁ svastimat* — *AV* 20.83.1.
18. *trivarūthaṁ trayāṇām śītātapavarṣāṇāṁ nivārakam, yadvā tribhūmikaṁ gṛham* — Sā on *ṚV* 8.18.21.
19. *apsu te rājan varuṇa gṛho hiraṇyayo mithaḥ* । — *AV* 7.83.1.
20. *sa ha saṁvatsaratamīṁ rātrim ājagāmeddhiraṇya vimitāni* — *ŚB* 11.5.1.11.
21. *Adbhuta Brāhmaṇa* 5.6.
22. *pūśca pṛthvī bahulā na urvī bhavā tokāya tanayāya śaṁ yo* — *ṚV* 1.189.2, 10.101.8.

mahāpura[23] signify that some of these fortifications were of considerable size. The Brāhmaṇas[24] in the context of *paśuparyagnikaraṇa* inform us of threefold strongholds. The *ŚB*[25] has declared this *tripura* as the best form of stronghold. Autumnal forts *śāradī pūḥ* (mentioned in the *ṚV*[26]) belonging to the Dāsas make us suppose that these fortresses were probably used as a place of refuge against the attack of enemies (specially the Aryan attack). But whether these were used as a place of permanent habitation is still questionable.

These castles were built with strong fences,[27] sometimes with hundred walls[28] and hundred gates[29] to make the security strong. Sometimes fire-parapet was kept burnt for the same purpose.[30]

From the phrase *aśma-pura*,[31] it appears that castles were built with stones. But *āyasī pūḥ*[32] occurring frequently in the Vedas suggest that iron fortresses also were built. Three castles of iron, silver and gold built by *asura*s have been recorded in the Yajurvedic Saṁhitā and Brāhmaṇas.[33]

Parallel with the idea of house as a regular dwelling place, concept of houses, built for some other purpose also has been

---

23. *upasadā vai mahāpuraṁ jayatīti* — *TS* 6.2.3.1; cf. *MS* 3.8.1; *KS* 24.10, 25.1; *KapKS* 38.3-4.
24. *AB* 1.23; *ŚB* 3.4.4.4.
25. *tasmād u haitat yat tripuraṁ sarve . . .* — *ŚB* 6.3.3.25.
26. *ṚV* 1.131.4, 1.174.2, 6.20.10, etc.
27. *ṚV* 7.99.5; *TS* 3.2.11.3.
28. *adhā mahī na āyasyanādhṛṣṭo nṛpītaye pūrbhavā śatabhuji* — *ṚV* 7.15.14.
29. *anarvā yacchatadurasya vedo . . .* — *ṚV* 10.99.3.
30. *ṚV* 7.3.7; *AB* 2.11; *ŚB* 6.3.3.25
31. *ṚV* 4.30.20; *ŚB* 3.1.3.11
32. *ṚV* 2.20.8, 7.3.7, 7.15.14, 7.95.1, 8.100.8.
33. *MS* 3.8.1-2; *KS* 24.10-25.1; *KapKS* 38.3-4; *TS* 6.2.3.1-2; *VS* 5.8; *AB* 1.23; *ŚB* 3.4.4.3-4.

traced in the Vedas through the terms like *garta* and *sabhā* (to mean gambling house), *vasudhānī* (treasury building) and *āvasatha* (guest house), etc. Though they were not meant for regular habitation, still they were concerned with some matters connected with people's everyday life, e.g., people went to the gambling house for the purpose of entertainment. The gambler's addiction to *sabhā*[34] makes its sense and purpose clear. In the *Nighaṇṭu* (3.4) *garta* is read as one of the house names; and Yāska[35] with a citation from the *ṚV*[36] explained *garta* as dicing hall.

The *CU*[37] has told us the story of King Jānaśruti Pautrāyaṇa who constructed many *āvasatha*s (guest house) in his domain with the intention that people would eat his food. Both the commentator[38] and translator[39] had taken the word *āvasatha* for guest house. Hence, we have been informed that at that time guest houses were built at various places for the refreshment of tired travellers.

Again *vasudhānī* occurring in the *TĀ*[40] help us to infer the existence of treasury building.

---

34. *sabhām eti kitavaḥ pṛcchamāno jeṣyāmītitanvā śuśujānaḥ* ı
akṣāso asya vitiranti kāmaṁ pratidīvne dadhata ā kṛtāni ıı
— *ṚV* 10.34.6.

35. *abhrātṛkeva puṁseva pitṝnetyabhimukhī santānakarmaṇe piṇḍadānāya na patiṁ* ı *gartārohiṇīva dhanalābhāya dakṣiṇājīgartaḥ sabhāsthāṇuḥ*
— *Nir* 3.5.

36. *abhrāteva puṁsa eti pratīci gartārugiva sanaye dhanānām*
— *ṚV* 1.124.7.

37. *jānaśrutir ha pautrāyaṇaḥ śraddhādeyo bahudāyī bahupākya āsa* ı
sa ha sarvata āvasathān māpayāñcakre, sarvata eva me 'nnamatsyantīti ıı
— *CU* 4.1.1.

38. *sa ha sarvataḥ sarvāsu dikṣu grāmeṣu nagareṣu cāvasathānetya vasanti yeṣvityāvasathāstān māpayāñcakre kāritavān . . .*
— Śaṅkarācārya on *CU loc. cit.*

39. Swami Gambhirananda (tr.) *Chāndogya Upaniṣad, loc. cit.*, pp. 244-45.

40. *suvarṇam kośaṁ rajasā parīvṛtam* ı *devānāṁ vasudhānīṁ virājam* ı
— *TĀ* 3.11.4.

Lay-out of the House/Building Plan

Names of various portions of house, e.g., *patnīnāṁ sadanam*, *sadas*, *agni-śālā*, *sadana/sādana/sadhastha*, *dhāman*, *koṣṭha*, etc., indicate that even at that ancient age house building was not anything casual. People built houses consisting of several rooms which served different purposes. Again *havirdhāna*, *goṣṭha*, *dharuṇī*, also formed various parts of the house.

In the *AV*, there are at least three hymns, which have been devoted entirely to the benediction of a newly built house (3.12, 9.3) and its glorification (7.60).

The passages like

ihaiva dhruvā pratitiṣṭha śāle 'śvāvatī gomatī sunṛtāvatī ।
ūrjasvatī ghṛtavatī payasvatyucchrayasva mahate saubhagāya ॥
dharuṇyasi śāle bṛhacchandāḥ pūtidhānyā ।

— *AV* 3.12.2-3.

or

ime gṛhā mayobhuva ūrjasvanta payasvantaḥ ।
pūrṇā vāmena tiṣṭhantas te no jānantvāyataḥ ॥
yeṣāmadhyeti pravasan yeṣu saumanaso bahu ।
. . . upahūtā bhūridhanāḥ svāduṁ samudaḥ ॥
. . . upahūtā iha gāva upahūtā ajāvayaḥ ।
atho annasya kīlāla upahūto gṛheṣu naḥ ॥
sunṛtāvantaḥ subhagā irāvanto hasāmudāḥ ।
atṛṣyā akṣudhyā sta gṛhā māsmad vibhītana ॥

— *AV* 7.60.2-6.

make us visualize the picture of an ideal house full of abundance and happiness. The house should be lofty-roofed, rich in corns, animals (cattle, horses, goat and sheep), food and drinks. It should be free from hunger and thirst. Many a friendly hearts reside therein. Delight and felicity should be there.

Again,

pūrṇaṁ nāri pra bhara kumbham etam ।
ghṛtasya dhārāmamṛtena saṁbhṛtām ॥

ima āpaḥ pra bharāmyayakṣmā yakṣmanāśanī ।
gṛhānupa prasīdāmyamṛtena sahāgninā ॥
— *AV* 3.12.8-9.

This is probably a description of the ceremony of householder's entering the new house with two important necessities of human life, i.e., fire and a well-filled pitcher, accompanied by his wife, clad in grass-robes (*tṛṇaṁ vasānā sumanā* — *AV* 3.12.5).

The text goes on describing the ideal house consisting of *havirdhāna* "store house," *agni-śālā* "fire-hall/sacrificial chamber," *patnīnāṁ sadana* "womens' apartment," *sadas* "dining hall cum drawing room,"[41] etc. *Patnīnāṁ sadana/patnī-śālā* appearing in late Vedic Saṁhitā and Brāhmaṇas suggests that a portion of house was kept apart for the female members especially on ritual occasions.

The names *agniśālā* (*AV* 9.3.7; *VS* 19.21), *dīkṣita vimita* (*AB* 1.3), *prācīnavaṁśa śālā* (*TS* 6.1.1.1; *ŚB* 3.1.1.7) meaning fire-shed or sacrificial campus indicate that separate fire-hall or sacrificial shed was built for the initiated sacrificer, where he established his ritual fire and performed various rites. In the context of Agniṣṭoma the *AB*[42] has instructed the sacrificer to stay within *dīkṣita vimita* after his initiation and prohibited to stay outside. From the *ŚB*[43] we have been informed that nobody other than consecrated sacrificer would be entitled to enter this sacrificial shade.

41. *havirdhānam agniśālaṁ patnīnāṁ sadanaṁ sadaḥ* ।
sado devānām asi devi śāle ॥ — *AV* 9.3.7.

42. *dīkṣitavimitaṁ prapādayanti . . . tasmāt dīkṣitaṁ nānyatra dīkṣitavimitādādityo 'bhyudiyātvā 'bhyastam iyādvā . . .* — *AB* 1.3.

43. *dīkṣitasyaiva prācīnavaṁśa nādīkṣitasya . . .* — *ŚB* 3.1.1.7.

According to the *ŚB*[44] *koṣṭha* was used as a store-room; though on ritual occasions, people used *havirdhāna* itself as the store-room.[45] For the preservation of corns use of granary was known to the people.[46] We are to remember here that though prayer hall, dining room, drawing room, ladies' apartment, etc., have been discussed in the ritual context, still in the everyday life also concept of these portions in connection with building construction was known to the people.

The house held not only people but also cattle and sheep at night.[47] From the *AV*'s[48] reference to *goṣṭha, vraja, saṁgavinī,*[49] etc., it can be assumed that well built cow-pen also was a part of human dwelling.

Construction of the House

As regards the construction of a house there are very few references, still in the context of different sacrificial rites various parts of the house,[50] e.g., door, door bolt, roof, etc., have been mentioned. Further the construction of sacrificial altar has been discussed in detail in the Yajurvedic Saṁhitā and Brāhmaṇas,[51] on basis of which we are to suppose roughly the construction of a house and its required materials of that period.

44. *anasa eva yajūṁṣi santi na koṣṭhasya* — *ŚB* 1.1.2.7.
45. *yajño vā 'anaḥ* I . . . *tasmād anasa eva gṛhṇīyāt* . . . — *ŚB* 1.1.2.7.
46. *dharuṇyasi śāle bṛhacchandā pūti dhānyā* I — *AV* 3.12.3.
47. *tṛṇair āvṛtā paladān vasānā rātrīvaśālā jagato niveśanī* I *mitā pṛthivyāṁ tiṣṭhasi hastinīva padvatī* II— *AV* 9.3.17.
48. *AV* 2.14.2-4, 4.21.1, 19.58.4.
49. *yasmāddhedaṁ bharatānāṁ paśavaḥ sāyaṁ goṣṭhaḥ santaḥ madhyandine saṁgavinīm āyanti* — *AB* 3.18.
50. *ṚV* 1.69.5, 1.91.19, 1.142.6, 10.40.12; *AV* 8.3.22, 10.8.43, 14.1.63; *VS* 5.30, 20.40, 21.16, 21.34, 21.49, 27.16, 28.5, 29.5, 30.10; *TS* 4.1.8.2; *ŚB* 1.6.1.19, 4.3.5.9, 4.6.7.9, 11.1.1.1-2, 11.4.4.2, etc.
51. *TS* 4.3.1-4.4.11; *MS* 2.8.8; *KS* 17.7; *KapKS* 26.6; *VS* 15.6-9; *ŚB* 6th-10th Kāṇḍa.

References to women's apartment, sacrificial chamber, store-room, etc., prove that the house consisted of several rooms; and *dvāra, dvāra-pidhāna, nahana*, etc., mentioned frequently suggest that these rooms were well fitted with doors, door posts and bolts most probably for security. Because of this *dvāra* in some places has been named as *duroṇa*,[52] that which is invincible.

In the context of consecration of a new house the *AV*[53] mentions names of *vaṁśa* (bamboo), *sthūṇā* (pillar), *upamit* (pillar), *parimit* (cross-beams), *pratimit* (beams), etc., from which we may guess that posts, beams and cross-beams were used for the framework of rooms. With reference to the construction of *prācīnavaṁśaśālā* the *ŚB*[54] has referred to a *sthūṇārāja*, the central beam.

The construction of *havirdhāna, prācīnavaṁśaśālā* and *sadas* has been discussed in the *TS* and the *ŚB*,[55] through the performance of rituals. With the aid of this discussion and Sāyaṇa's commentary thereon, we may have a rough idea how these structures were built up. At first a central post was erected. Both the *havirdhāna* and *sadas* should have doors on both sides.[56] Therefore, for the front and back doors four other pillars were set up and beams both long ways and cross ways

---

52. (i) *adrau cid asmā antar duroṇe viśāṁ na viśvo amṛtaḥ svādhīḥ* ||
— *ṚV* 1.70.2.

(ii) . . . *duroṇe dustaryagṛhe* — Sā. *ibid.*

53. (i) *ṛtena sthūṇāmadhiroha vaṁśogro virājannapa vṛṁkṣava śatrūn* |
— *AV* 3.12.6.

(ii) *upamitaṁ pratimitam atho parimitāmuta* |
śālayā viśvavārayā naddhāni vicṛtām asi || — *AV* 9.3.1.

54. *tad ya eṣa pūrvārdhyo varṣiṣṭhaḥ sthūṇārājo bhavati* — *ŚB* 3.5.1.1.

55. *TS* 1.3.1, 6.1.1; *ŚB* 3.1.1.6-8, 3.5.3.9, 3.6.1.23, etc.

56. *ubhayato dvāraṁ havirdhānaṁ bhavati* | *ubhayato dvāraṁ sadaḥ* |
— *ŚB* 3.5.3.7.

were leant and connected. For the construction of *sadas* and *havirdhāna*, the proper position of the beams has been directed in the *ŚB* —

> *tad udīcīna vaṁśaṁ sado bhavati, prācīnavaṁśaṁ havirdhānam*
> — *ŚB* 3.6.1.23

In this connection, the *ŚB* has remarked "in the human practice hall or hut should be constructed with the top beams running from south to north."

> *tasmān manuṣyā udīcīna vaṁśam eva śālāṁ vā vimitaṁ vā minvanti.* — *ŚB* 3.1.1.7

It is interesting to observe that in later ages some Western scholars also have opined in similar language regarding the construction of this framework. "A chief post was erected at the central position and four other pillars were set in the four corners of the room. Against them beams were leant at angles as props and then those upright pillars were connected by cross-beams" (Zimmer's view cited by Macdonell & Keith, VI, I, p. 230).

Now, for the roof we see in the Yajurvedic Saṁhitā and Brāhmaṇas, some terms like *chadis*,[57] *viṣuvant*,[58] *akṣu*;[59] from the textual context it appears that these were used as roof materials. Against the framework of bamboo or bamboo-ribs, a ridge called *viṣuvant*, a net called *akṣu* and covering mats named *chadis* were thatched. From the *TS* we have been informed that in case of constructing sacrificial hall, the number of these covering mats may vary according to the desire of the sacrificer.

---

57. *ṚV* 10.85.10; *AV* 3.12.3; *VS* 5.28; *TS* 4.4.3.3, 6.2.10.5-6; *AB* 1.29; *ŚB* 3.5.3.9.

58. *akṣum opaśaṁ vitataṁ sahasrākṣaṁ viṣuvati* |
avanaddham abhihitam brahmaṇā vi cṛtām asi || — *AV* 9.3.8.

59. *ṚV* 1.180.5; *AV* 8.8.18, 9.3.8, etc.

The walls were filled up with bundles of grass[60] and the whole structure was held together with various types of knots and ties, viz., *nahana, praṇāha, sandaṁśa, pariṣvañjalya,*[61] etc. Most probably side posts were called *pakṣa*. A house erected on two/four/six/eight/ten side posts has been described in the *AV*.[62] "Clay was used for smearing and minor finishing of the walls." (Muir, *Original Sanskrit Texts*, V, p. 461).

From these statements, it appears that in the early Vedic age generally houses were built of wood, bamboo ribs, grass, etc. Though time and again *trivarūtha gṛha* explained by the commentator[63] as "three storeyed building or that triply defended from heat, cold and rain," has been mentioned in the *ṚV*; still on the basis of this much it is difficult to ascertain whether the technique of fashioning brick-built house was developed in the Ṛgvedic age (in parallel with the fashion of wood and grass-made house) or not.

However, in the context of five layered (*pañca-citika*) and seven-layered (*sapta-citika*) fire-altar the Yajurvedic Saṁhitā and Brāhmaṇas[64] present before us names of various types of bricks. Though it is true that in the context of *citi-nirmāṇa* brick is a technical name for any required material, e.g., animal-bricks, food-bricks, etc. still, use of bricks burnt by chaff-fire

---

60. *AV* 9.3.4, 9.3.17.

61. *vaṁśānāṁ te nahanānāṁ praṇāhasya tṛnasya* ǀ
pakṣāṇāṁ viśvavāre te naddhāni vi cṛtām asi ǁ
sandaṁśānāṁ paladānāṁ pariṣvañjalyasya ca ǀ
idaṁ mānasya patnyā naddhāni vi cṛtām asi ǁ
— *AV* 9.3.4-5.

62. *yā dvipakṣā catuṣpakṣā ṣaṭpakṣā yā nimīyate* ǀ
aṣṭāpakṣāṁ daśapakṣāṁ śālāṁ mānasya patnīm agnigarbha ivā śaye ǁ
— *AV* 9.3.21.

63. Sā on *ṚV* 8.18.20-21, 8.42.2, 10.142.1, etc.

64. *TS* 4.3.1-4.3.5; (names of various types of bricks) *retaḥsic* — *ŚB* 7.4.2.22; *dviyajus* — *ŚB* 7.4.2.16; *ṛtavya* — *ŚB* 7.4.2.29; *apasyā* — *ŚB* 7.4.2.35; animal-bricks and food-bricks — *ŚB* 6.1.2.30.

has been mentioned in *TS*[65] (in the context of piling Gārhapatya fire. Again the process of brick-making (*ŚB* 6.2.1.8-9) and brick-makers (*ŚB* 6.5.3.1) have been mentioned which prove that actual bricks also were used. Apart from bricks, sand of grovel, stone, iron dust also were used for preparing fire-pan[66] (*ukhā-nirmāṇa*). Though there is hardly any direct reference to the use of these materials for the construction of a house, still it may not be wrong to suppose that at least use of these ingredients as building materials was known to the people. Thus, it may be safely stated that brick-built houses were fashioned in the late Vedic age but whether this idea was known in the early Vedic period — is still a question.

The expressions *aśmanmaya nahana* (*ṚV* 10.67.3), and *aśmapura* (*ŚB* 3.1.3.11) are proofs of building stony castles or castles with stony ramparts. That the use of iron and gold as building materials may be supposed from the expressions like *ayohataṁ yonim* (*VS* 26.26) or *hiraṇyaya gṛha* (*AV* 7.83-1) scattered in the Vedic Saṁhitās. Three castles of *asuras* (as already mentioned before) built of iron, gold and silver prove the validity of this statement.

Household Furniture

After the completion of house construction, people require some furniture for their own comfort and house decoration as well. References scattered in the Vedic literature provide us some information about the use of various furniture, viz., beds/cots, seats (mats or plank), throne, etc.

Now as regards beds/cots, we find in the *ṚV*[67] there are at least three names, i.e., *talpa, vahya*, and *proṣṭha*. Description

65. *nair̄tī kṛṣṇāstisras tuṣapakvā bhavanti* — *TS* 5.2.4.21.
66. *athaitat trayaṁ piṣṭaṁ bhavati — śarkarā — śma 'syorasaḥ* ı *tena saṁsṛjati* ı — *ŚB* 6.5.1.6.
67. *proṣṭheśayā vahyeśayā narīr yā talpaśīvariḥ* ı
striyo yā puṇyagandhāstā sarvāḥ svāpayāmasi ıı — *ṚV* 7.55.8.

of the ladies lying on *talpa*, *vahya* and *proṣṭha* indicates that use of different types of cots was prevalent from the early Vedic period. Co-existence of these three terms in the same verse, signifies their difference, which is difficult to ascertain from the text. From Sāyaṇācārya's commentary on the *TB*[68] *proṣṭha* appears to be a bench whereas *vahya* has been explained as bed/cot by some Western scholars (Macdonell & Keith, VI, I, p. 301, II. 278).

For the seats late Vedic literature presents before us several names like *āsandī*,[69] *phalaka*,[70] *paryaṅka*,[71] etc., used mainly for ritual purpose. Apart from this, *upadhāna*, *upavāsana*,[72] *upabarhaṇa*,[73] *āsāda*,[74] *kūrca*,[75] *kaśipu*,[76] etc., were also used as seats, though actually they are the parts of a throne. The fifteenth chapter of *AV* (15.2) describes Lord Ekavrātya's throne from which we can roughly form an idea about the construction of a throne. Its four feet length-wise and cross-pieces, forward and cross-tapes suggest wooden boards and cords. It had a seat (*āsāda*) and a support (*upaśraya*) which was covered with pillow (*upabarhaṇa*) and a cushion (*āstaraṇa*/*upastaraṇa*). In another place the *AV* has called this cushion and coverlet by different names, i.e., *upadhāna* and *upavāsana*.

---

68. (i) *āroha proṣṭhaṁ viṣahasva śatrūn . . .* I — *TB* 2.7.17.1.
    (ii) *he rājan 'proṣṭham āsandīrūpaṁ pañcakam āroha* — Sā *ibid.*
69. *AV* 14.2.65, 15.3.2; *TS* 5.2.1.5, 5.6.9.1; *MS* 3.2.1; *KS* 19.11; *VS* 7.56, 19.16; *AB* 8.5-6, 8.12; *PB* 5.5.1-3; *ŚB* 5.2.1.22, 5.4.4.1; *JB* 2.4.18.
70. *PB* 5.5.11; *ŚB* 3.3.4.9, 13.4.3.1; *AĀ* 1.2.3.
71. *sa āgacchatyamitaujasaṁ paryaṅkam* — *Kauṣ* 1.5.
72. *yad āsandyām upadhāne yadvopavāsane kṛtam* I — *AV* 14.2.65.
73. *veda āstaraṇaṁ brahmopabarhaṇam* I — *AV* 15.3.7.
74. *sāmāsāda udogītho 'paśrayaḥ* — *AV* 15.3.8.
75. *TS* 7.5.8.5; *PB* 5.5.12; *ŚB* 11.5.3.4, 11.5.3.7, etc.
76. *AB* 7.18; *ŚB* 13.4.3.1, etc.

In the context of royal consecration Brāhmaṇa[77] literature has described a king's throne in a similar language with slight variations. Size and shape of the feet and seat and height of the throne, everything has been stated in a distinct language. This height and size may vary according to the purpose, e.g., at the Sautrāmaṇī[78] rite throne should be made of fig-wood and knee-high, of unlimited width and depth and covered with plaited reed work, whereas in the coronation[79] ceremony imperial seat should be of shoulder high and wound all over with grass cords. In other cases, e.g., the singer's throne (*PB* 5.5.1-3) or that, on which fire pan should be placed, should be of span high, a cubit in width and covered with cords of reed-grass and smeared with clay.[80] The *Kauṣ* has given another name for throne, i.e., *paryaṅka* (*Kauṣ* 1.5).

Besides these various formed thrones, some sort of mats, cushions (in some cases wooden planks) were used as different forms of seats, i.e., *kaśipu*, *kūrca*, etc. A *kaśipu* made of reed-grass has been recorded in the *AV*.[81] In the context of Mahāvrata rite the *TS* (7.5.8.5) refers to the use of grass-made *kūrca*s by Adhvaryu. From the *ŚB*[82] we have been informed that mats and cushions wrought with golden threads were in

---

77. *AB* 8.5; *ŚB* 14.1.3.8.

78. *audumbarī bhavati . . . jānusaṁmitā bhavati . . . kṣatramu vā eṣa bhavati* । *yaḥ sautrāmaṇyām abhiṣicyate* । *tasmāt jānu-saṁmitā* । *tasmāt tiraścī* । . . . *muñja vivayanā bhavati* ॥ — *ŚB* 12.8.3.4-6.

79. *samrāḍāsandīṁ paryāhṛtya dakṣiṇataḥ . . . aṁsadadhnā bhavati* । . . *bālvajībhīrajjubhirvyūtā bhavati* — *ŚB* 14.1.3.9-11

80. *athainam āsandyā bibharti* । . . . *audumbarī bhavati* । . . . *prādeśamātryūrdhvā bhavati* । . . . *aratnimatrī tiraścī* । . . . *catuḥsraktayaḥ pādā bhavanti* । . . . *mauñjībhi rajjubhir vyutā bhavati trivṛdbhiḥ* । . . . *mṛdā digdhā* । — *ŚB* 6.3.1.12-15.

81. *yathā naḍaṁ kaśipune striyo bhindantyaśmanā* । — *AV* 6.138.5.

82. *hiraṇmayaṁ kaśipum āstṛṇāti . . . hiraṇmaye kūrce yajamāno . . .* — *ŚB* 13.4.3-1.

use (most probably on special occasions). Apart from these grass mats, use of wooden planks as seats was prevalent.[83] In the context of horse sacrifice the *ŚB*[84] has told us of a golden plank as seat of the Adhvaryu priest.

83. *AB* 7.70; *PB* 17.1.14; *ŚB* 3.3.4.9, etc.

84. *pratyaṅṅadhvaryur hiraṇmaye vā kūrce hiraṇmaye vā phalake* ।
— *ŚB* 13.4.3-1.

4

Mode of Production and Other Occupations

A MAJOR part of people's everyday life was devoted to their earning. In order to do so people followed different modes of production which influenced his life style strongly. From the study of Vedic literature it becomes evident that at that period the mainstay of the society was agriculture and cattle rearing, though there are some other references, which indicate that trade also was practised simultaneously. Further, references to weaving, carpentry, pottery, fishery, etc., inform us that from the early Vedic period all these were practised as means of earning livelihood.

Agriculture

Among all these modes agriculture comes first. References to farmers,[1] cornfield,[2] granary,[3] cultivation,[4] and preservation[5]

1. *ṚV* 1.168.7, 4.57.8, 10.94.13; *AV* 3.17.5, 4.11.10, 6.30.1, 6.116.1; *VS* 30.11; *AB* 5.3; *ŚB* 1.6.1.3; *TB* 2.4.8.7, etc.
2. *dyaur na ya indrābhiḥ bhūmār yastasthau rayiḥ śavasā pṛtsu janān* ।
tam naḥ sahasrabharam urvarāsāṁ daddhi sūno sahaso vṛtraturaṁ ॥
— *ṚV* 6.20.1, 10.142.3
3. *ṚV* 2.14.11, 10.68.3; *AV* 2.14.2; *VS* 29.1; *Nir* 3.20.
4. *ṚV* 1.23.15, 1.117.21, 1.168.7, 1.176.2, 3.3.7, 4.57.8, 8.20.19, 8.22.6, 10.34.13, 10.94.13, 10.101.3-6, 10.117.7, 10.131.2; *AV* 3.17.1-9, 6.30.1, 8.10.24, 10.125.2, 12.1.42; *VS* 12.68-69, 12.71, 19.6; *TS* 4.2.5.5-6, 4.2.6.5.
5. *tad id badanty adrayo vimocane yam annañjaspā iva ghedupabdibhiḥ* । →

of seeds help us to form a rough idea about agricultural system of that period. That agriculture was a settled practice, has been suggested in the constant praise of agriculture[6] and its required implements[7] as well as in the prayers to the deities for ample rain[8] and harvest,[9] etc. Two entire hymns have been addressed to *Kṣetrapati,* in order to achieve success in cultivation.[10] The Dice hymn of *ṚV* advises people to practice agriculture as a means of gaining wealth :

> *akṣair mā dīvyaḥ kṛṣim it kṛṣasva*
> *vitte ramasva bahu manyamānaḥ* ।
> — *ṚV* 10.34.13

IMPORTANCE OF AGRICULTURE

In the context of preparing sacrificial altar, while narrating the mode of ploughing, the *ŚB* declares agriculture as food. From the Yajurvedic Saṁhitā and Brāhmaṇas[12] we have been informed that in the Coronation ceremony the king designate was crowned for the sake of agriculture, common good, prosperity and progress. From this, importance attached to agriculture can be assumed easily.

→ *bapanto bījam iva dhānyakṛtaḥ pṛñcanti somaṁ na minanti bapsataḥ* ॥
— *ṚV* 10.94.13

6. *ṚV* 4.57.3, 4.57.8, 10.34.13, 10.101.7, 10.117.7; *AV* 3.17.1, 3.17.9, etc.
7. *ṚV* 1.179.6, 2.14.11, 4.57.4-8, 8.78.10, 10.48.7, 10.71.2, 10.101.3-6, 10.117.7, 10.131.2; *AV* 2.8.4-5, 3.17.3-7, 6.91.1, 8.9.16, 10.6.33; *VS* 12.68-69, 12.71; *MS* 2.7.12; *KS* 16.11; *TS* 4.2.5.5-6, 4.2.6.1-6, 5.2.5.2, etc.
8. *ṚV* 8.22.6; *AV* 4.15.1-16, 7.18.1-2.
9. *ṚV* 3.3.7, 4.57.3, 4.57.6, 4.57.8, 8.22.6; *AV* 3.17.2, 3.17.5, 3.17.9, etc.
10. *ṚV* 4.57; *AV* 3.17.
11. *annaṁ vai kṛṣiḥ* — *ŚB* 7.3.2.6
12. *MS* 1.2.2, 3.6.8; *TS* 7.1.11.1; *VS* 4.10, 9.22; *ŚB* 5.2.1.25.

In order to get plentiful crops, ample rain as well as to avoid the damages caused by natural calamities like drought, lightning, etc., prayers have been offered to the deities in the *AV*.[13] In this connection, we may mention here the deities, e.g., Maruts and Aśvins who were concerned with cultivation.[14] The *AV*[15] has described Indra as the Lord of plough, *Sīrapatiḥ*. The *ŚB*'s[16] reference to *śūrpamān yavamān kṛṣir uddālavān dhānāntarvān gandharvas*, makes us presume that *gandharvas* were competent cultivators.

STAGES OF CULTIVATION

In the Vedic literature, there are numerous references to cultivation,[17] from which we find that in the total processing there were four stages of operations, viz., (1) ploughing the field, (2) sowing of seeds, (3) harvesting ripe corn, and (4) threshing and separating the straws from corn. The *ŚB*[18] has neatly summed up all these stages in a sentence. Beside this, in the context of Cayana the Yajurvedic Saṁhitā and Brāhmaṇas[19] have described the total processing in detail, which provide us various information, e.g., shape and size[20] of the

13. *AV* 3.17.2, 3.17.5, 3.17.9, 6.142.1, 7.11.1, 7.18.1-2.

14. *ṚV* 1.117.21, 1.168.7, 8.22.6; *AV* 6.30.1.

15. *indra āsīt sīrapatiḥ śatakratuḥ kīnāśa āsan marutaḥ sudānavaḥ* ।
— *AV* 6.30.1

16. *te ha te gandharvā āsuḥ śūrpam yavamān kṛṣir uddālavān dhānāntarvān. . .*
— *ŚB* 11.2.3.9

17. *ṚV* 1.23.15, 1.117.21, 1.168.7, 1.176.2, 3.3.7, 4.57, 8.20.19, 8.22.6, 10.34.13, 10.94.13, 10.101.3-6, 10.117.7, 10.131.2-3; *AV* 3.17.1-9, 6.10.1, 8.10.24, 10.125.2, 12.1.42; *MS* 3.2.4; *KS* 20.3; *KapKS* 32.5; *TS* 5.2.5.2-5; *ŚB* 7.2.2.1ff-7.2.4.26.

18. *kṛṣanto ha smaiva pūrve bapanto yanti lūnanto 'pare mṛṇantaḥ śaśvaddhebhyo 'kṛṣṭapacyā 'evauṣadhaya pecire* — *ŚB* 1.6.1.3

19. *TS* 5.2.5.2-5; *ŚB* 7.2.2.1, 7.2.4.26.

20. (i) *puruṣamātreṇa vimimīte, yajñena vai puruṣaḥ sammito yajñapuruṣaivainaṁ vimimīte yāvān puruṣa ūrdhvabāhus tāvān bhavati*
— *TS* 5.2.5.1

→

ground to be ploughed, the mode and number of ploughing,[21] watering,[22] etc. Though details mentioned are applicable for ritual purpose, from them we may have a fair idea about the process of cultivation followed at that period.

As regards ploughing the ground we find that a team of six or eight[23] or twelve[24] oxen was employed to draw the plough. The *ŚB*[25] has recorded the use of a plough drawn by twenty-four animals. On the contrary it was found that sometimes sheep were employed for the same purpose.[26]

According to the late Vedic Saṁhitās and Brāhmaṇas,[27] it appears that the use of roller was known to the people, probably for levelling the soil and making it ready for sowing.

That manures were used for fertilizing the soil has been known from the use of terms, e.g., *śakṛt*,[28] *śaka*,[29] *karīṣa*,[30] etc. Cowdung was used to serve this purpose. The *AV*[31] appreciates

---

→ (ii) *vācam visṛjya stamba yajur harati* ।
stamba yajur hṛtvā pūrveṇa parigraheṇa likhitvā 'ha
— *ŚB* 7.2.2.1

21. *TS* 5.2.5.3-5; *ŚB* 7.2.2.2-21.
22. *ŚB* 7.2.4.1-12.
23. *AV* 6.91.1; *MS* 3.2.4; *KS* 20.3; *KapKS* 32.5; *TS* 5.2.5.2; *ŚB* 7.2.2.6, etc.
24. *yad dvādaśagavena saṁvatsareṇeveyaṁ* — *TS* 5.2.5.2; cf. *ŚB* 7.2.2.6
25. *caturviṁśati gavaṁ vā samvatsaram evābhisampadam* । — *ŚB* 7.2.2.6
26. *indrāgnībhyāṁ baladābhyāṁ sīravāhāvavi* . . . — *TS* 5.6.21.1
27. (i) *yajñāyaiva prabhinnāya matyam anvavāsyati śāntyai* — *TS* 6.6.7.4
(ii) *tadyathā duṣkṛṣṭaṁ durmatīkṛtam sukṛṣṭaṁ sumatīkṛtam*
— *AB* 3.88
28. *ṚV* 1.161.10; *AV* 12.4.4, 12.4.9; *TS* 7.1.19.3.
29. *AV* 3.14.4, 12.4.4.
30. *AV* 3.14.3, 19.31.3; *ŚB* 2.1.1.7.
31. *saṁjagmānā avibhyuṣīr asmin goṣṭhe karīṣiṇīḥ* ।
vibhratīḥ somyaṁ madhvanamīvā upetana ॥
ihaiva gāva eteneho śakeva puṣyata ।
ihaivota prajāyadhvam mayi saṁjñānam astu vaḥ ॥
— *AV* 3.14.3-4

the animals as a source of natural manure. According to the *ŚB*[32] cowdung surcharges the soil with savour, that is why cowdung was collected for cultivation.

People's prayer for heavy rainfall suggests that for watering the field people mainly depended on rain.[33] In the context of ritual cultivation, the *ŚB*[34] has instructed to pour twelve jars of water in the field from four directions, which appears to be a symbol of rainfall throughout the year. From this, it has been evident that people had to depend on rainfall for watering the cornfield. Still, the expressions like *hradaṁ kulyā* (*ṚV* 3.45.3) or *khanitrimā āpaḥ* (*ṚV* 7.49.2) prove that irrigation system (both the artificial and natural ones) was not unknown since the early Vedic period.

After having prepared the ground ready, the seeds were sown. The *ŚB*'s[35] reference to the sowing of both the domestic and wild seeds on both the ploughed and unploughed ground indicates that use of both kinds of seeds was conventional. According to the *TS*[36] cultivation of at least fourteen types of corn was known to the people. In the context of Vasordhārā rite the *VS*[37] has given an enumeration of corn, viz., *vrīhi, yava, tila, māṣa, aṇu, priyaṅguḥ, mudga, khalva, śyāmāka, nīvāra, godhūma* and *masūra*. The *MS* (4.3.2) and the *KS* (12.7) while enumerating

---

32. *tad asya evainam etat pṛthivyai rasena samardhayati tasmād ākhukarīṣaṁ sambharati purīṣyā iti* — *ŚB* 2.1.1.7
33. *AS* 4.15.1-9, 7.18.1-2.
34. *dvādaśodacamasān kṛṣṭe ninayati* । *dvādaśa māsā saṁvatsaraḥ* । . . . *tvataivāsminnetad vṛṣṭim dadhāti* । — *ŚB* 7.2.4.4, 7.2.4.9
35. *MS* 3.2.5; *KS* 20.4; *KapKS* 32.6; *TS* 5.2.5.2-5; *ŚB* 7.2.2.1-4, 7.2.2.28.
36. *caturdaśabhir vapati sapta grāmyā oṣadhayaḥ saptā 'raṇyāḥ* । — *TS* 5.2.5.5
37. *vrīhayaśca me, yavāśca me, māṣāśca me, tilāśca me, mudgāśca me, khalvāśca me, priyaṅgavaśca me, 'ṇavaśca me, śyāmākāśca me, nīvārāśca me, godhūmāśca me, masūrāśca me, yajñena kalpantām* ॥ — *VS* 18.12

corn, have given almost the same list with a slight variation. *Daśa grāmyāṇi dhānyāni bhavanti* (*BU* 6.3.13), clearly shows that by the time of Upaniṣads people learnt to grow some more species of domestic corn.

Names of cutting implements[38] and the description of cutting corn[39] have made it clear that ripe corn were cut with a sickle and after that they were threshed on the floor of the granary.[40] There the grains were separated from straws by winnowing them with the help of a sieve[41] (*titaü*) or a basket[42] (*śūrpa*).

According to the *TS*[43] there are two harvests in a year while the *ŚB*[44] has declared herbs grow thrice in a year in the spring, rainy season and in the autumn. In the context of *Dvādaśarātra* sacrifice the *TS*,[45] in a single sentence has summed up the times of ripening corn, e.g., summer for barley, autumn for rice, winter and cool season for bean and sesamum. The month of Caitra has been recorded in the *KB*[46] as the time of harvesting corn.

From the *ṚV*,[47] it appears that seeds were preserved for the next season. For this preservation, use of granary was

38. *ṚV* 8.78.10, 10.101.3; *AV* 3.17.2; *VS* 12.68; *TS* 4.2.5.5.
39. *ṚV* 10.101.3, 10.131.2; *AV* 10.125.2; *VS* 19.6; *TS* 1.8.2.1, etc.
40. *khale na parṣān hanmi bhūri kiṁ mā nindanti śatravo 'nindrāḥ* ।
— *ṚV* 10.48.7
41. *saktum iva titaünā punanto yatra dhīrā vācam akrata* । — *ṚV* 10.71.2
42. *varṣa vṛddham upayaccha śūrpaṁ tuṣam palāvanapa tad vinaktu* ।
— *AV* 12.3.19
43. *dviḥ samvatsarasya sasyaṁ pacyate* — *TS* 5.1.7.2
44. *tebhyaḥ etāstriḥ purā jāyante vasantā prāvṛṣi śaradi* — *ŚB* 7.2.4.26
45. *yavam grīṣmāyauṣadhīr varṣābhyo vrīhiñcharade māṣatilau hemanta-śiśirābhyām* — *TS* 7.2.10.2
46. *caitrasyāmāvāsyāyā ekāha upariṣṭād dīkṣerannāgataṁ sasyaṁ bhavati* ।
— *KB* 19.3
47. *vapanto bījamiva dhānyakṛtaḥ pṛñcanti somaṁ na minanti vapsataḥ* ।
— *ṚV* 10.94.13

known to the people. In the range of Vedic literature, we find at least four names to mean granary, viz., *upānasa, sthivi, ūrdara, kṛdara,* etc. From the textual context the term *upānasa*[48] appears to mean wagon body. However, the commentator has explained the term as granary. From the description of collecting barely from *sthivi* it may not be wrong to take *sthivi* in the sense of granary.[49] *Ūrdara* occurs only once in the *ṚV* (2.14.11). From the expression *tam ūrdaraṁ na pṛṇatā yavena* (*ūrdara,* filled with barley) we are to guess the meaning of *ūrdara* as granary. Yāska in his *Nirukta*[50] has explained the term *ūrdara* and *kṛdara* as synonyms for granary. In later ages, Sāyaṇācārya[51] also agreed with him on this point.

FARMERS

As regards farmers, we find in the Vedic literature, they have been called by four or five names, viz., *kīnāśa, kārṣīvaṇa, vapa* and *iḍavāh.* These names have occurred in Vedas to mean cultivator or farmer in its general sense, or the persons who were somehow involved in the process of cultivation.

Kīnāśa,[52] appearing in the *ṚV* as well as in the *AV,* means cultivator, sometimes ploughman only. The *AV*[53] has supplied another name for plougher, i.e., *kārṣīvaṇa.* From the textual context, *dhānyakṛt*[54] indicates cultivator though the term has

---

48. *ṚV* 10.105.4; *AV* 2.14.2.
49. *bṛhaspatiḥ parvatebhyo vituryā nirgā upeyavam iva ṣthivibhyaḥ* ।
— *ṚV* 10.68.3
50. *ūrdaraṁ kṛdaram ityāvapanasya, ūrdaram uddīrṇam bhavati , urje dīrṇam vā* — *Nir* 3.20
51. *ūrdhvaṁ dīrṇam ūrdaraṁ kusūlam* — Sā on *ṚV* 2.14.11
52. *ṚV* 4.57.8; *AV* 4.11.10, 6.30.1; *VS* 30.11; *TB* 2.4.8.7
53. *yad yāmaṁ cakrur nikhananto agre kārṣīvaṇā annavido na vidyayā* ।
— *AV* 6.116.1
54. *vapanto bījamiva dhānyakṛtaḥ pṛñcanti somaṁ na minanti vapsataḥ* ।
— *ṚV* 10.94.13

been rendered as winnower by some Western scholars.[55] From the *AB*,[56] we have got a picture of farmers who are delighted at the advent of rainy season. Here we find another name of farmer, i.e., *iḍavāh*, which has been explained as farmers by Sāyaṇa.[57] The *VS* and the *TB*[58] in the context of human sacrifice have recorded the name of *vapa* as one of the sacrificial victims, which means sower.

AGRICULTURAL IMPLEMENTS

In order to go through these various stages of operations, the farmer required different implements at different stages, viz., plough, sickle, goad, etc. Vedic Saṁhitā and Brāhmaṇas provide us at least three words to mean plough, e.g., *sīra*[59] (otherwise read as *śīla* — *KapKS* 28.8), *lāṅgala*[60] and *phāla*.[61] From the use of these terms (*lāṅgala, phāla* and *sīra*) occurring separately in consequent verses,[62] it may not be wrong to interpret *sīra* as the whole plough while *lāṅgala* and *phāla* as its parts. *Sīra* or *śīla* was dragged by a team of oxen (six or eight or twelve or even sometimes by twenty-four also) which were yoked and harnessed with traces and controlled by *aṣṭrā*[63] the

---

55. Keith & Macdonell, *Vedic Index*, I, p. 182, 399, Monier-Williams.
56. *annaṁ vai nyuṅkho yadeḍavā abhigeṣṇāścaranti . . .* — *AB* 5.3
57. *iḍāśabdo 'nnavāci, tad yeśāṁ karṣakāṇām asti te karṣakāḥ iḍavāḥ* ।
— Sā on *AB* 5.3
58. *VS* 30.7; *TB* 3.4.3.1.
59. *R̥V* 4.57.8, 10.131.3-4; *AV* 3.17.7, 6.30.1, 6.91.1, 8.9.16; *MS* 2.6.2, 2.11.4; *TS* 4.2.5.5; *VS* 18.7; *TB* 1.7.1.2, etc.
60. *R̥V* 4.57.4; *AV* 2.8.4, 3.17.6; *MS* 2.7.12; *KS* 16.11; *TS* 4.2.5.6; *VS* 12.71.
61. *R̥V* 4.57.8, 10.117.7; *AV* 3.17.5, 10.6.33; *VS* 12.69.
62. *R̥V* 4.57.7-8; *AV* 3.17.3-6.
63. *śunaṁ vāhāḥ śunaṁ naraḥ śunaṁ kṛṣatu lāṅgalam* ।
śunaṁ varatrā badhyantāṁ śunamaṣṭrām udīṅgayaḥ ॥
— *R̥V* 4.57.4; *AV* 3.17.6

goad, held by the ploughman. The *ŚB*,[64] while discussing the expiatory rites connected with *Agnihotra* has referred to *tottra* (another name of goad) used for driving cattles.

From the fact of its being drawn by a large number of animals, it appears that large and heavy ploughs were used for tilling the ground. The *TS* in the context of Horse Sacrifice referred to the plough drawn by two sheep (*sīravāhāvavī* — *TS* 5.6.21.1). Are we to suppose here that a lighter variety (of the plough) also was used in cultivation?

The term *lāṅgala* appearing frequently in the *ṚV* and in the late Vedic Saṁhitās as well, has been described as having a smooth handle (*tsaru*), lance-pointed (*pavīravat*), and well-lying (*suśevam*). The *phāla* appears to mean share (carved blade, which actually tills the soil), though somewhere it means the whole plough (*AV* 10.6.33; *TS* 4.2.5.6).

In the context of animal offerings in the "Soma Sacrifice" the *TS* (6.6.7.4) has mentioned use of *matya* in the ploughed field, which has been explained as roller by some Western scholars. Again reference to *laya* (*VS* 18.7) read as *layu* (*MS* 2.11.4) and *lāya* (*KS* 16.11) indicates harrow or hoe, which served more or less the same purpose.

The terms like *sṛṇi* and *dātra* (sickles) indicate that these were used for cutting corns. The winnowers required *śūrpa* (winnowing basket) or *titaü* (sieve) for winnowing and unhusking the threshed corn.

Cattle Rearing

Besides agriculture, cattle rearing was practised with equal importance. In the *ṚV*, two hymns (6.28, 10.169) have been

---

64. *balībardo vā yuktaḥ tena daṇḍaprajitena tottraprajitena yam-adhvānaṁ samīpsati . . .* — *ŚB* 12.4.1.10

addressed entirely to the cows.[65] Frequent references to cows, prayer to the deities for their protection,[66] safe shelter[67] and food[68] as well, suggest that these animals were regarded as wealth. In the *R̥V*[69] cows have been eulogized in an exalted tone, in some places they have been addressed as deities.[70]

Prayers have been offered to the deities for having a large number of animals[71] (specially cows) and good pasturage.[72] In the *AV* (3.14) there is a benedictory hymn of cow-pen. Apart from this, in some other passages also cow-pen has been addressed in a glorified language.[73] All this suggests that at that time people could not think of a home without cattle. In the Brāhmaṇa literature, we find that people having realized the utility of cattle described it in terms of food,[74] home,[75] nourishment[76] and wealth.[77] Cattle were necessary for cultivation, therefore cattle meant food and wealth to them. In trade, cows were used as medium of exchange.[78] Use of cattle as sacrificial fee was known to the people from the

---

65. *R̥V* 1.42.8, 1.43.2, 4.24.10, 6.28.1, 6.53.10, 6.54.5, 10.169.1-4; *AV* 6.77.2-3, 7.77.6-7; *VS* 8.54-55; *TS* 3.1.2.1.
66. *R̥V* 6.28.3, 6.54.5, 6.54.7, 10.169.2; *AV* 6.141.1, 7.75.1-2, 11.2.9.
67. *R̥V* 10.101.8, 10.169.4; *AV* 3.14.1, 19.58.4.
68. *R̥V* 1.42.8, 6.28.7, 8.45.16, 10.106.2, 10.169.1; *AV* 7.73.11, etc.
69. *R̥V* 4.58.4, 6.28.6-7, 10.169.2-3.
70. *gāvo bhago gāva indro me acchān gāvaḥ somasya prathamasya bhakṣaḥ* ।
imā yā gāvaḥ sajanāsa indra icchāmīddhr̥dā manasā cid indram ॥
— *R̥V* 6.28.5
71. *R̥V* 6.28.2, 6.53.10; *AV* 3.14.1, 3.14.5, 6.141.1, 11.2.9.
72. *R̥V* 1.42.8, 6.28.7, 8.45.16, 10.106.8; *AV* 7.73.11, 7.75.1-2, etc.
73. *R̥V* 6.28.2, 10.101.8, 10.169.2; *AV* 6.77.1, 7.75.2, 19.58.4.
74. *paśavo hi annam* — *ŚB* 3.7.1.20
75. *gr̥hā hi paśavaḥ* — *ŚB* 1.8.2.14
76. *puṣṭiḥ paśavaḥ* — *ŚB* 3.1.4.14
77. *paśavo vasuḥ* — *ŚB* 3.7.3.13
78. *R̥V* 4.24.10, 8.1.5; *AV* 8.7.11; *VS* 8.53-54; *TS* 3.1.2.1, etc.

Ṛgvedic[79] age. Moreover, cattle were given in the form of prize in debates/discourses, held on the sacrificial occasions.[80]

As regards persons involved in cattle rearing, there are references to *paśupā, gopā, godhuk, dogdhṛ* meaning herdsman, milkman, etc., which indicate that cattle rearing was practised as a major occupation since the early Vedic[81] age. According to the Brāhmaṇas (*ŚB* 3.6.2.12; *AĀ* 3.1.6; *ŚĀ* 7.19) and Upaniṣads (*CU* 4.4.5; *BU* 3.1.1) cattle-tending was one of the daily duties of a student.

Besides cattle farming, other animals like horses, goats, sheep, etc. were tended.[82] In the Vedic Saṁhitās there are references to prayers offered to the deities for protection[83] (of these animals) and increase in number,[84] which suggest that all these animals were regarded as property. Dogs were tamed specially to guard the house.[85] Two watch-dogs kept in Yama's house have been mentioned in the *ṚV* (10.14.11). Camels also were domesticated, most probably for carrying loads from one place to another.[86]

Trade & Commerce

In the Vedic literature there are references to the traders,[87] sale and purchase,[88] trading commodities,[89] articles used as

79. *ṚV* 1.126.2, 1.126.5, 6.27.8, 6.47.23-24, 7.90.6, 8.4.20-21.
80. *BU* 3.1.1, 4.11.2.
81. *ṚV* 1.4.1, 1.144.6, 3.45.3, 4.6.4, 5.31.1, 6.19.3, 10.19.4-5; *AV* 3.8.4, 6.77.2, 7.73.6, 8.9.1; *VS* 17.58, etc.
82. *ṚV* 6.53.4, 6.54.5; *AV* 4.14.1, 6.77.1; *VS* 30.11; *TB* 3.4.9.
83. *ṚV* 1.43.2, 6.28.3, 6.54.5, 6.54.7, 10.169.2; *AV* 6.141.1, 7.75.1-2, 11.2.9.
84. *ṚV* 6.28.2; *AV* 3.14.1, 3.14.5-6.
85. *ṚV* 7.55.1-8, 10.14.10; *VS* 16.28; *TS* 4.5.4.2.
86. *ṣaṣṭiṁ sahasrāśvasyayutāsanam uṣṭrāṇāṁ viṁśatiṁ śatā* — *ṚV* 8.46.22
87. *ṚV* 1.33.3, 1.56.2, 1.112.11, 4.55.11, 4.55.6, 5.45.6, 8.45.14, 10.156.3; *AV* 3.15.1; *VS* 16.19; *AB* 1.12; *TB* 3.4.14.1, etc.
88. *ṚV* 4.24.9-10; *AV* 3.15.2; *VS* 3.49, 8.54-55; *TS* 3.1.2.1, 6.1.3.3, etc.
89. *AV* 4.7.6; *TS* 6.1.10.1-2; *ŚB* 12.7.2.10.

mediums of exchange,[90] etc., which clearly indicates that since early Vedic age trade was practised as a means of earning livelihood. The *AV* 4.15 is actually a merchant's prayer uttered for achieving success in the business.

Though the term *kraya* (purchasing) or *vikraya* (sale) is absent in the *R̥V* and the root/*krī* from which the term has been derived occurs rarely in the *R̥V*[91] (but it occurs frequently in the later Saṁhitās),[92] the concept of selling and purchasing was not unknown; e.g., the *R̥V*[93] has fixed ten milch-cows as the price for Indra's fetish. In another passage the same text could not ascertain any price adequate for the purchase of Indra.[94] Even the haggling of market was known to the R̥gvedic[95] people. In the context of purchasing Soma, the *ŚB*[96] has remarked at first people bargain and then come to the terms.

From the early Vedic period, there are references to the sea-voyages[97] and sea-going strong vessels[98] from which we can infer the existence of maritime trade.

---

90. *Ibid.*
91. *AV* 3.15.2, 4.27.6, 8.7.11; *VS* 3.49, 8.54-55, 19.13; *TS* 3.1.3.1.
92. *AV* 3.15.2, 4.27.6, 8.7.11; *VS* 3.49, 8.54-55, 19.13; *TS* 3.1.2.1.
93. *ka imaṁ daśabhir mamendraṁ krīṇāti dhenubhiḥ* । — *R̥V* 4.24.10
94. *mahecana tvam adrivaḥ parā śulkāya deyam* ।
    na sahasrāya nāyutāya vajrivo na śatāya śatam agha ॥
    — *R̥V* 8.1.5
95. *bhūyasā vasram acarat kanīyo 'vikrītam akāniṣaṁ punar yan* ।
    sa bhūyasā kanīyo nārirecī hīnā dakṣā viduhanti pra vāṇam ॥
    — *R̥V* 4.24.9
96. *tasmād idam sakr̥t sarvaṁ paṇyam arvāk paṇanta paraḥ sampādayanti*
    — *ŚB* 3.3.3.4
97. *R̥V* 1.56.2, 4.55.6; *AV* 3.6.3, 6.105.3.
98. *AB* 1.3.2, 6.29.5.

According to the *AV*,[99] garments (*dūrśa*), coverlets (*pavasta*), animal skin (*ajina*) were business commodities. The Yajurvedic Saṁhitā and Brāhmaṇas[100] have mentioned some other names, e.g., lead, wool, thread, garments, gold and animals as business articles.

Vedic Saṁhitās[101] inform us that in the early Vedic period trade consisted in the form of barter. The expression *somakrayaṇī gauḥ* referred to in the *YS*[102] suggests importance of cows, as medium of exchange. In this connection we may refer to the *AB* (1.27) where goddess Vāc converted herself into a cow and instructed gods to purchase Soma with that. In the *TS* (6.1.10.1-2) we find a list of nine items, at the cost of which Soma was purchased. The *ŚB* (12.7.2.10) while discussing on the *Sautrāmaṇī* rite, mentions lead, wool, thread and food grains as mediums of exchange.

As regards traders, we see in the Vedic literature there are some names, e.g., *vaṇij*,[103] *vāṇija*,[104] *paṇi*,[105] *śreṣṭhī*[106] which occur to mean merchant. In the *Ṛ̥V* and later Saṁhitās, *vaṇij* appears to mean merchant. Indra has been described as a merchant in the *AV*.[107] It is difficult to ascertain the exact

---

99. *pavastaistvā paryakrīṇan dūrśebhir ajinairuta । prakrīrasi tvam oṣadhe 'bhrikhāte narūrupaḥ ॥* — *AV* 4.7.6

100. (i) . . . *ajayā krīṇāti . . . hiraṇyena krīṇāti . . . dhenvā krīṇāti . . . ṛṣabheṇa krīṇāti . . . anaḍuhā krīṇāti . . . mithunābhyāṁ krīṇāti . . . vāsasā krīṇati* — *TS* 3.7.7.8, 6.1.10.1-2

(ii) *sīsena śaṣpāṇi krīṇāti ūrṇābhiḥ tokmāni sūtrair vrīhīn* — *ŚB* 12.7.2.10

101. *Ṛ̥V* 4.24.9-10, 8.1.5; *VS* 8.54-55; *TS* 3.1.2.1, etc.

102. *VS* 3.49, 8.54-55; *TS* 3.1.2.1, 6.1.10.1-2.

103. *Ṛ̥V* 1.112.11, 5.45.6; *AV* 3.15.1.

104. *VS* 16.19, 30.17; *TB* 3.4.14.1.

105. *Ṛ̥V* 1.32.2, 1.33.3, 1.180.7, 8.15.14, 8.64.2, etc.

106. *tasmād u śreṣṭhī rocayatyeva yaṁ kāmayate* — *AB* 3.30

107. *indram ahaṁ vaṇijaṁ codayāmi* — *AV* 3.15.1

meaning of the term *paṇi*. Still from the description of *paṇis* in some places, it appears that greedy traffickers are meant by the term.[108] Yāska[109] also, on account of its being derived from the root √*paṇ* (to trade) has explained the term as merchant. In the *AB śreṣṭhī* appears to mean a merchant-prince or the headman of a guild.

Other Modes of Production

Along with agriculture, animal husbandry, trade and commerce, hunting and fishing also were practised simultaneously, as other modes of production.

HUNTING

Hunting of various animals, hunting implements, modes of hunting, etc., have been mentioned in various passages of the *ṚV* and *AV*, from which we may infer that hunting was practised from early Vedic period, though its purpose has not been clear from the said references. It is noteworthy that Keith and Macdonell[110] in their work have opined,

> It is not probable that even in the Vedic period hunting formed the main source of livelihood for any of the Vedic tribes: pastoral pursuits and agriculture were no doubt the mainstay of their existence.

On the basis of this statement it may not be wrong to infer that hunting was the mainstay of the society in the pre-Vedic age when people were nomads. In course of time, they settled in fixed places and learnt to practise agriculture. Gradually their lifestyle was changed.

---

108. *ṚV* 1.33.3, 1.180.7, 5.61.8, 6.53.3, 8.64.2, 10.60.6.
109. (i) *paṇir vaṇig bhavati* । *paṇih pananāt* । *vaṇik paṇyam nenekti* — *Nir* 2.17

 (ii) *paṇīṁśca vaṇijaḥ* — *Nir.* 6.26
110. Keith & Macdonell, *Vedic Index*, II, p. 173.

Hunting Implements

In this task, they required some implements. Various types of nets/traps were used, viz., *nidhā,*[111] *pāśa,*[112] *mukṣija,*[113] *jāla/jālaka,*[114] etc. The phrase *gṛbhnāti-ripuṁ nidhayā nidhāpatiḥ* (*ṚV* 9.83.4) proves use of *nidhā,* a sort of snare/net mainly for catching birds. *Mukṣija* was another name for snare which served more or less the same purpose. From Śunaḥśepa's repeated prayer for being released from *pāśa bandhana* we are to guess use of *pāśa* was prevalent for fastening animals.[115] The picture of wild steer captured in leather straps (*ṚV* 10.28.10) make us suppose use of leather straps (for tying the animals). Description of wild beasts flying away from the bowman suggests arrows were used for hunting.[116] Use of an arrow having the shape of trident (*iṣustrikāṇḍā*) has been recorded in the *AB* (3.33).

Mode of Hunting

Various modes of hunting have been mentioned in the range of Vedic Saṁhitās. Birds were caught mainly in nets.[117] Reference to *ṛśyada* meaning pits (literally translated as antelope catcher), suggests the use of pits for catching antelopes.[118] From the *AV* (5.14.11) it appears that elephants were caught with the instrumentality of tame female ones. The expression *avaruddhaḥ paripadaṁ na siṁhaḥ* (*ṚV* 10.28.10)

---

111. *ṚV* 9.83.4, 10.73.11; *AV* 8.8.5; *AB* 3.19.
112. *ṚV* 1.24.13, 1.24.15, 2.27.16, 2.29.5; *AV* 2.12.2, 9.3.2; *VS* 6.8; *AB* 4.10; *TB* 2.2.4.5, 2.2.5.1, etc.
113. *ṚV* 1.125.2.
114. *AV* 8.8.5, 8.8.8, 10.1.30; *BU* 4.2.3.
115. *ṚV* 1.24.13, 1.24.15.
116. *tasmād bhiyāvaruṇā dūramāyaṁ gauro na kṣepṇor avijyāyāḥ* ।
— *ṚV* 10.51-6
117. *ṚV* 1.125.2, 9.83.4, 10.73.11, etc.
118. *yuvaṁ vandanamṛśadyādupathur yuvaṁ sadyo* . . . — *ṚV* 10.39.8

make us infer that lions were caught in ambuscade (hidden pitfalls). Sometimes they were surrounded by the hunters and slain.[119] Hunting dogs were used to capture boars.[120] Buffaloes were caught by throwing leather straps/ropes.[121] Desciption of a wild steer trembling at the bowstring of an archer indicates that steers were shot with arrows and caught.[122] According to the *AV*,[123] it seems that after having shot the animal, the hunter chased the foot-prints of the wounded game, most probably to collect the carcass.

Hunters/Fishermen

Now, it may not be irrelevant to discuss about the persons who were involved in hunting/fishing professionally.

In the context of Human sacrifice the Yajurvedic Saṁhitā and Brāhmaṇas[124] enumerate a large number of people (at least ten), viz., *ānda, bainda, dāśa, dhaivara, kaivarta, mārgāra, maināla, pauñjiṣṭha, parṇaka* and *śauṣkala* who have been explained as fishermen by the commentator.[125]

But as regards the mode of their work or required implements there is hardly any evidence in the said textbooks.

---

119. *sa navajātastuturyāt siṁhaṁ na kruddham abhitaḥ pariṣṭuḥ* ।
— *ṚV* 5.15.3

120. *yam imaṁ tvaṁ vṛṣākapiṁ priyam indrābhirakṣasi* ।
nvasya jambhiṣad api karṇe varāhayur viśvasmād indra uttaraḥ ॥
— *ṚV* 10.86.4

121. *niruddhaścin mahiṣas tarṣyāvān godhā tasmā ayathaṁ karṣad etat* ॥
— *ṚV* 10.28.10

122. *tasmād bhiyā varuṇa dūramāyaṁ gauro na kṣepṇor avijyāyāḥ* ।
— *ṚV* 10.51.6

123. *AV* 10.1.26, 11.213.

124. *sarobhyo dhaivaram* । *vaiśantābhyo dāśam* । *upasthāvarībhyo baindam* । *naḍbalābhyaḥ śauṣkalam* । *pāryāya kaivartam* । *avāryāya mārgāram* । *tīrthebhya āndam* । *viṣamebhyo mainālam* । *svanebhyaḥ parṇakam* । *guhābhyaḥ kirātam* । — *VS* 30.16; *TB* 3.4.12.1

125. Sā on *TB, loc. cit.*

Further, some other names, viz., *mṛgayu, kirāta, pāśin, goghāta, govyaccha, govikarta*, etc. (whose names have been marked as hunters[126]), have been recorded in the said texts. *Niṣādas* also are said to have earned their livelihood by hunting/fishing (*PB* 16.6.7; *TB* 3.4.5).

Existence of these people suggests that hunting was practised by some people as a means of earning. The name of Nirṛti "the goddess of destruction" has been mentioned in the *AB*[127] as *pāśinī* (one, having a noose). The *TMB*[128] in the legend of Prajāpati and his daughter has recorded the name of Rudra as *mṛgavyādha* (a huntsman).

FISHERY

Fish and its being caught in nets have been referred to in the *ṚV*[129] which make us guess that catching of fish was in practice since the Ṛgvedic age.

Existence of fishery, as a separate vocation can be presumed from the list of people, who have been explained by the commentator as fishermen and enumerated in the Yajurvedic texts (*VS* 30.16; *TB* 3.4.12.1 — names have already been mentioned in the section on Hunting). As regards the mode of hunting very little is known as because the only available evidence on this point are commentaries of the said texts. However, J. Auboyer[130] in her work has remarked:

> As for the fishermen, they used hooks, nets and basket traps. The Indian coastal waters were teeming with fish and the fishermen had no difficulty in filling their boats with the catch.

---

126. *VS* 30.17-18; *TB* 3.4.17.1.
127. *nirṛtir ha pāśinyupāste . . .* — *AB* 4.10
128. *ya u eva mṛgavyādhaḥ* । — *AB* 3.33
129. *puroḷā intur vaśo yakṣurāsīdrāye matsyāso niśitā apītā* । — *ṚV* 10.68.8
130. J. Auboyer, *Daily Life in Ancient India*, Part I, Ch. 4, p. 101.

Vocations Related to Cottage Industries

Besides these, weaving, carpentry, pottery, etc., were known to the people of that period, which developed as cottage-industries.

WEAVING

Weaving was a well-known occupation from early Vedic age[131] and was practised by a particular sect of people who were neither brāhmaṇas nor preparers of libations. Existence of female weaver, e.g., *vayantī* (*R̥V* 2.3.6, 2.38.4; *VS* 20.41), *sirī* (*R̥V* 10.71.9), *vayitrī* (*PB* 7.8.9), indicates that work of weaving was done mainly by the special care of women.[132] Still from the expression *vāsovāyo 'vīnām ā* (the weaver of woollen cloth — *R̥V* 10.26.6) we may infer that occasionally men also practised it.

The discussion on various dress-materials (which we have done already under "Dress Arrangement, Ch. 2") bespeaks of high standard of clothing and weaving of that period. Cotton, silk, wool and animal skin were used as dress material, even grass and feathers also were woven.

Weaving technique has been recorded in the *AV*[133] through a metaphor. Weaver's loom was termed as *veman*.[134] Two persons were required to handle it most probably for weaving

---

131. *ime nārvāṅ parāñcaranti na brāhmaṇāso na sutekarāsaḥ* ।
ta ete pāpam abhipadya pāpayā sirītantraṁ tanvate aprajajñayaḥ ॥
— *R̥V* 10.71.9

132. *R̥V* 2.3.6, 2.38.4; *AV* 10.7.42, 14.2.51; *TS* 2.5.5.3.

133. *tantram eke yuvatī virūpe abhyākrāmaṁ vayataḥ ṣaṇmayūkham* ।
prānyā tantūṁstirate dhatte anyā nāpavr̥ñjāte na gamāto antam ॥
— *AV* 10.7.42

134. *sarasvatī manasā peśalaṁ vasu nāsatyābhyāṁ vayati darśataṁ vapuḥ* ।
rasaṁ parisrutā na rohitaṁ nagnahudhīstasaram na vema ॥
— *VS* 19.83

forwards and backwards.[135] They streched out warps (*otu*[136]) of the cloth and were weaving with the aid of wooden pegs (*mayūkha*[137]). In the weaving process a shuttle (*tasara*[138]) was used. Lead was used probably as a weight.[139]

SMITH

Vocation of blacksmith was equally important for providing so many types of instruments and tools required for continuing the task of other professionals.

In the *ṚV*[140] there are at least three terms, viz., *karmāra, dhmātā* and *dravi* which occur to mean blacksmith or smelter. In the context of Human sacrifice the *VS* and the *TB*[141] present another name for smelter, i.e., *ayastāpa*.

The smith has been described as a cunning worker in the *AV*[142]. The names *dhmātṛ* and *dravi* indicate his task of smelting ore on the fire. Out of hammered metals he produced kettles[143] fashioned with *ayas*, Soma-cups of beaten *ayas*,[144] arrows

---

135. (i) *ime vayanti pitaro ya āyayuḥ pravayāpavayetyāsate tate* ।
— *ṚV* 10.130.2

(ii) *pumām enaṁ tanuta utkṛṇanti pumān vitatne adhināke 'smin*
— *ṚV* 10.131.2

136. *ṚV* 6.9.2-3, 10.130.2; *AV* 14.2.51; *TS* 6.1.1.7.

137. *ime mayūkhā upa sedurū sadaḥ sāmāni cakruṣtasarāṇyotave* ।
— *ṚV* 10.130.2

138. *VS* 19.83; *MS* 3.11.9; *KS* 38.3., etc.

139. *sīsena tantraṁ manasā manīṣiṇa ūrṇāsūtreṇa kavayo vayanti*
— *VS* 19.80

140. *ṚV* 5.9.5, 6.3.4, 9.112.2, 10.72.2, etc.

141. *manyave 'yastāpam* — *VS* 30.14; cf. *TB* 3.4.10.1

142. *ye dhīvāno rathakārā karmāro ye manīṣiṇaḥ* । *upastīn parṇa mahyaṁ tvaṁ sarvān kṛṇvabhitojanān* ॥ — *AV* 3.5.6

143. *gharmaścittaptaḥ pravṛje ya āsīdayasmayastambā dāma viprāḥ* ।
— *ṚV* 5.30.15

144. *rakṣohā viśvacarṣaṇir abhi yonim ayohatam* । *druṇā sadhastham āsadat* ।
— *RV* 9.1.2

pointed with *ayas*,[145] etc. Further, shovel, spade, ploughshare, sickle, axe, etc., were his other products. But his working method and tools can be hardly known from the texts. Only the bellow of birds' wings which he used to fan the flames of fire, has been mentioned.[146]

The earliest record of the name of goldsmith *hiraṇyakāra* and jeweller *maṇikāra* as professional figures can be traced in the *VS*[147] but use of varieties of ornaments and jewelleries has been attested from the *ṚV* onwards — on the basis of this evidence, existence of these crafts and craftsmen as well may be presumed from early Vedic period. (See Ornaments under Dress Arrangement, Chapter 2).

CARPENTRY

In the Vedic literature, there are references to the carpenter and chariot-wright (*tvaṣṭṛ*,[148] *taṣṭṛ*,[149] *takṣan*[150]) and their products, which prove the importance of their service. In the *ṚV* the skill of a carpenter has been expressed in a distinct language:

> *abhi vyayasva khadirasya sāramojo dhehi spandane śiṁśapāyām* ।
> *akṣa-vīlo vīḷito vīḷayasva mā yāmādasmādava jīhipo naḥ* ॥
> — *ṚV* 3.53.19

He manufactured various types of wooden implements and utensils, viz., varieties of wooden jars[151] (*kośa, dru, droṇa, sadhastha*) and ladles[152] (*juhū, darvī, upabhṛt, upasecanī, sruk, sruva,*

---

145. *ālāktā yā ruruśīrṣṇyatho yasyā ayomukham* ।
idaṁ parjanyaretasa iṣvyai devyai bṛhannamaḥ ॥ — *ṚV* 6.75.15
146. *jaratībhir oṣadhībhiḥ parṇebhiḥ śakunānām* । — *ṚV* 9.112.2
147. *VS* 30.7, 30.17; *TB* 3.4.3.1, 3.4.13.1.
148. *ṚV* 1.85.9; *AV* 12.3.44.
149. *ṚV* 1.20.6, 1.61.4, 1.105.18, 1.130.4, 3.38.1, 7.32.20, 10.119.5, etc.
150. *ṚV* 9.112.1; *AV* 10.6.3; *MS* 3.9.5; *KS* 12.10; *VS* 16.27; *TB* 3.4.2.1, etc.
151. *ṚV* 3.62.15, 7.101.4, 8.20.8, 9.1.2, 9.15.7, 9.17.8, 9.33.2, 9.98.2, etc.
152. *ṚV* 1.20.6, 1.84.18, 1.110.6, 1.116.24, 1.121.6, 1.144.1, 8.45.5, 10.21.3, *AV* 8.6.17; *TS* 6.5.10.5, etc.

camasa) which were used to serve mainly ritual purposes. Besides these, he manufactured various types of furniture, e.g., beds[153] (*talpa, vahya, śayana proṣṭha*), chairs and seats[154] (*āsandī, paryaṅka*), cradles[155] (*preṅkha*), etc.

In the context of Coronation ceremony the Br[156] texts have discussed his another production, i.e., king's throne (which were made of either *udumbara* or *khadira* wood) in detail, including its material, shape, size and the process of manufacturing. Moreover from the Vedic texts, we find that *takṣan*[157] manufactured chariots, wagons and sometimes carved with finer works also. In this task he used axe[158] (*kuliśa, paraśu* and *svadhiti*) and scissors[159] (*bhūrij*) as necessary instruments.

Takṣan and *rathakāra*[160] being the members of kingmakers had earned important position in the society.

POTTERY

Though the name of potter (*kulāla, kaulāla, mṛtpaca*) as a separate professional and his equipment wheel have been mentioned for the first time in the Yajurvedic Saṁhitās,[161] still the use of various earthenware utensils and implements, viz., *kumbha*,[162] *kalaśa*,[163] *sthālī*,[164] etc., to serve both domestic and ritual purpose,

---

153. *proṣṭheśayā vahyeśayā nārīr yā talpaśīvarīḥ* ı
striyoyā puṇyagandhāstāḥ sarvāḥ svāpayāmasi ıı — *ṚV* 7.55.8
154. *AV* 14.2.65, 15.3.2; *TS* 7.5.8.5; *VS* 8.56; *Kauṣ* 1.5.
155. *KS* 34.5; *PB* 5.5.7; *AĀ* 1.2.3-4.
156. *AB* 8.5-6; *ŚB* 3.3.4.26, 5.2.1.22, 5.4.4.1, etc.
157. *imā brahmāṇi bardhanāśvibhyāṁ santu śantamā* ı
yā takṣāma rathā̐ ivāvocāma bṛhannamaḥ ıı — *ṚV* 5.73.10
158. *ṚV* 1.162.9, 1.162.18, 1.162.20, 3.2.1, *KS* 12.10.
159. *ṚV* 4.2.14, 8.4.16, 9.26.4; *AV* 20.127.4, etc.
160. *MS* 2.6.5, 4.3.8; *ŚB* 5.3.1.1ff.
161. *MS* 16.27, 30.7; *MS* 2.9.5; *KS* 17.13; *TS* 4.5.4.2.
162. *ṚV* 1.116.7, 1.117.6, 7.33.13, 10.89.7; *AV* 1.6.4, 3.12.7; *VS* 29.87.
163. *ṚV* 1.117.12, 3.12.15, 4.27.5, 4.32.19; *AV* 9.1.6, 9.4.5; *TS* 1.1.8.1.
164. *ṚV* 8.6.17; *TS* 6.5.10.5; *VS* 19.27; *AĀ* 1.11.8, 3.2.4; *ŚĀ* 11.6.

has been attested in the early Vedic Saṁhitās. On the basis of this evidence, we are to suppose existence of pottery (as a small industry) since early Vedic age. In the context of *Agnihotra* the *MS*[165] prohibits (esp. in the sacrifice) the use of the pot manufactured by the potter on account of its being wrought by using wheel. The *MS* has called it *asuryaṁ pātram* and prescribed to use *ūrdhvakapāla pātra* (the pot having a lid) in the sacrifice, made by the Aryans. From this, it may not be wrong to suppose that both the technique of manufacturing pots (i.e., by using wheels and connecting two different shreds as well) were known to the people of that age. In the *Maitrī*[166] movement of human body has been compared with the constant movement of potter's wheel from which we may easily infer that products of potter were in constant demand.

Apart from these, the Yajurvedic Saṁhitā and Brāhmaṇas have recorded names of some other vocations related with cottage-industries,* viz., wine maker *surākāra*[167] (*ṚV* 1.191.20), arrow maker *iṣukāra*[168] (*ṚV* 1.184.3), bow maker *dhanuṣkāra*,[169] bowstring maker *jyākāra*,[170] rope maker *rajjusarja*,[171] etc.

Some of these cottage industries were conducted by womenfolk, e.g., basket makers *bidala-karī*,[172] thorn workers

---

165. *āryakṛtī bhavaty ūrdhvakapālā sadevatvāya sā hi sadevā 'suryaṁ vā etat pātraṁ yat kulālakṛtam cakravṛttam* I — *MS* 1.8.3

166. *paribhramatīdaṁ śarīraṁ cakramiva mṛtapacena* I — *Maitrī* 2.6, 3.3

* A point should be mentioned here that some of these professionals are already met with in the *ṚV*, e.g., *surākāra*, *upalaprakṣiṇī* and some others.

167. *kīlālāya surā-kāram* — *VS* 30.11; *TB* 3.4.7.1

168. (i) *nama iṣu-kṛdbhyo* . . . — *VS* 16.46; *TS* 4.5.4.2

(ii) *śaravyāya iṣukāram* — *VS* 30.7; *TB* 3.4.3.1

169. *dhanuṣkṛdbhyo vo namaḥ* — *VS* 16.46

170. *karmaṇe jyākāram* — *VS* 30.7; *TB* 3.4.3.1

171. *diṣṭāya rajjusarjam* — *VS* 30.7; *TB* 3.4.3.1

172. *piśācebhyo bidalakārīm* — *VS* 30.8; *TB* 3.4.5.1

kaṇṭakīkarī,[173] ointment maker *āñjana karī,*[174] female embroiderer *peśaskarī,*[175] scabbard maker *kośa karī,*[176] weaver *sirī*[177] (*ṚV* 10.71.9), *vayitrī,*[178] launderess *vāsaḥpalpulī,*[179] female dyer *rajayitrī,*[180] female grinder of corns *upalaprakṣiṇī* (*ṚV* 9.112.3).

They provided articles of basic necessities, e.g., the cane worker produced baskets and sieves (*śūrpa*),[181] various types of seats and mats made of plaited grass (*kūrca*),[182] *upastaraṇa,*[183] *peśaskarī** beautified garments and cushions (used in thrones) with her cunning work,[184] ointment maker *āñjanakarī* produced different types of ointments,[185] perfumes, etc., *rajayitrī* dyed clothes and *upalaprakṣiṇī* ground corns. Further, the name *smarakārī* (traced in the *TB*[186]) which has been rendered as "a woman who deals in love-charms" — (Griffith) suggests the existence of another vocation conducted by women.

---

173. *yātudhānebhyaḥ kaṇṭakī-kārīm* — *VS* 30.8; *TB* 3.4.5.1
174. *śīlāyāñjanakārīm* — *VS* 30.14; *TB* 3.4.10.1
175. *niṣkṛtyai peśaskārīm* — *VS* 30.9; *TB* 3.4.5.1
176. *nirṛtyai kośakārīm* — *VS* 30.14; *TB* 3.4.10.1
177. *tatra te pāpam abhipadya pāpayā sirītantraṁ tanvate aprajajñayaḥ* ।
— *ṚV* 10.71.9
178. *gnāstvā kṛntannapaso tanvata vayitro vayan* — *PB* 1.8.9
179. *medhāya vāsaḥ-palpūlīm* — *VS* 30.12; *TB* 3.4.7.1
180. *prakāmāya rajayitrīm* — *VS* 30.12; *TB* 3.4.7.1
181. *AV* 9.6.16, 10.9.26, 12.3.19; *TS* 1.6.4.5, 3.2.5.11.
182. *TS* 7.5.8.5; *ŚB* 11.5.3.4, 11.5.3.7.
183. *ṚV* 9.69.5; *AV* 5.19.12; *Kauṣ* 1.5.

* The name *peśaskarī* has been recorded in the *VS* for the first time but her production, i.e., embroidered garment and clothes have been mentioned throughout Vedic Saṁhitā and later texts (see Dress Arrangement, Ch. 2).

184. *ṚV* 10.18.7, 10.146.6; *AV* 6.124.3, 20.128.7; *ŚB* 13.8.4.7.
185. *śīlāyāñjanakārīm* . . . — *VS* 30.14; cf. *TB* 3.4.10
186. *saṁjñānaya smarakārīm* — *VS* 30.9; *TB* 3.4.5.1

The term *śilpa* appearing in the *AB*[187] (6.27) has been described as the imitation of *devaśilpa*. In order to give an illustration of *śilpa,* toy-making, weaving, glassworks, works of gold and chariot-wright have been mentioned.

According to the information of the *JB*[188] (1.263) vocations, adopted by people of different castes may be classified into two sections, i.e., (1) *śilpa,* conducted by kṣatriyas, viz., *hasti, niṣka, aśvatarīratha, aśvaratha, rukma,* and (2) those conducted by vaiśyas, viz., cattle, horse, goat, sheep (i.e., animal husbandry), *hasti* (toy-making), *vrīhi, yava, tila, māṣa* (practice of agriculture), *hiraṇya* (works of gold), *sarpiṣ, kṣīram* (preparing milk products), *rayi, puṣṭi* (to earn wealth by practising trade with these materials).

Miscellaneous Vocations

BARBER & WASHER

The profession of barber (*vaptṛ*) was known from the Ṛgvedic age. The name *vaptṛ,*[189] on account of its being derived from the root $\sqrt{vap}$ "to shave" indicates his duty, i.e., task of shaving. The late Vedic literature[190] has given us two more names *vapa* and *nāpita* to mean barber.

The sentence, *keśaśmaśru vapate, nakhāni nikṛntate, mṛtā vā eṣā tvagamedhyā yat keśaśmaśru mṛtam eva tvacam amedhyāmapahatya yajñīyo bhūtvā medham upaitya* (*TS* 6.1.2.2), clearly indicates that people considered nails and hair impure

---

187. *devaśilpāny eteṣāṁ vai śilpānām anukṛtīha śilpam adhigamyate — hastī kaṁso vāso hiraṇyam aśvatarīrathaḥ śilpam* — *AB* 6.27

188. *etāni vai kṣatre śilpāni hastiniṣko 'śvatarīratho 'śvaratho rukmaḥ kaṁsaḥ. . . etāni vai viśi śilpāni go 'śvaṁ hasti hiraṇyam ajāvikaṁ vrīhiyavās tilamāṣāḥ sarpikṣīraṁ rayiḥ puṣṭiḥ* — *JB* 1.263

189. *yad udvato niatoyāsi vapsat pragardhinīva senā* ।
yadā te vāto anuvāti śocir vapteva śmaśru vapasi prabhūma ॥
— *ṚV* 10.142.4

190. *AV* 6.68.1-3, 8.2.17; *ŚB* 3.1.2.2.

parts of body. Therefore, the sacrificer had to become purified by trimming his nails and shaving his hair and beard before his initiation in the *Agniṣṭoma* sacrifice. Shaving process (i.e., how to comb and moisten the whisker before shaving, etc.) has been recorded in the *ŚB* (3.1.2.2-9). In this connection the *ŚB* (3.1.2.4-5) has mentioned human practice on this point, i.e., out of ritual purpose normally people were habituated to trimming their nails from left side at first and similarly to shave the hair from left side. Before seasonal offerings (*cāturmāsya*) also the sacrificer had to shave his head all round.[191] In this ritual shaving, copper razor and three spotted porcupine's quills were used as shaving instruments.[192] It is noteworthy that there was a system of shaving the dead person also before his cremation.[193]

The names *malaga*,[194] *vāsaḥpalpūlī*[195] to mean launder and launderess prove that laundering was practised by both men and women.

OCCUPATIONS RELATED WITH HOUSEHOLD

In the late Vedic literature (esp. in the Brāhmaṇa and Upaniṣads) names of some other persons have been scattered, from which it appears that in order to maintain regular routine of the household people required the help of some types of attendants, viz., servants/attendants (*anucara*,[196] *anucarī*,[197]

191. *ŚB* 2.6.3.14-17, 2.6.4.5-7.

192. *tattryenī śalalī bhavati lohaḥ kṣuraḥ . . . tena parivartayate* ।
— *ŚB* 2.6.4.5-7

193. *keśa-śmaśru-nakha-loma nikṛntanāni kṛtvā vipurīṣaṁ cecchan* ।
keśādi nikhāya sarpiṣāntaraktvā citāvenaṁ ādadhāti kṛṣṇajinam āstīrya prākśirasam
— *KŚS* 25.7.18-19

194. *etaṁ tvacaṁ lohinīm tām nudasva grāva śumbhāti malaga iva vastrā*
— *AV* 12.3.21

195. *medhāya vāsaḥpalpūlīm* . . . — *VS* 30.12; *TB* 3.4.7.1

196. *balāya anucaram* — *VS* 30.13; *TB* 3.4.13.1

197. *ŚB* 13.5.2.4-8, 13.5.4.27.

paricara,[198] *dāsī,* etc.), doorkeeper (*anukṣattā*[199]), announcer of visitors (*saṁśrāvayitr̥*[200]), cook (*paktr̥,*[201] *srapayitr̥,*[202] *śamitr̥*[203]), and waiter/handmaid (*pariveṣṭrī*[204]), etc. In the context of *Mahāvrata* ceremony, dancing and singing of female attendants have been mentioned in the *TS.*[205] In the context of Horse-sacrifice the *ŚB*[206] has recorded the appearance of four queens in the sacrificial campus accompanied by their four hundred attendants.

OCCUPATIONS RELATED TO THE KING/ADMINISTRATION

Further, names of some other vocations which were probably concerned with administration have been recorded in various places of Vedic literature. They are as follows: officer *karaṇa,*[207] minister *mantrin,*[208] minstrel* *sūta,*[209] architect *sthapati,*[210]

---

198. *ŚB* 4.3.5.9; *CU* 4.10.1-4, 7.8.1, etc.
199. *aupadaṣṭrāyānukṣattāram* — *VS* 30.13; *TB* 3.4.13.1
200. *śrotraṁ saṁśrāvayitr̥* — *Kaus.* 2.1.
201. *AV* 10.9.7, 10.9.11, 11.1.17; *ŚB* 3.3.4.17, 10.4.2.19.
202. *na vā etasya manuṣyaḥ srapayitā devo hyeṣaḥ* — *ŚB* 1.2.2.14
203. *AV* 10.9.7; *AB* 7.1; *PB* 25.18.4.
204. *AV* 9.6.51; *MS* 1.2.16; *TS* 6.3.1.3; *VS* 6.13, 30.12; *ŚB* 13.4.5.6; *TB* 3.4.8.1, etc.
205. *parikumbhinyo dāsyo mārjālīyaṁ parinr̥tyanti* — *TS* 7.5.10.1
206. *udavasanīyāyāṁ saṁsthitāyāṁ catasraśca jāyāḥ kumārīṁ pañcamīṁ catvāri ca śatāni anucarīṇāṁ yathā samuditam* — *ŚB* 13.5.4.27
207. *vidma te svapnaṁ janitraṁ grāhyāḥ putro 'si yamasya karaṇaḥ* — *AV* 16.5.1
208. *nama mantriṇe vāṇijāya* — *VS* 16.27; *TS* 4.5.2.2

* *Sūta,* the ministrel, being one of the eleven king-makers had earned an important position (on account of his easy access to the king) in the society. However, in the later ages the Sūtra texts have marked his profession as condemned. It is interesting to note here that the same term denotes charioteer (in some places) also, another *ratnin.*

209. *AV* 3.5.7; *TS* 1.8.9.1, 4.5.2.7; *MS* 2.9.3; *KS* 15.4; *VS* 16.18, etc.
210. *VS* 16.19; *TS* 4.5.4.2.

chamberlain *kṣattṛ,*[211] treasurer *saṁgrāhītṛ,*[212] tax collector *bhāgadhuk,*[213] supervisor of gambling house *akṣāvāpa,*[214] courier *pālāgala,*[215] commander *senānī,*[216] village headman *grāmaṇī/ grāmyavādin,*[217] car fighter *mahāratha/ratheṣṭhāḥ,*[218] warrior *śūra,*[219] archer *dhanvasaha* (*ṚV* 1.127.3)/*dhanvacara* (*ṚV* 6.36.1), boxer *muṣṭihā* (*ṚV* 8.20.20), announcer *anukrośaka,*[220] executor *nisara,*[221] ambassador*/envoy *dūta/arati* (passim in the *ṚV*), spies *piśuna,*[222] (*ṚV* 7.104.20), *spaśa,*[223] (*ṚV* 1.25.13), police officer *ugra* (*ṚV* 7.38.6), *jīvagṛbh,*[224] (*ṚV* 10.97.11), guard *pāyu,*[225] forest guard *vanapa,*[226] etc.

---

211. *VS* 16.26; *TS* 4.5.4.1; *MS* 2.6.5, 4.3.8; *ŚB* 5.3.1.1, etc.
212. *MS* 2.6.5, 4.3.8; *VS* 16.26; *TS* 4.5.4.1; *ŚB* 5.3.1.1.
213. *MS* 2.6.5, 4.3.8; *TS* 1.8.9.1; *ŚB* 5.3.1; *TB* 1.7.3.1.
214. *MS* 2.6.5, 4.3.8; *KS* 15.4; *TS* 1.8.9.1; *ŚB* 5.3.1.1, etc.
215. *pālāgalasya gṛhān paretya caturgṛhītam ājyaṁ gṛhītvā* — *ŚB* 5.3.1.11
216. *MS* 2.6.5, 4.3.8; *KS* 15.4; *VS* 16.26; *TS* 1.8.9.1.
217. *TS* 1.8.9.1, 2.3.1.3; *TB* 1.7.3.1.
218. *mahāratho jāyatām . . . jiṣṇu ratheṣṭhāḥ* — *TS* 7.5.18.1
219. *mā 'smin rāṣṭre iṣavyaḥ śūro* — *TS* 7.5.18.1
220. *modāyānukrośakam* — *TB* 3.4.15.1
221. (i) *krodhāya nisaram* — *TB* 3.4.10.1

     (ii) *nisaraṁ badhyānāṁ bahirniḥsārayitāram* — Sā on *TB loc. cit*

* Frequent references to spies *spaśa/piśuna* and messenger *dūta/ arati* indicate the importance of the service rendered by spies and ambassadors, required for administrative purposes. The phrase *indrasya dūtīr iṣitā carāmi* (*ṚV* 10.108.2) makes us suppose that at that time women also were appointed as mesengers.

222. *VS* 30.13, *TB* 3.4.7.1; *CU* 7.6.1.
223. *ṚV* 1.33.8, 4.4.3, 6.67.5, 7.61.3, 7.87.3, etc.
224. *ātmā yakṣasya naśyati purā jīvargṛbho yathā* — *ṚV* 10.97.11
225. *ṚV* 1.147.3, 2.1.7, 4.2.6, 4.4.6, 4.4.12, etc.
226. *banāya banapam* — *VS* 30.19; *TB* 3.4.11.1, etc.

OCCUPATIONS RELATED TO CONVEYANCE

Moreover, the vocations of charioteer *rathin,*[227]/*sārathi,*[228] *sūta,*[229] *rathagṛtsa*[230] (a skilled charioteer), yoker and unyoker of horses *yoktṛ/vimoktṛ,*[231] boatman *nāvāja,*[232] poleman/ferryman *śambin,*[233] rower *aritṛ,*[234] have been recorded in the range of Vedic literature.

PROFESSIONS RELATED WITH MUSIC AND DANCE

From the discussion on cultivation of music and dance (for details see under Cultivation of Fine Arts, Entertainment, Ch. 5) it becomes clear that some people were professionally involved in the practice of music and dance. According to their subject they may be classified into three groups:

(i) singer/musicians,

(ii) dancers, and

(iii) instrumental hands.

From the *ṚV* onwards, besides the singer priests, some professional singers have been mentioned. They have been called by varieties of names in various texts, e.g., *kāru* (*ṚV* 9.112.3), *jaritā* and *sūta* (*AV* 5.11.8; *VS* 16.18), *gāyana* (*GB* 1.1.9). Further, in the context of Human sacrifice names of *kimpuruṣa* and *talava* have been recorded in the *YS* and *Brs*, who were explained by the commentators as some sorts of singers or musicians.

227. *ṚV* 1.25.3, 1.122.8, 2.39.2, 3.3.6, 5.83.3, 5.57.8; *AV* 4.34.4, 7.62.1, *VS* 16.26; *TS* 4.7.15.3, 5.2.2.3, etc.

228. *ṚV* 1.55.7, 1.144.3, 2.19.6, 6.20.5; *AV* 15.2.1; *MS* 4.3.8; *AB* 2.25, etc.

229. *AV* 3.5.7; *MS* 2.6.5, 2.9.3; *KS* 15.4; *TS* 1.8.9.1; *ŚB* 5.3.1.5.

230. *TS* 4.4.3.1; *VS* 15.15; *AB* 3.4.8-9.

231. *yogāya yoktāraṁ kṣemāya vimoktāram* — *VS* 30.14; *TB* 3.4.10.1

232. *athaiṣa eva nāvājo yat kṣīrahotā* — *ŚB* 2.3.3.15

233. *agner hotreṇa pra ṇude sapatnāṁchambina nāvam udekeṣu dhīraḥ*
— *AV* 9.2.6

234. *ṚV* 2.42.1, 9.95.2, etc.

Though cultivation of dance was prevalent since the early Vedic period, the dancer as a professional figure has been mentioned for the first time in the Yajurvedic Saṁhitās, viz., *vaṁśanartin* "pole-dancer" and *śailūṣa* "a public dancer/actor."

Apart from the singers and dancers, names of some instrumental hands also have been traced in the context of Human sacrifice, they are drummers (*dundubhyāghāta* — *TB* 3.4.13.1, *āḍambarāghāta* — *VS* 30.19); flute player (*tūṇavadhma* — *VS* 30.19); lute players (*vīṇā-vāda* — *VS* 30.19; *TB* 3.4.15.1); *vīṇāgaṇagina* (*ŚB* 12.4.2.8); etc. The Yajurvedic expression: *pāṇisaṅghātam vīṇāvādaṁ tūṇavadhmaṁ tānnṛttāya* (*VS* 30.20) rendered as "a *tāla* man, lutist, a flutist to be staked to the dance" (Vatsyayan, *CIDLA*) indicates the existence of professional musical accompanists.

Apart from these, some other vocations also are met with, in the context of Human sacrifice, viz., theologian,[235] reciter *chandoga*,[236] orator *pravāditṛ*,[237] astronomer *nakṣatradarśa*,[238] money lender *kusīdin*,[239] wood cutter *dārvāhāra*,[240] fire kindler *agnyedha*,[241] hand clapper *pāṇighna*,[242] conch blower *śaṅkha-dhma*,[243] etc., from which we came to know that by the close of Vedic period reciting, fire kindling, hand clapping, etc., were known professions to the people. It is really amazing to note the existence of such a large number of vocations in India at such a hoary antiquity.

235. *AV* 9.6.37, 10.7.20; *KS* 23.4; *AB* 25.15; *ŚB* 5.4.4.5.
236. *sāma iti chāndogāḥ* — *ŚB* 10.5.2.10
237. *vācaḥ pravaditāsyāmiti* — *TS* 7.1.10.1
238. *prajñānāya nakṣatradarśam* — *VS* 30.10; *TB* 3.4.4.1
239. *ṚV* 8.66.10; *ŚB* 13.4.3.11.
240. *bhāyai dārvāhāram* — *VS* 30.12; *TB* 3.4.8.1
241. *prabhāyāgnyedham* — *VS* 30.12; *TB* 3.4.8.1.
242. *pāṇighnaṁ tūṇavadhmaṁ tānnṛttāya* — *VS* 30.30; *TB* 3.4.15.1.
243. *avasparāya śaṅkhadhmam* — *VS* 30.19; *TB* 3.4.12.1.

Forbidden Professions

While discussing professions, the Sūtra[244] texts have declared some professions condemned for brāhmaṇas. According to their injunction, trade, cattle rearing, acting, theft, practice of medicine, money lending, following the vocations of artisans, bards and servants, were forbidden.

Besides these, one who lives by the use of arms (i.e., a soldier), by letting lodgings/land, a professional messenger, spy, surgeon, fowler, police officer, a jailor, a servant of a guild, a false witness, a doorkeeper, musical accompanists, dancer, singer, *soma* seller, washerman, cobbler, a dealer of spirituous liquor, servant of śūdra — all these people were denounced like śūdras on account of their contemptible occupations.[245] The Sūtra[246] literature (especially *VDS*) has prohibited the brāhmaṇas to follow these vocations on violation of which brāhmaṇas were to lose their status and be considered condemnable.

Now, this prohibition on brāhmaṇas to follow these professions and at the same time their existence in society clearly indicates that these were followed by lower caste people (especially śūdras).

---

244. *GDS* 2.8.17; *ĀpDS* 1.6.18. 18-33, 1.6.19.1ff.
245. *ĀpDS* 1.6.18.18-33.
246. *VDS* 14.41-45.

5

Entertainment

AFTER a whole day's hard work (which people had to do in order to meet the basic requirements of their day-to-day life), they required some entertainment for relaxation. During their leisure they practised dicing, racing, hunting, etc. Besides, cultivation of fine arts, i.e., music (both vocal and instrumental) and dance were other forms of entertainment.

Dicing

Frequent references to the game of dice,[1] dicing nuts,[2] names of various throws,[3] gaming board/ground,[4] names of gamesters,[5] etc., suggest the popularity of this game. The story of penniless, unfortunate gambler, narrated in the Dice-hymn (of the *ṚV* 10.34) is not only a prohibition from the practice of gambling but also an example of people's irresistible attraction for dice.

---

1. *ṚV* 10.27.17, 10.34, 10.42.9, 10.43.5; *AV* 4.38, 6.118, 7.50, 7.109, 12.3.52; *TS* 1.8.6; *ŚB* 5.4.4.6, etc.
2. *ṚV* 10.27.17, 10.34.1, 10.34.5; *AV* 7.109.7, 20.34.4-5; *TS* 4.3.3.2; *ŚB* 5.4.4.6; *CU* 7.3.1, etc.
3. *ṚV* 10.42.7; *VS* 30.18; *TS* 4.3.3.1-2; *TB* 3.4.16.1; *ŚB* 13.3.2.1; *CU* 4.1.4, etc.
4. *ṚV* 8.4.3, 8.87.1, 8.87.4, 10.34.1, 10.34.9; *AV* 4.15.12; *KS* 9.16; *TS* 2.5.1.3, 3.4.8.5; *ŚB* 5.3.1.10, 5.4.4.20.23.
5. *ṚV* 1.92.10, 2.12.4-5, 10.34.3, 10.34.6, 10.34.10-11; *VS* 30.18; *TB* 3.4.16.1; *AB* 2.19.

MYTHOLOGICAL BACKGROUND OF DICING

Dice had its influence not only on men but also on the divine beings (like gods, nymphs, *gandharvas*). From the *ṚV* onwards gods (especially Indra)[6] have been frequently mentioned as competent gamblers. Prayers (wishing victory in the game of dice) offered to Agni, Maruts (*AV* 7.50.3) and Aśvins (*ṚV* 1.112.34; *VS* 34.29) indicate the connection of these deities with dice. Sāyaṇa while commenting on the *AV*[7] (4.38.1; 7.109.3, 5) has mentioned the nymphs and *gandharvas* as presiding deities of dice. People believed that success and failure in dice depends on their favour or wrath.[8] The descriptions of *apsarases* *udbhindantīṁ sañjayantīm apsarāṁ sādhudevinīm* (*AV* 4.38/1) or that of *gandharvas*, *sa no devo haviridaṁ juṣāṇo gandharvebhiḥ sadhamādaṁmadema* (*AV* 7.109.5) inform us of the nymphs and *gandharvas* as expert dicers. All these prove that dice, as a form of entertainment, was prevalent among gods and demi-gods as well.

People, with a desire to procure success and to avert ill-luck in the game, offered prayers to these deities[9] and nymphs.[10] Further, they have been invoked under the notion that all the evil conditions and miseries should go to the rival gamester.[11] Not only prayers, but sometimes witchcraft and magic rites also were employed to make the success invariable.[12] The *ĀpDS* (2.7.16.12) prescribes *ṣaṣṭhe 'dhavaśīlo*

6. *ṚV* 1.92.10, 2.12.4-5; *AV* 20.34.4-5, etc.
7. (i) *dyūta-krīḍādhi-devatām apsarojātīyām* — Sā on *AV* 4.38.1
   (ii) *apsarasaḥ dyūtakriyā devatāḥ* — Sā on *AV* 7.109.3
   (iii) *gandharvebhiḥ gandharvaiḥ akṣādhiṣṭhāyakaiḥ* — Sā on *AV* 7.109.5
8. *yā akṣeṣu pramodante śucaṁ krodhaṁ ca bibhratī* ।
   ānadinīṁ pramodinīm apsarām tām iha huve ॥ — *AV* 4.38.4
9. *ṚV* 1.112.24; *AV* 7.50.1-4, 7.50.7-8; *VS* 34.29.
10. *AV* 4.38.1ff, 7.109.2-3.
11. *AV* 4.38.1-4, 7.50.1ff, 7.109.1ff.
12. *ṚV* 10.34.7; *AV* 5.31.6, 19.34.2; *TS* 3.4.8.2; *Kauṣ* 7.10, 41.10-13.

'kṣaśīlaśca, one who desires to become a competent dicer should offer funeral oblations to his Manes on the sixth day of the latter half of the month. This prescription helps us guess that people offered ancestral rites also to become a competent gambler.

During the game, practice of cheating and telling lies was very common since the Ṛgvedic[13] period. In the *AV* (6/118) there is an entire hymn which is actually a prayer, asking forgiveness against offence of cheating at dice.

THE GAME — ITS CLASSIFICATION

On the basis of references to the game of dice, scattered in the Vedic literature, the game played by people may be divided into two classes, i.e., ritual[14] and secular games.[15] Apart from these, game of dice has been recorded in the Sūtra literature as a method of treatment. The *ĀpGS*[16] has mentioned the game of dice in connection with the treatment of a boy who has been attacked by a dog-demon, i.e., epilepsy. From this, we may infer that besides having entertainment value, dice was somehow connected with the treatment of disease.

Secular Game

The story narrated in the Dice-hymn of the *ṚV* may be mentioned as an instance of a secular game. The seer Kavaṣa Ailūṣa was a gambler whose excessive addiction to dice

---

13. *ṚV* 5.85.8; *AV* 6.118, 12.3.52.
14. *MS* 4.4.6; *TS* 1.8.16; *VS* 10.28; *TB* 1.5.11.1, 1.7.10.5; *ŚB* 5.4.4.6, 13.3.2.1; *BŚS* 2.7.10, 2.8.11-13, 2.9.12-28; *LŚS* 4.10.22-23; *KŚS* 5.6.2, 15.7.5-21, etc.
15. *ṚV* 10.34; *AB* 2.16; *KB* 12.1.3; *Nir* 9.8.
16. *śvagraha gṛhītaṁ kumāraṁ tapoyukto jālena pracchādya . . . devanam uddhṛtyāvokṣyākṣānnupākṣeṣūttānaṁ nipātya dadhnā lavaṇamiśreṇāñjalinottarair avokṣet prātar madhyandine sāyaṁ . . .* — *ĀpGS* 7.18.1

created a fatal effect in his surroundings. He did not hesitate to repulse his loving wife just for the sake of dice.

akṣasyāham eka parasya hetor anuvratām apajāyām arodham
— *ṚV* 10.34.2

As a result of his dangerous addiction he has lost everything and become almost a deserted person not only from the society but from his own people also.

dveṣṭi śvaśrūr apajāyā ruṇaddhi . . . — *ṚV* 10.34.3

Nobody relies on him, even his parents refuse to protect him.

pitā mātā bhrātara enam āhur na jānīmo nayatā baddham etam ।
— *ṚV* 10.34.4

In spite of his extreme misfortune he has attended the gaming ground regularly to win his rival in a counter-game but his luck betrays each time.

sabhām eti kitavaḥ pṛcchamānaḥ jeṣyāmīti tanvā śuśujānaḥ ।
akṣāso asya vitiranti kāmaṁ pratidīvne dadhata ā kṛtāni ॥
— *ṚV* 10.34.6

Being refused and insulted by everyone he has become disillusioned and decided not to participate in gambling but before the imperial voice of dice all his pious resolutions break down and he succumbs to the temptation of the moment.

yad ādīdhye na daviṣāṇyebhiḥ parāyadbhyo 'ava hīye sakhibhyaḥ ।
nyuptāśca babhravo vācamakrata emīdeṣāṁ niṣkṛtaṁ jāriṇīva ॥
— *ṚV* 10.34.5

Ultimately the poor fellow has become a physical and moral wreck.

Thus, we see that through this story the *ṚV* directly prohibits men from gambling. In some other passages also dicing has been mentioned in the same line with wine, meat, wrath, etc., as a source of vice and leading men[17] astray.

From the description of a gamester, as he is depicted in the Dice-hymn, we can easily guess his social status. He has been grouped with *māgadha* and *puṁścalī* and denounced as a non-brāhmaṇa eunuch in the *VS*.[18] The incident of Kavaṣa Ailūṣa's abandonment from the sacrificial ground by the fellow members confirms this notion.[19]

But in spite of these repeated denouncement and warning against practice of gambling, people's attraction for dice has been increased gradually. In the *ṚV*[20] the gamester appears by the name *kitava* and *śvaghnin* only, whereas in the Yajurvedic Saṁhitā and Brāhmaṇas[21] he has been called by various names, e.g., *ādinavadarśa, kalpin, adhikalpin, bahis-sada, sabhāsthāṇu* (probably named so, on account of his constant presence in the gaming ground), etc.

It is to be remembered here that from the said texts it is hardly possible to explain these names safely. However, according to the commentator, these terms appear to be various technical names of gamblers. Further, in the same context we find two other persons *sabhāvin*,[22] "a keeper of gambling hall" and *akṣāvāpa*[23] "superintendent of dice." Appearance of this swarm of gamblers makes us suppose that by this time people's addiction to dice increased so much,

---

17. (i) *na sa svo dakṣo varuṇaḥ dhrutiḥ*
sā surā manyuḥ vibhīdako acittiḥ I — *ṚV* 7.86.6
(ii) *yathā māṁsaṁ yathā surā yathā 'kṣā adhidevane* I — *AV* 6.70.1
18. . . . *māgadhaḥ puṁścalī kitavaḥ klīvo 'śūdrā abrāhmaṇāste prājāpatyāḥ* . . . — *VS* 30.22
19. *AB* 2.19; cf. *KB* 12.1.3.
20. *ṚV* 1.92.10, 2.12.4, 2.29.5, 4.20.3, 4.20.5, 5.05.8, 8.45.38, 10.34.3, 10.34.7, 10.34.10-13, etc.
21. *VS* 30.18; *TB* 3.4.16.1; *ŚB* 13.6.2.20 (9).
22. *kṛtāya sabhāvinam* — *TB* 3.4.16.1
23. *atha śvobhūte 'kṣāvāpasya ca gṛhebhyo govikartasya ca* — *ŚB* 5.3.1.10

that two separate officials (*akṣāvāpa* and *sabhāvin*) were to be appointed, most probably to control the game. Among them, *akṣāvāpa* being a member of king-makers (*ratnins*) enjoyed a special status in the society.

Ritual Game

Though dicing has been denounced in the *R̥V*, from the references to the ritual game of dice (as they have been scattered in the Vedic literature) we find that game of dice had an important role in the rituals. It is noteworthy that in spite of frequent mention of the game in the Vedic literature, specific details (of the game) are not always available from the description of secular games. However, later Vedic Saṁhitās and Brāhmaṇas provide us some expression connected with dice, e.g., dicing nuts, their number and material, etc. (but everything has been traced in the context of ritual games). Therefore, in order to gather a rough idea of the same we have to collect information from the ritual context.

As regards the ritual game at first we should mention the game of dice to be played on the occasion of the *Vājapeya* and *Rājasūya* sacrifice by the king which formed a part of his coronation.[24] Again, another ritual game has been mentioned in the *ŚB* (2.2.1.1) in the context of *Agnyādheya* ceremony, to be played by the priests which is an integral part of laying down of the *sabhya*-fire.

The ritual game differs from the secular one in one respect, that is, in the former case the players merely picked up the required number of dice[25] most probably to avoid the errors, which would be unavoidable, if a real game had been played.

---

24. *MS* 4.4.6; *TS* 1.8.16, 4.3.3.1-2; *VS* 10.28; *ŚB* 5.3.1.10, 5.4.4.6, 13.3.2.1.
25. *athāsmi pañcākṣān pāṇāvāvapati* . . . — *ŚB* 5.4.4.6

The expressions like *nīcā vartanta upari sphuranty . . .* or *divyā aṅgārā iriṇe nyuptāḥ* in the *R̥V* (10.34.9) make it clear that in the secular game dice were thrown.

DICE: ITS MATERIAL

Though the term *akṣa* primarily means game of dice,[26] still in some places the same term indicates dicing nuts, also named as *babhru* and *vibhīdaka*.[27]

Normally, dicing nuts used in secular games were made of the fruits of *vibhīdaka*, a tree (*Terminallia bellerica*) born on windy spot, which were uneven in shape and had no numerals marked on them (VI, I, p. 4).

So far as the texts are concerned, there is no specific mention of the material of dice, used for ritual games (e.g., in the coronation of the king). However, the commentators in later ages have tried to focus on this point. The expressions like *akṣā nāma kapardakāḥ suvarṇa-nirmitāḥ, vibhītakaphalāni sauvarṇānīva* in Sāyaṇa's commentary on the *TS*[28] and *ŚB*[29] or *sauvarṇa kapardāḥ* mentioned in Mahīdhara's commentary on the *VS*[30] in connection with *Rājasūya* sacrifice make us suppose that in the ritual games the use of golden dice was prevalent. Further, the use of golden, silver, ivory and *vibhītaka* nuts became prevalent in the Sūtra period.[31]

---

26. *R̥V* 10.34.2, 10.34.6; *AV* 4.17.7, 6.118.2, 12.3.52.
27. *R̥V* 7.86.6, 10.34.1, 10.34.4-5; *TS* 2.1.5.8, 2.1.7.3; *ŚB* 13.8.1.16.
28. *akṣāḥ kapardakāḥ suvarṇanirmitāḥ vibhītakaphalāni sauvarṇānītyeke* । *te cākṣā dyūtasthāne nivapanīyāḥ* । — Sā on *TS* 1.8.16.2
29. *yajamāna-haste pañcākṣāvāpaṁ ca vidhatte — athā 'smā iti* ।
akṣā nāma kapardakāḥ suvarṇanirmitāḥ vibhītakaphalāni sauvarṇāni vetyeke । *te cākṣā dyūtasthāne nivapanīyāḥ* । — Sā on *ŚB* 5.4.4.6
30. *yajamāna-haste dyūtasādhanabhūtan pañcākṣān sauvarṇa-kapardān nidadhyāt . . .* — Mahī on *VS* 30.18
31. *sauvarṇāḥ syuriti baudhāyanāḥ* । *rajatā iti śālīkiḥ* । *nāgadantā ityaupamanyavaḥ* । *vaibhītakā ityaupamanyavīputrāḥ* ।
— *BŚS*.22.19.11

Dice : Its Number

As regards the number of dice, we see in the *ṚV*[32] the gambler has been described as the leader of a great horde, from which it appears that a large number of dice were used. According to the information of Vedic Saṁhitās, we find the expression *tripañcāśat*[33] which indicates the total number of dice used in the game. But the scholars are not unanimous regarding the exact meaning of the term. Some of them have rendered it as fifteen (Ludwig, Weber, Zimmer[34]) while others considered it as fifty-three (Roth, Grassmann[35]).

In the ritual game, the priest handed over five dice to the king to indicate his victory over the quarters.[36]

Gambling hall

sabhām eti kitavaḥ pṛcchamānaḥ jeṣyāmīti tanvā śuśujānaḥ ।
— *ṚV* 10.34.6

The gamester's regular visit to *sabhā* indicates the existence of a separate gambling hall, built for the particular purpose. In order to maintain this hall an officer-in-charge *sabhāvin* was appointed. The name *sabhāsthāṇu* (as already mentioned) clearly indicates the person's excessive addiction to this place.

---

32. *yo vaḥ senānīr mahatogaṇasya rājā vrātasya prathamo babhūva*
— *ṚV* 10.34.12
33. *tripañcāśaḥ krīḍati vrāta eṣāṁ deva iva savitāsatyadharmā* ।
— *ṚV* 10.34.8
34. Ludwig, Weber and Zimmer's view referred to by Macdonell & Keith, VI, I, p. 2.
35. (i) Roth, *Sanskrit Wörterbuch*, III, p. 434.
(ii) Grassmann, *Wörterbuch zum Ṛgveda*, p. 558.
36. *athāsmai pañcākṣān pāṇāvāvapati* . . . — *ŚB* 5.4.4.6

According to the information of the *ĀpDS*[37] the king must provide a gambling hall open to the truthful. Moreover, if the people were to participate in the game, they should play in the hall meant for the very purpose. Those who would play elsewhere should be penalised with heavy fine.

Gaming Ground/Board

Now, the gaming ground/board, where dice were thrown. To mean this gaming ground we find two terms *iriṇa* and *adhidevana* occurring in the Vedic Saṁhitās.[38] In spite of having some other meanings, e.g., natural hole/cleft *svakṛta iriṇa* (*KS* 9.16) or that made by water *apākṛtam iriṇam* (*ṚV* 8.4.5), the expressions *pravāteja iriṇe varvṛtānāḥ* (*ṚV* 10.34.1), *divyā aṅgārā iriṇe nyuptāḥ* (*ṚV* 10.34.9), *yathā 'kṣā adhidevane* (*AV* 6.70.1); etc., clearly indicate *iriṇa/adhidevana* to be the place, where dice were thrown.

According to some Western[39] scholars dice-board also may be named so (*iriṇa*) on account of having similar holes in it. It is really very difficult to ascertain whether a dice board or only a dug-out space was used for the actual game. According to Keith and Macdonell "no board appears to have been used but a depression on which dice were thrown" (Keith & Macdonell, VI, I, p. 4).

---

37. (i) *sabhāyā madhye adhidevanamuddhṛtyāvokṣyā 'kṣānnivapedyugmān vaibhītakān yathārthān | āryāḥ śucayaḥ satyaśīlāḥ dīvitāraḥ syuḥ |*
— *ĀpDS*, 2.10.25.12-13

(ii) *te ca tatra devitvā yathābhāṣitaṁ paṇaṁ sabhikāya dattvā gaccheyuḥ . . . sa eva ca sthānāntare dīvyato daṇḍayet |*
— Haradatta on *ĀpDS*, *loc. cit*

38. *ṚV* 8.4.3, 8.87.1, 8.87.4, 10.34.1, 10.34.9; *AV* 4.15.12; *KS* 9.16; *TS* 2.5.1.3, 3.4.8.2, etc.

39. Pischel, *Vedische Studien* referred to by Macdonell & Keith, VI, I, p. 80.

Dice Box

Use of dice box can be hardly traced in the Vedic literature. Still, the *ŚB*,[40] in the context of *Rājasūya* sacrifice, refers to *akṣāvapana* used as honorarium to be paid to *akṣāvāpa* (the superintendent of dice) which has been explained by the commentator as a dice box.[41]

Throw of Dice

The Yajurvedic Saṁhitā and Brāhmaṇas[42] in connection with the human sacrifice, enumerate several professional persons, to be dedicated to something, which appear from the textual context to be the names of various sorts of gamesters and throws of dice. Those are as follows: *kṛta, tretā, dvāpara, āskanda* and *abhibhū*. Almost the same list appears in the *TB*,[43] with a slight change, i.e., *akṣarāja, kṛta, tretā, dvāpara* and *kali*. From the *ŚB* (13.6.2.20), *kali* appears to be another name of *abhibhū*, whereas *abhibhū* and *akṣarāja* seem to be identical in the *VS*[44] and *TS*.[45]

Names of some of these throws can be traced back from early Vedic Saṁhitās also. The throw of dice was generally

---

40. *tasya dvirūpo gaurdakṣiṇā śitibāhur vā 'śitivālo vā sirnakharāḥ vāladāmnā 'kṣāvapanaṁ prabaddham etadu hi tayor bhavati* — *ŚB* 5.3.1.10

41. *akṣāvapanaṁ pātram akṣā upyante 'sminniti akṣāvapanam akṣasthānāvapanaṁ pātram* I — Sā on *ŚB, loc. cit*

42. *TS* 4.3.3.1-2; *VS* 30.18; *TB* 3.4.16.1; *ŚB* 13.6.2.20 (9).

43. *akṣarājāya kitavam* I *kṛtāya sabhāvinam* I *tretāya ādinavadarśam* I *dvāparāya bahis-sadam* I *kalaye sabhāsthāṇum* II — *TB* 3.4.16.1

44. *akṣarājāya kitavam* I *kṛtāyādinavadarśam* I *tretāyai kalpinam* I *dvāparāyadhikalpinam* I *āskandāya sabhāsthāṇum* . . . — *VS* 30.18

45. *āskando 'yānām . . . abhibhūrayānām* . . . — *TS* 4.3.3.2

named as *ayā*[46] and *graha*[47] in the early Vedic Saṁhitās which was called *grābha*[48] in later Saṁhitās.

The phrase *ayā iva paricaranti devā* (*ṚV* 10.116.9) indicates that people were aware of more than one throw since the time of *Ṛgveda,* where gods have been compared to the throws of dice giving or destroying wealth.

As regards the nature of these throws our textbooks help very little. However, the commentators have given some explanations on this point. According to Sāyaṇācārya *kṛta* is the winning throw and *kali* is just opposite to it.[49] But the passage *ghṛtena kaliṁ śikṣāmi* . . . (*AV* 7.109.1) makes us infer that probably the *AV* suggests *kali* as the winning throw.

According to Ānandagiri on the *Chāndogyopaniṣad Bhāṣya,*[50] *kṛta, tretā, dvāpara* and *kali* should be applied to the sides of dice marked with numbers/dots four, three, two and one. Rudradatta on the *ĀpDS*[51] opined:

> *Kṛta* is a number of thrown dice usually divisible by four, while other three throws then being *tretā,* when three remained over after being divided, the *dvāpara,* when two

---

46. *ṚV* 10.116.9; *AV* 4.28.3; *MS* 2.7.20; *KS* 39.7, etc.

47. *udbhindantīṁ sañjayantīm apsarāṁ sādhudevinīm* ।
glahe kṛtāni kṛṇvānām apsarām tāṁ iha huve ॥

48. *ṚV* 8.81.1, 9.106.3.

49. (i) *kṛtaśabdavācyaṁ lābhahetum ayaṁ vicinotu* — Sā on *AV* 7.50.3
(ii) *kaliśabdavācyasyāyasya patane parājayo bhavatītyakṣasamayaḥ* — Sā on *AV* (P) 1.49.4

50. *akṣasya yasmin bhāge catvāro 'ṅkāḥ sa kṛta-nāmāyo bhavati, yasmin bhāge trayo 'ṅkāḥ sā tretā nāmāyo bhavati, yatra tu dvāvaṅkau sa dvāpara nāmakaḥ* । *yatraiko 'ṅkaḥ sa kalisaṁjña iti bhāgaḥ* ।
— Ānandagiri on *CUBh* 4.1.4

51. *nyupteṣvakṣeṣu catuṣkaśo vibhajyamāneṣu yatra sarve bhāgāḥ samānāḥ bhavanti tat kṛtaṁ nāma* । *atha yatrāntatas trayo 'vaśiṣyante sā tretā, yatra dvau sa dvāparaḥ, yatraiko sa kaliḥ* ।
— Rudradatta on *ĀpDS* 5.20.1

becomes remainder and *kali* is that when one remained. If five were the dividing number then the throw which showed no remainder, should go by the name *kali* and in that case *kṛta* would be that when four was left.

RELATION BETWEEN NAMES OF AGES AND DICE

The names of all the four throws appear in the late Vedic literature and somewhere they have been related with four ages and compared to four states of a man, i.e., *nidrā, sañjihāna, utthāna* and *carat/calat* stage.[52]

Pandurangabhatta[53] in his own work has presented the opinions of both the traditional and Western scholars and he opined:

> probably the proportion of virtue and the length of each *yuga* are relative with numbers marked on the sides of dice. During *kṛtayuga* virtue was fully present in men, when *dharmadevatā* the metaphysical cow stood on four feet; similarly the dice having four dots marked on it, is named *kṛta*. A general decline of virtue was seen gradually in *tretā, dvāpara* and *kali yugas*, when the said cow stood on her three, two and one foot respectively.[54]

It is noteworthy that number of dots also decreased on the dice, named *tretā, dvāpara* and *kali*. Hence, it can be safely said that sides of dice were named after the names of *yugas*.

Western scholars have put forth their opinion just reverse to it. In their view the famous four ages described in the Hindu literature have been named after the sides of a dice. A.B. Keith in his *Rigveda Brāhmaṇas*[55] declared the terms *kṛta, tretā, dvāpara*

---

52. *kaliḥ śayāno bhavati sañjihānastu dvāparaḥ* ।
uttiṣṭhaṁstretā bhavati kṛtastu sampadyate caraṁścaraiveti ॥ — *AB* 7.15
53. Pandurangabhatta, *DPSL*, p. 81.
54. *Ibid.*, p. 82.
55. A.B. Keith, *RB*, p. 302, n. 6.

and *kali* indicate the dice and not ages because the concept of ages is rather modern and not of the Vedic period.

Racing

CHARIOT RACE AND HORSE RACE

Chariot racing was another form of popular entertainment of the Vedic period. We are to suppose people's attraction for it from the references (scattered in Vedic literature) to races,[56] race course,[57] racing horse[58] and chariots,[59] prizes,[60] etc.

Besides chariot race there are some other references (mainly in the *ṚV*[61]) which, according to some scholars,[62] are clear references to horse racing in the Vedic period. Occurrence of the term *vāja*[63] in its application with horses, invocation of deities[64] in the sacrificial ground for achieving success in these races, make us believe the existence of horse race also as a separate mode of entertainment. The Ṛgvedic passage *aruṣo na vājī kāṣṭhā bhindannūrmibhiḥ* (*ṚV* 4.58.7; cf. *VS* 1.9.75) appears to present before us the picture of a horse bursting through the fences. It is a notable thing that though there is hardly any direct reference to the racing in the early Vedic period, there

---

56. *ṚV* 5.35.7, 6.24.6, 10.102; *AV* 10.4.1; *VS* 9.5-12; *TS* 1.7.8, 5.2.3.2, 7.5.9.2; *MS* 3.2.9; *KS* 20.11; *KapKS* 32.13; *AB* 2.25, 4.7-8; *ŚB* 5.1.1.3-4, etc.
57. *ṚV* 8.80.8; *AV* 2.14.6; *VS* 27.37; *TS* 2.4.14.3; *AB* 4.7; *PB* 9.1.35, etc.
58. *ṚV* 1.73.9, 2.14.3, 9.100.10; *AV* 4.27.1, 4.27.3; *VS* 29.1-3; *TS* 7.1.12.1.
59. *ṚV* 1.148.3, 2.2.3, 2.8.1, 5.60.1, 5.60.4; *AB* 4.9; *ŚB* 5.1.5.10.
60. *ṚV* 1.81.3, 6.45.2, 8.80.8, 9.53.2, 9.109.10, 10.156.1, etc.
61. *ṚV* 1.162.17, 2.23.13, 3.11.9, 3.37.6, 3.42.6, 5.35.1, 5.61.1-3; *TS* 3.4.7.1, etc.
62. Macdonell & Keith, VI, II, p. 444.
    Gonda, *HIL*, I, p. 80.
63. *ṚV* 2.23.13, 3.11.9, 3.37.6, 3.42.6, 5.35.1, 5.86.2, etc.
64. *ṚV* 1.27.7-9.

are references (scattered mainly in the Yajurvedic Saṁhitā and Brāhmaṇas[65] connected with various rituals) which appear to be praise of horses probably to inspire them just before the race.

Moreover, horse riders have been mentioned more than once. The *AĀ*[66] instructs how to ride a horse. From all these we may assume that both the horse race and chariot race might have been practised as forms of entertainments.

MYTHOLOGICAL BACKGROUND OF RACES

It is true that chariot races are found mostly in the ritual context. Still, in the context of *Vājapeya*, the *ŚB* instructs on the manner of yoking horses to the chariot (just before the actual race) used in secular purpose.

> *sa dakṣiṇāyugyam evāgre yunakti savyāyugyaṁ vā 'gre mānuṣe*
> — *ŚB* 5.1.4.7; cf. 5.1.4.9, 5.1.4.11

On the basis of this evidence it can be presumed that apart from ritual purpose races were held just for the sake of entertainment.

Chariot races, as have been recorded in the Vedas, prove that races were equally popular among divine beings (gods, metres, etc.). The *R̥V* refers to Aśvins travelling frequently in chariots. The earliest record of chariot race can be traced in the *R̥V*[67] (1.116.17) where Aśvins after having run a race won Sūryā as their wife. In this connection Mudgala hymn of the *R̥V* (10.102) may be mentioned, which has been considered by

---

65. *MS* 3.2.9; *KS* 15.8; *TS* 1.3.4.1, 1.3.13.2, 1.4.46.3, 1.7.8.1, 1.7.8, 1.8.15, 7.1.2.1; *VS* 10.19; *ŚB* 5.1.1.3-4, 5.1.5.10; *TB* 3.4.7.1, etc.

66. *tiryañcam adhirohed ityāhus tiryañcaṁ vā aśvam adhirohanti . . .*
— *AĀ* 1.2.4

67. *ā vāṁ rathaṁ duhitā sūryasya kārṣmevātiṣṭhadarvatājayantī* ।
viśve devā anvamanyanta hr̥dbhiḥ samuśriyā nāsatyā sacathe ।
— *R̥V* 1.116.17

some scholars[68] as a description of chariot race undertaken by an old gentleman Mudgala in an ordinary cart drawn by a single bullock. An imaginary chariot race among gods and serpents has been recorded in the *AV*[69] (10.4.1) to show the supremacy of gods.

Presentation of various narratives (scattered in the Saṁhitā and Brāhmaṇas[70]) describing races indicates the importance attached to it. In the context of Dvidevatyagraha libations the *AB* (2.25) presents before us a story where gods ran a race in order to settle the dispute of having the prestigious privilege of drinking *soma* at first. Another narrative of gods' race has been recorded in the *AB* (4.7-8) which was held in order to win Āśvinaśastra. Description of a race between metres has been traced in the Yajurvedic Saṁhitā and Brāhmaṇas[71] (cf. *PB* 7.6.11) which they (metres) joined in order to win the cattle. According to the *ŚB* (5.1.1.3-4) gods ran a race among themselves to determine the ownership of sacrifice. Similar description of races among gods has been found in the *PB*.[72] From these it may not be wrong to suppose that people were habituated to settle different disputed matters through running races.

Besides, on the day of king's coronation, at the mid-day *soma* feast a chariot race was celebrated as a ceremonial item.[73] Seventeen chariots participated in this race. It was run accompanied with the chanting of *sāman* and beatings of

---

68. (i) Geldner, referred to by Macdonell & Keith, VI, I, p. 54.
    (ii) Gonda, *HIL*, I, p. 80.
69. *indrasya prathamo ratho devānām aparo ratho varuṇsya tṛtīyait* ı
    ahīnāmapamā ratha sthāṇu ıı — *AV* 10.4.1
70. *ṚV* 1.116.17, 10.102; *AV* 10.4.1; *TS* 5.3.2.2.3, 7.5.9.2; *AB* 2.25; 4.7-8; *PB* 7.2.1-2, 9.1.35-36; *ŚB* 5.1.1.3-4, etc.
71. *MS* 3.2.9; *KS* 20.11; *KapKS* 32.13; *PB* 7.6.11; *ŚB* 8.3.1.1, etc.
72. *PB* 7.2.1-2, 9.1.35-36.
73. *ŚB* 5.1.4.4 – 5.1.5.10.

seventeen drums[74] (*ŚB* 5.1.5.6). The expressions, e.g., *bṛhaspate vājaṁ jaya* (5.1.5.8) or *indra vājaṁjaya* (5.1.5.9), clearly indicate during race the brāhmaṇa priest inspired the king. Total distance of the race was fixed, a range of seventeen arrows between the *udumbara* post fixed at *cātvāla* and *utkara* (the heap of rubbish).[75] Another ritual race has been prescribed as a part of *Mahāvrata* rite.[76] The *TB*'s[77] reference to the chariot race in connection with *Odanasava* rite is another specimen of ritual race.

RACING HORSE

Swift moving steeds, viz., *atya*, *vājin*, etc., were used for running races.[78] Though there are some other names for horses (found in the *YS* and Brāhmaṇas[79] in the context of *Aśvamedha* sacrifice), *atya*, "the runner" and *vājin* "the racer" appearing in connection with race make us suppose that probably these swift moving horses were used in the races.

The expressions like *nikto vāji* (*ṚV* 9.109.10) and *ukṣante aśvā̆ atyā ivājiṣu* (*ṚV* 2.4.3) make us infer that before a race horses were given a good wash. Description of well decorated

---

74. (i) *atha saptadaśa dundubhīn anuvedyantaṁ samminvanti* ।
— *ŚB* 5.1.5.6

(ii) *dhāvantyājim āghnanti dundubhinābhi sāma gāyati*
— *ŚB* 5.1.5.17

75. (i) *te saptadaśa pravyādhān ājiṁ dhāvanti* — *TB* 1.3.6.3

(ii) *prakarṣeṇa balādhikyena vidhyante mucyante vāṇā yāvatparimāṇeṣu tāvatparimāṇa deśa pravyādhāste ca saptadaśasaṁkhyakāḥ* । *teṣām ante avadhitvadyotanāya kācid audumbarī śākhā nikhanyante* । *tat kāṣṭhāyukto 'vadhir ājiḥ* । *tatparyantaṁ rathārūḍha dhāveyuḥ* ।
— Sā on *TB loc. cit*

76. *TS* 7.5.9.2; *AĀ* 5.1.5.

77. *TB* 2.7.8.1ff.

78. *ṚV* 2.34.3, 9.109.10, 10.68.11; *VS* 29.1-3; *TS* 7.1.12.1, etc.

79. *TS* 1.3.4.1, 1.3.13.2, 1.4.46.3, 7.1.12.1, etc.

horses indicates a system of decorating the racing horse with gold and pearl ornaments and trappings.[80]

Apart from horses, other animals like ass, mule, cows, even sometimes ox, were used for chariot races. The *AB*,[81] while describing Āśvinaśastra has mentioned gods' racing, chariots drawn by ass, she-mule, cow, etc.

Generally two horses were used for drawing racing, chariots but there are some other references to the chariots, drawn by three (*R̥V* 10.33.5), four (*R̥V* 2.18.1), five (*KS* 15.2) even six (*R̥V* 1.116.4) horses. The name *praṣṭivāhī* rendered as "a chariot drawn by a team of side-horse" indicates employment of side-horses in the chariot in addition to yoke-horses.[82]

On the contrary, it is very interesting to note the use of *sthūri* meaning the chariot drawn by a single steed, which probably indicated the inferior status of the rider.[83]

Now, the race course. Though the term *āji* primarily means race, in some cases the same term stands for race course,[84] also named as *kāṣṭhā*[85] and *saptya*.[86]

---

80. *R̥V* 1.126.4, 1.162.2, 4.2.8, 9.109.10; *AV* 20.16.11; *VS* 25.39; *TS* 4.6.9.2, etc.

81. *aśvatarīrathenāgnir ājim adhāvat* I . . . *gobhiraruṇair ūṣā ājimadhāvat* I. . . *aśvarathenendra ājim adhāvat* I . . . *gardabha-rathenāśvinā udajayatām aśnuvatām* . . . — *AB* 4.9

82. *praṣṭivāhinaṁ yunakti, praṣṭivāhī vai devarathaḥ* I — *TB* 1.3.6.4

83. *R̥V* 10.131.1; *AB* 5.30; *PB* 16.13.2, 18.9.7; *ŚB* 13.3.3.9; *TB* 1.8.2.4; 3.8.2.13, etc.

84. *R̥V* 4.24.8; *AV* 2.14.6.

85. *R̥V* 6.46.1, 8.80.8; *AV* 2.14.6; *VS* 27.37; *TS* 2.4.14.3; *AB* 4.7; *PB* 9.1.35, etc.

86. *yaḥ kakubho nidhāraya pr̥thivyām abhidarśataḥ* I
sa mātā pūrvyāṁ padaṁ tadvaruṇasya saptyaṁ mahī II — *R̥V* 8.4.4.

The phrase *ūrvī kāṣṭhā*, mentioned in the *R̥V* (8.80.8) indicates this course as broad. According to the *AV*[87] shape of this course appears to be quasi-circular (2.14.6).

From the description of races (scattered in the Saṁhitā and Brāhmaṇas[88]) it becomes clear that distance was measured out. Regarding this point the textbooks opine differently. The *AB*[89] states that gods fixed the course of their race from fire "the Lord of house" (*gārhapatyāgni*) to the Sun (*āditya*). The measurement of this distance has been specified in the *TB*;[90] this distance should be so far as the range of seventeen arrows. On this point the *ŚB* keeps silence, but Sāyaṇa,[91] while commenting on *ājidhāvanakathā* (narrated in the *TB* in the context of *Vājapeya*) mentions the course of race between the *cātvāla* and *udumbara* post set in the heap of rubbish.

Occurrence of the terms *dhana* and *vāja*[92] in their application with races indicate that in these races prizes were offered to the winner. People contended with zealous interest to win those prizes.[93] Other words used in the *R̥V*[94] to denote victory and prize are the *kāra* and *bhara*.

---

87. *paridhāmānyāsām āśurgāṣṭhābhivāsaram* । — *AV* 2.14.6
88. *AB* 4.7; *PB* 9.1.35; *ŚB* 5.1.4.4; *TB* 1.3.6.3.
89. *te 'gner evādhi gr̥hapater ādityaṁ kāṣṭhāṁ kurvata* — *AB* 4.7
90. *te saptadaśapravyādhān ājiṁ dhāvanti* — *TB* 1.3.6.3
91. *sapatadaśa pravyādha karaṇaṁ prajāpatiśarīra parimitatvāt* । . . . *tadante yā audumbarī śākhā sthāpitā tasyām avasthitena yajamānenājidhāvanaṁ kurvata* . . . — Sā on *ŚB* 5.1.5.14
92. *dhana* : *R̥V* 1.81.3, 6.45.2, 8.80.8, 9.53.2, 9.109.10; *vāja*: *R̥V* 7.38.8; *TS* 1.1.14.2, 1.7.8.4.
93. *R̥V* 1.81.3, 1.112.7, 1.112.10, 1.116.5, 2.10.6, 8.3.15, etc.
94. *kāraṁ na viśve ahvantaḥ devāḥ* ।
bharam indrāya yad ahiṁ jaghāna ॥ — *R̥V* 5.29.8

Contests of Skill/Pre-eminence

Besides chariot and horse races, some other contests of skill have been traced in the Vedic Saṁhitās. According to the *AV*[95] (3.8.3) it appears that such contests were held in order to settle pre-eminence among others, where prizes were staked[96] (*AV* 20.9.3). In this connection the Yajurvedic Saṁhitās[97] may be referred to, which have recorded some contests, which were held particularly in the sacrificial grounds. From this it can be considered that probably these contests formed a part of ritual.

Plays/Games

Moreover the *R̥V*'s[98] reference to playful Maruts make us suppose the existence of sports/games which were practised as forms of entertainment. The Yajurvedic Saṁhitās[99] refer repeatedly to the terms *krīḍā, moda,* etc., from which people's attraction towards the games can be safely assumed. But it is true that from these references, it is difficult to ascertain the nature of these games.

---

95. *huve somaṁ savitāraṁ namobhi viśvānādityā uttarattve* ।
ayam agnirdīdāyaddīrghameva sajātair iddho 'pratibruvadbhiḥ ॥
— *AV* 3.8.3

96. *tanvāyāmi suvīryaṁ tad brahma pūrvacittaye* ।
yenāyatibhyo bhr̥gave dhane hite yena praskaṇvam āvitha ॥
— *AV* 20.9.3

97. *TS* 1.3.4.1, 1.3.13.2, 1.3.14.7, 1.4.46.3, 1.7.8.1, 1.7.8.4, 4.1.2.1, 4.1.11.4, 4.2.11.3, etc.

98. (i) *krīḍaṁ vā śardho mārutam anarvāṇaṁ rathe śubham* ।
kaṇvā abhi pragāyata ॥ — *R̥V* 1.37.1
(ii) *praśaṁsā goṣvaghnyaṁ krīḍam yacchardhomārutam* ।
jambhe rasasya vāvr̥dhe ॥ — *R̥V* 1.37.5

99. *krīḍa ca me modaśca me* . . . — *MS* 2.11.3; *KS* 18.8; *KapKS* 28.7; *VS* 18.5; 18.11; *TS* 4.7.2.2.

Lottery Contest

Apart from this, in the context of three day rite of Garga, the *TMB*[100] presents before us a narrative of gods' *aṁśāharaṇa* where the term *aṁśāharaṇa* has been rendered as drawing of the lots. The story appears to be a picture of lottery contest from which it can be assumed that system of settling any disputed matter through lottery contest was known to the people of that period.

Hunting

Practice of hunting was prevalent since the time of *ṚV*. But as regards the purpose of hunting, it is really difficult to ascertain anything convincingly. Still from the references to hunting implements, hunters, and different modes of hunting it can be presumed that hunting might have been practised as a mode of entertainment in addition to its value as a mode of production, which have been discussed already (for details see under Hunting and Fishing, Mode of Production and Other Occupations, Ch. 4).

Cultivation of Fine Arts

It is true that ritual music is not directly concerned with people's everyday life. But as regards technical details of music, information (which have been reflected in the classical music) are not available from the descriptions of secular music. Therefore, we have to collect information on the same from the ritual context.

Music and Dance

Cultivation of fine arts, i.e., practice of both the vocal and instrumental music and dance was also considered as popular

100. *tayā vā idaṁ sahasraṁ vikalpayāmahā ityabruvaṁstām udake praveśayāmṣte- 'bruvannaṁśāharāmahai yasmai na iyam prathamāyodeṣyati iti te aṁśān āharante . . .* — *PB* 21.1.2

form of entertainment. Singing[101] and dancing,[102] different forms of music,[103] its participants[104] (singers, musicians and dancers), musical instruments,[105] employment of music and dance for both the ritual[106] and secular[107] purpose (as they have been recorded in the Vedas) indicate that singing and dancing were practised not only as forms of entertainment but also as the means of earning livelihood at least of some sects of people. Existence of dancing and singing as separate vocations like any other has added an additional degree to it and at the same time indicates a change or development in the society. Further, these were regarded as important features of ritual performances. On the basis of these references traced so far

101. *ṚV* 1.4.10, 1.5.1, 1.5.4, 1.5.8, 1.8.10, 1.10.1, 1.10.5, 1.107.2, 1.147.1, 2.41.1-2, 8.63.5, 8.66.1; *AV* 4.15.5, 5.11.8-9, 12.1.41, 19.1.1, etc.

102. *ṚV* 1.10.1, 1.92.4, 8.20.22, 8.24.9, 8.24.12, 10.72.6; *AV* 4.38.1 ff, 10.7.43, 12.1.41, 20.76.2, etc.

103. *arka*: *ṚV* 1.71.1, 1.83.6, 1.167.6, 6.21.4, 7.24.5, etc.
gātu: *ṚV* 1.15.2, 2.20.5, 3.4.4, 4.4.6, 5.57.8, etc.
uktha: *ṚV* 1.8.10, 1.10.86, 1.100.14, 3.53.3.
gir: *ṚV* 1.3.2, 1.3.5, 1.6.6, 1.6.9, 1.9.4, etc.
gāthā: *ṚV* 1.167.6, 8.32.1, 8.71.14, 8.98.9, 9.11.4, 9.99.4, 10.85.6; *MS* 3.7.3 (wedding song); passim in *JB* and *PB*.
raibhī, nārāśaṁsī : *ṚV* 10.85.6.

104. *ṚV* 1.6.6, 1.7.1, 1.83.6, 8.1.7-8, 10.71.11; *AV* 7.73.1, 20.110.1; *VS* 33.18; *TS* 4.6.2.2, etc.

105. Drum: *ṚV* 1.28.5, 6.47.29, 6.47.31; *AV* 5.20.1ff, 5.21.1ff, 6.38.4, 12.1.41; *VS* 16.35; *KS* 34.5; *TS* 7.5.9.3; *TB* 3.4.13.1; *ŚB* 5.1.5.6, etc.
Flute: *ṚV* 10.135.7; *MS* 3.6.8; *KS* 23.4, 34.5; *TS* 6.1.4.1; *PB* 6.5.13; *TB* 3.4.13.1, 3.4.15.1, etc.
Lute: *ṚV* 2.43.3; *AV* 4.37.5, 20.132.3; *TS* 6.1.4.1; *MS* 3.6.8; *KS* 34.5; *ŚB* 3.2.4.6, 13.1.5.1; *JB* 1.42, etc.

106. *ṚV* 1.4.10, 1.5.4, 1.5.8, 1.21.2, 1.107.2, 1.167.6, 1.173.1, 7.102.1-3, 8.63.5, 8.66.1; *AV* 5.11.8-9, 6.1.1, 19.1.1; *ŚB* 5.1.5.17, 13.1.5.3, 13.4.2.8, etc.

107. *AV* 5.12.7, 12.1.41; *MS* 3.7.3-4; *KS* 23.10, 24.1; *KapKS* 37.2; *TS* 6.1.6.6; *ŚB* 3.2.4.1-6.

in the Vedic literature, music and dance can be divided mainly under two heads; (i) ritual, and (ii) secular/social.

But, whether ritual or social, whatever the purpose may have been, it can be stated safely that music and dance were the spontaneous expressions of people's delight and perfection. That is why the role of music and dance in their everyday life was a vital one. A close relationship between delight, enjoyment, rapturous ecstacies, pleasures, laughter and dance has been shown in the *AV*.[108] In this connection, the *ŚB*[109] has remarked that whosoever thinks himself perfect either sings or delights in song.

It is interesting to note that a modern scholar also has remarked in the same manner:

> people following any happy occurrence demanded expression in the happy rhythmic movements of limbs; men and women of the community joined in the carnival of mirth.[110]

In the *KB*[111] dancing, singing and playing with music have been declared as *trivṛt/śilpa*, the fine arts consisting of three faculties. Inclusion of *devajanavidyā* referred to in the *CU*[112] (7.1.2, ff.)

108. *ānandā modāḥ pramudo 'bhīmoda mudaśca me* ।
haso nariṣṭā nṛttāni śarīramanu prāviśan ॥
— *AV* 11.8.24

109. *tasmād u haitad yaḥ sarvaḥ kṛtsna manyate gāyativaiva gīte vā ramate* ।
— *ŚB* 6.1.1.15

110. Vatsyayan, *CIDLA*, p. 12.

111. *trivṛddhai śilpaṁ nṛttaṁ gītaṁ vāditram iti* । — *KB* 29.5

112. (i) *ṛgvedaṁ bhagavo 'dhyemi yajurvedaṁ sāmavedaṁ ātharvaṇaṁ caturtham itihāsapurāṇaṁ pañcamaṁ vedānāṁ vedaṁ pitryaṁ, rāśiṁ, daivaṁ, nidhiṁ, vākovākyam ekāyanaṁ devavidyāṁ brahmavidyāṁ bhūtavidyāṁ kṣatravidyāṁ, nakṣatravidyāṁ sarpadevajanavidyāṁ etad bhagavo 'dhyemi* — *CU* 7.1.2

(ii) *sarpa-devajanavidyāṁ sarpavidyāṁ gāruḍaṁ devajanavidyāṁ gandhayukti nṛtyagīta-vādyśilpādi vijñānāni* ।. . .
— Śaṅkara on *CU*, *loc. cit.*

which has been interpreted by Śaṅkara as consisting of music, dance and science of perfumery works indicates music and dance as separate branches of learning, which were to be studied regularly.

MUSIC & DANCE — ITS MYTHOLOGICAL BACKGROUND

Uṣas

Regular arrival of dawn in the early morning with all her charms appeared as a beautiful dancing maiden before the eyes of the R̥gvedic seer.[113]

Description of her beautiful embroidered garment throws light on the dress and costumes of a dancer prevalent at that time.[114] Her arrival and departure, display of her beauty with all her boldness and frankness, everything may be considered as rhythmic movements of a dancer.[115] From the *AB*'s[116] reference to the rotation of day and night in a rhythmic manner we are to suppose that there must have been some prescribed rules for dancing even in that ancient period.

In the *R̥V*,[117] thunder-god Indra has been frequently mentioned as the leader of dancers and somewhere as a lover of song. His close associates Maruts and Aśvins also appear as gay singers and dancers.[118] In the scenery of thunderstorm the Vedic seer could visualize Maruts as dancing and singing and playing with musical instruments (*R̥V* 1.85.10). Actually they (Maruts) are the divine singers. Description of Maruts as

---

113. *adhi peśāṁsi vapate nr̥tūrivāporṇute vakṣa usreva barjaham* ।
jyotirviśvasmai bhuvanāya kr̥ṇavatī gāvo na brajaṁ vyuṣā āvartamaḥ ॥
— *R̥V* 1.92.4

114. Vatsyayan, *CIDLA*, p. 15.

115. *ā ghā yoṣeva sūnar yūṣā yāti pramuñjatī* ।
jarayantī vr̥janaṁ padvadīyata utpātayati pakṣiṇaḥ ॥ — *R̥V* 1.48.5

116. *prati padaśca ahaśceti punar āvr̥ttaṁ punar ninr̥ttam* ॥ — *AB* 5.15

117. *R̥V* 2.22.4, 8.24.9, 8.24.12, etc.

118. *chandaḥ stubhaḥ kubhanyava utsamā kīrino nr̥tuḥ* । — *R̥V* 5.52.12

leaders of a troupe of dancers and the story of the origin of this world (according to which, thickening cloud of dusts arising from the steppings of dancing gods created this world) help us imagine the picture of a group dance.[119]

Apart from these deities, *gandharva*s and *apsarase*s have been described as competent singers and dancers. Description of *gandharva*s' and *apsarase*s' dancing, accompanied by the music of lutes and cymbals has been recorded in the *AV*.[120] In the late Vedic literature also dancing nymphs have been mentioned very often. The *JB*[121] has described the region of dancing and singing nymphs and *gandharva*s, which Bhṛgu visited at his father's command. In the *ŚB*[122] (3.2.4.6) their addiction to singing and dancing has been mentioned explicitly. In this connection, we may refer to the Kaṭha,[123] where Yama tried to allure Naciketas by providing him dancing nymphs, seated in divine chariots and playing on harps.

From the study of Vedic Saṁhitā and Brāhmaṇas we find that Vedic seers had keen power of observation. They tried to catch elements of music and dance in various sights and sounds of natural phenomena.

The sound of wings of a flying vulture appeared to the Vedic seer similar to the music produced by playing on *karkari* —

> *yad ut patan vadasi karkariryathā bṛhad vadema vidathe subīrāḥ*
> — *ṚV* 2.43.3

---

119. *ṚV* 8.20.22, 10.72.6, etc.

120. *AV* 4.37.1-12, 4.38.1, 4.38.3, etc.

121. *ṣaṣṭham ājagāma* ı *pañca nadīḥ puṣkariṇīḥ puṇḍarīkiṇīr madhūdkās syandamānāḥ* ı *tāsu nṛtta-gītaṁ vīṇāghoṣo 'psarasāṁ gaṇās surabhir gandho mahān ghoṣo babhūva* ı . . . — *JB* 1.42. cf. 1.44

122. *ŚB* 3.2.4.6.

123. *imā rāmāḥ sarathāḥ satūryāḥ na hīdṛśā lambhanīyā manuṣyaiḥ* ı
ābhir matprattābhiḥ paricārayasva naciketo maraṇaṁ mā 'nuprākṣiḥ ıı
— *Kaṭha* 1.1.25

Similarly in the sound of thunderstorm they have heard the music of playing on the harp.

> *ūrdhvaṁ nunudre 'vataṁ ta ojasā dādṛhāṇaṁ cid vibhidur vi parvatam,*
> *dhamanto vāṇaṁ marutaḥ sudānavo made somasyāraṇyāni cakrire.*
> — *ṚV* 1.85.10

Again, in the thunderstorm the Atharvavedic seer has heard the chorus delivered by Maruts:

> *gaṇāstvopa gāyanti mārutaḥ parjanya ghoṣiṇaḥ pṛthak*
> — *AV* 4.15.4

The crackling sound of frogs appeared to them as chanting of *sāmans* by brāhmaṇas:

> *brāhmaṇāso somino vācamakrata brahmakṛṇvantaḥ parivatsarīṇam* ।
> — *ṚV* 7.103.8

The *ŚB*[124] in the context of *Darśapūrṇamāsa* rite has remarked, when it rains hard the musical sound as that of *sāman* chant is heard.

Before the poetic vision and keen aesthetic sense of Vedic seers natural events like rhythmic rotation of day and night or arrival of dawn or scenery of thunderstorm were reflected as dancing figures. Quite naturally these natural phenomena have been described in the Vedic literature in terms of music and dance.

DANCE AND MUSIC IN SOCIAL LIFE

Practice of music and dance in the social life of people has been traced in the Vedic literature. From the study of these passages it appears that music and dance were considered as an integral part of human life.

---

124. *yadā balavad varṣati sāma ivopabdiṁ kriyate* — *ŚB* 11.2.7.32

The providing occasions of their dancing and singing were sometimes communal gatherings or any festival occasion or sometimes ceremonies like marriage or funeral rite. Even minor events like finding out a source of water provoked their joy and inspired them to dance and sing on. The *ṚV*[125] has referred to some Pārāvatas, who while seeking water danced about the spring. Singing and dancing of common people have been traced in the Bhūmi-sūkta of the *AV*.[126]

References to the dancing and singing (as they have been traced in the Vedas) suggest that music and dance programmes (not in the modern sense) were held in solo,[127] duet,[128] sometimes in chorus[129]/community form also. Description of god's dancing from which this world was originated may be mentioned as an example of community dance.[130] Another similar passage may be cited from the *ṚV*[131] as community dance along with song in which people joined with all their vigour and vivacity. The atmosphere resounded with the happy cries of dancers. The picture of this collective dance in the form of a couple embracing each other makes us presume a festive occasion.

---

125. *chandaḥ stubhaḥ kubhanyava utsamā kīriṇo nṛtuḥ* ।
te ye kecinna tāyava ubhā āsandṛśi tviṣe ॥ — *ṚV* 5.52.12

126. *yasyāṁ gāyanti nṛtyanti bhūmyāṁ martyā byaiḷavāḥ* ।
yudhyante yasyām ākrando yasyāṁ vadati dundubhiḥ ॥ — *AV* 12.1.41

127. *ṚV* 1.83.6, 10.71.11; *ṚV* 1.92.4.

128. *ṚV* 6.63.5; *AV* 5.12.7.

129. (i) *ṚV* 1.6.6, 1.7.1; *AV* 4.15.5; *CU* 1.12.1ff.
(ii) *ṚV* 8.20.22, 8.24.9, 8.24.12, 10.94.4-5.

130. *yad devā adaḥ salile susaṁrabdhā atiṣṭhata* ।
atrā vo nṛtyatām iva tīvro reṇur apāyata ॥ — *ṚV* 10.72.6

131. *bṛhad vadanti madireṇa mandinendraṁ krośanto 'vidannavā madhu* ।
saṁrabhyādhīrāḥ svasṛbhir anartiṣvrāghoṣayantaḥ pṛthivīm upabdibhiḥ ।
suparṇā vācamakratopa dyāvyākhare kṛṣṇā iṣirā avartiṣuḥ ।
nyaraṅkti yantyuparasya niṣkṛtam purureto dadhire sūryaśvitaḥ ॥
— *ṚV* 10.94.4-5

In the sound of thunderstorm the Vedic seer has discovered song of Maruts' troupe (as has been mentioned already) which conveys the idea of a chorus song. The *śauva udgītha* (recorded in the *CU* 1.12.1) is another instance of a chorus song. The phrase *pracodayantā vidatheṣu kāru prācīnaṁ jyotiḥ pradiśā diśantā* (*AV* 5.12.7) appears to present before us the picture of a duet song delivered by two minstrels in the assembly.

The funeral hymn of the *ṚV*[132] has instructed the relatives of the dead to go forth, sing, dance, laugh and prolong the span of their own life after having rendered duties to the departed soul. The expression *prāñco agāma nṛtaye hasāya* (we have gone forth for dancing and laughter) may indicate that laughter and dance were associated with each other even at the moment of sorrow and death. In the Gṛhya-Sūtras singing and dancing has been prescribed on the occasion of marriage ceremony, *Sīmantonnayana*, etc. We will discuss it under the section "Employment of music and dance in the rituals."

As regards the participants, we find from the references (scattered in the Vedic literature) both men and women indulged in the practice of dancing and singing,[133] though in the Brāhmaṇic[134] passages womens' special attraction for music and dance has been mentioned distinctly. Further, existence of the passage, e.g., *patnī-karmaiva ete atra udgātāraḥ kurvanti* indicates that formerly wives of sacrificers were entrusted

---

132. *ime jīva vimṛtair avavṛtrannabhad bhadra devahūtir no adya* ।
prāñco agāma nṛtaye hasāya drāghīya āyuḥ prataraṁ dadhānāḥ ।
— *ṚV* 10.18

133. (dance of male candidates) *ṚV* 8.20.22, 8.24.12; *AV* 4.15.4, 5.12.7.
(dance of female candidates) *AV* 4.37.1ff; *TS* 7.5.8-2; *PB* 15.12.6, etc.

134. (i) *nṛttaṁ gītaṁ strīṇām karma* — *ŚB* 3.2.4.6
(ii) *patnīkarmaiva ete atra yad udgātāraḥ kurvanti* — *ŚB* 14.3.1.35
(iii) *ya eva gāyati yo nṛtyati tasminnevaitā nimiślatamā eva* ।
— *ŚB* 3.2.4.6

with the chanting of *sāman*; in later ages they were replaced by the Udgātṛ priests. Apart from festivals or ritual occasion, practice of music and dance has been recorded as means of entertaining another person (especially women). In this connection, we may refer to a story (narrated in the *ŚB*), where gods recovered Soma with the help of Vāc and (recovered) her through the aid of music and dance.

MUSICAL INSTRUMENTS

While singing and dancing people required some instruments as their accompaniments. The instruments used by the people may be classified into some groups, e.g., drums, flute, lute, cymbal, harp, etc. Besides these there are references to some other names, viz., *gargara, godhā, piṅgā, vāṇīcī,*[135] etc., which appear to be some sort of musical instruments, but it is very difficult to ascertain their exact nature.

As regards the drums, we see from the *ṚV* onwards, there are at least four/five names for drums, viz., *dundubhi*[136] (kettle-drum), *bhūmi dundubhi*[137] (earth drum), *vanaspati*[138] (wooden drum), *āḍambara,*[139] *lambara,*[140] etc., which indicates use of varieties of drums. On the basis of these references we may easily infer wide use of drums in both the times of war and peace.

---

135. (i) *ava svarāti gargaro godhāpariṇiṣvaṇat* ।
piṅgā pari ca niṣkadad indrāya brahmodyatam ॥ — *ṚV* 8.69.9
(ii) *suṣṭuto vṛṣṇvasū rathe vāṇīcyāhitā* । — *ṚV* 5.75.4

136. *ṚV* 1.28.5, 6.47.29, 6.47.31; *AV* 5.20.1ff, 5.21.1ff, 12.1.41; *VS* 16.35; *TB* 1.3.6.2; *ŚB* 5.1.5.6, etc.

137. *bhūmidundubhir bhavati* . . . — *KS* 34.5

138. *ṚV* 1.166.5, 3.34.10; *AV* 5.20.1, 5.21.3

139. *śabdāya āḍambarāghātam* . . . — *VS* 30.19; *ŚB* 14.4.8.1

140. *tasmai sa tatra vijihīte yathā lambarasya khaṁ* . . . — *BU* 5.12.1

Usually the drum was wrought of wood and compact with leather straps.[141] *Bhūmidundubhi* has been mentioned in the Yajurvedic Saṁhitā and Brāhmaṇas. It is a special kind of drum, which was made by digging hole in the ground and covered with hide to be used in the *Mahāvrata* rite, which was performed at the winter solstice to drive away the influences, hostile to the return of the Sun (Hillebrandt, *VM* I, p. 148; Macdonell, VI, II, p. 368).

Normally drums were beaten with music[142]/dance[143] or to announce victory[144] or any other important news. From the description of a rushing woman grasping her son, who has been awakened and puzzled to hear the sound of drum beatings of enemy camp, it appears that another purpose of drum beating was to threaten the enemies.

> *dundubher vācaṁ prayatāṁ vadantīṁ āśṛṇvatī nāthitā ghoṣabuddhā* ।
> *nārī putraṁ dhāvatu hastagṛhyāmitrī bhītāsamare badhānām* ॥
> — *AV* 5.20.5

In the *AV* there are two hymns (5.20, 5.21) which have been entirely devoted to the war drum. All these indicate that drums were used to produce war-music. Another instrument, which was used to serve the same purpose was *bakura* (occurring in the *ṚV* and later texts). The description of Aśvins playing with *bakura* at the time of their expedition against *dasyus*, indicates its (*bakura*) use at the time of war.[145] The phrase *bākuraṁ dṛtim*

141. (i) *uccair ghoṣo dundubhiḥ satvanāyan vānaspatyaḥ saṁbhṛtā usriyābhiḥ* । — *AV* 5.20.1

(ii) *vānaspatyaḥ saṁbhṛtā usriyābhir viśvagotrīyāḥ* । — *AV* 5.21.3

142. *ŚB* 5.1.5.6, 5.1.5.17.

143. *TS* 7.5.10.1; *PB* 5.6.15.

144. (i) *iha dyumattamaṁ vadajayatām iva dundubhiḥ* । — *ṚV* 1.28.5

(ii) *AV* 5.20.4, 5.21.4-8, 5.21.11, etc.

145. *yavaṁ vṛkeṇāśvinā bapanteṣaṁ duhantā mahiṣena dasrā* ।
abhi dasyuṁ bakureṇādhamantorū jyotiścakrathuḥ ॥ — *ṚV* 1.117.21

(*ṚV* 9.1.8) seems to indicate *bakura* as a wind instrument. As regards its name, texts are not unanimous. From the textual context, it appears that the same name has been read differently in different texts, viz., *bakura/bākura* (*ṚV* 1.117.21, 9.1.8), *bekuri* (*TS* 3.4.7.1), *bhekuri* (*KS* 18.14), *bhakuri* (*VS* 18.40), *bhekura/bhākura* (*ŚB* 9.4.1.9) and *bekurā* (*PB* 6.7.8). It has been identified with Goddess Vāc in the *PB*.[146]

Flutes (*nāḍī*) were used as musical accompaniments. References to *tūṇava* and *nāḍī*, mentioned separately in the same line (in the Yajurvedic Saṁhitā and Brāhmaṇas[147]) indicate that use of various sorts of flutes was known to the people.

Lutes (*vīṇā*) have been mentioned very often.[148] In the *ŚB*,[149] it has been identified with Śrī. Most probably that is why it was looked upon as a graceful and sacred instrument. The *ŚB* (13.1.5.1) has remarked *yadā vai puruṣo śriyaṁ gacchati vīṇā 'smai bādyate*, when a person attains grace lutes are played to him. Its divine origin has been narrated in the *ŚB*.[150] In the Ṛgvedic Āraṇyakas,[151] human lute has been described as the imitation of this divine lute. Its various parts, viz., head (*śiras*), cavity (*udara*), sounding board (*ambhaṇa*), strings (*tantra*), and plectrum (*vādana*) have been mentioned in the said texts.[152]

146. *bekurā nāmāsi juṣṭā devebhyo namo vāce namo vācaspataye । devi vāg yatte madhumat tasmin mā dhāḥ । . . .* — *PB* 1.3.1

147. *MS* 3.6.8; *KS* 23.4, 34.5; *TS* 6.1.4.1; *PB* 6.5.13; *TB* 3.4.13.1, 3.4.15.1, etc.

148. *MS* 3.6.8; *KS* 3.4; *TS* 6.1.4.1; *ŚB* 3.2.4.6.

149. *śrīyai vā etadrūpam yadvīṇa . . .* — *ŚB* 13.1.5.1

150. *atha devā vīṇāṁ eva sṛṣṭvā vādayanto hi gāyanto niṣedur iti* — *ŚB* 3.2.4.6

151. *atha khalviyaṁ daivī vīṇa bhavati tadanukṛtīrasau mānuṣī vīṇā bhavati . . .* — *AĀ* 3.2.5; *SĀ* 8.9

152. *yathāsyā śiraḥ evam amuṣyāḥ śiro yathāsyā udaramevamamuṣya ambhaṇaṁ yathāsyai jihvaivamamuṣyai vādanaṁ yathāsyā tantrayaḥ evamamuṣyā aṅgulayo yathasyā svarā evam amuṣyā svarā . . . romaśena carmaṇā pihitaṁ bhavati . . .* — *AĀ* 3.2.5; cf. *SĀ* 8.9

The instrument was covered with hairy skin. The *JB*[153] has compared these various parts with ritual implements, viz., *raśanā, droṇa-kalaśa, adhiṣavaṇa-carma, grāvā,* etc.

Kāṇḍavīṇā mentioned in the *KS* (34.5), appears to be the name of a sort of lute made out of joints of reed. According to the *AĀ*, women played on this instrument (*patnyaśca kāṇḍavīṇā* — *AĀ* 5.1.4). In the *JB*[154] we find a list providing varieties of lute names, viz., *karkari-alābuḥ, vakrā kapiśīrṣṇī, aiṣīkī apaghāṭalīkā, kaśyapī-vīṇā* (probably named so on account of its shape, similar to a tortoise) and *śatatantrī vāṇaḥ*. From the study of Brāhmaṇa and Āraṇyaka texts, it appears that *aiṣīkī apaghāṭalīkā* of the *JB*, and *apaghāṭilā* of the *PB* are the same instrument called differently in different texts. *Karkari* and *āghāṭi* (occurring in the *R̥V* and the *AV*) were used to accompany dancers. The expression *karkarikarṇyaḥ* (*MS* 4.2.9) rendered as "cattle branded on the ear with a mark similar to lute" (Macdonell *VI*, I, p. 139) makes us assume that *karkari* was a type of lute.

Vāṇa mentioned from the *R̥V*[155] onwards indicates the name of harp/lyre having one hundred strings. Maruts have been described in the *R̥V* (1.85.10) singing and playing on this harp. The *AĀ* (5.1.4) refers to the use of *audumbara vāṇa* in *Mahāvrata* rite.

---

153. *atha ya yūpa āsīdya evaiṣa vīṇāyā daṇḍās eva saḥ* ।
atha ya raśanā asau yānyevaitāni vīṇāyā upavāṇānī tā eva tāḥ ।
atha yo droṇa kalaśa āsīt yaivaiṣa vīṇāyai sunā sa eva saḥ ।
atha yad adhiṣavaṇaṁ carmāsīt yadevaitat vīṇāyai carma tadeva tat ।
atha ya uparavā āsan ya evai te vīṇāyā ākāśās ta eva te ।
atha ye grāvāṇa āsan yanyevaitāni vīṇāyā vādanāni ta eva te ।
— *JB* 2.70

154. *karkarī cā lābuśca vakrā ca kapiśīrṣṇī caiṣiki cāpaghāṭalīkā, vīṇā ca kaśyapī . . . vāṇaśca śatatantrī . . .* — *JB* 2.404

155. *R̥V* 1.85.40, 8.20.8, 9.97.8, 10.32.8; *AV* 10.2.17; *TS* 7.5.9.2; *KS* 34.5; *PB* 5.6.12, 14.7-8, etc.

EMPLOYMENT OF MUSIC AND DANCE IN RITUALS

Music and dance beside having their entertainment value had a vital role in the ritual performances.

Vocal Music

Numerous occurrences of prayer songs in the *ṚV* uttered by the singer priests indicate that singing was practised in the early Vedic period, mainly for religious purpose, i.e., to entertain gods, who were invoked repeatedly to appear in the sacrificial ground. Existence of various kinds of laudatory verses, viz., *arka, gātu, gāthā, gāyatra, kuṁbyā, nārāśaṁsī, raibhī,*[156] etc. (traced in Vedic Saṁhitās) lend support to this view. In the Brāhmaṇa literature also, there are references to music, which formed important parts of ritual performances.

The Sāmavedic Saṁhitā and Brāhmaṇas may be considered as the source book of vocal music practised by Vedic people. Mainly the Ṛgvedic verses have been adapted in the texts of Sāmasaṁhitā for the purpose of singing them in various rites. The songs have been compiled in four works called *gānagranthas*, viz., *grāmageya, āraṇyageya, ūha,* and *ūhya* texts. The *grāmageya* text divided into 17 *prapāṭhakas*, contains *sāmans*, which are sung upon *ṛcs* in the same order in which they appear in the *pūrvārcika*.[157] The name *grāmageya* indicates that they could be studied within a village.

The *āraṇyageya* divided into six *prapāṭhakas* describes the *sāmans* which are sung upon the *ṛcs* appearing in the

---

156. *ṚV* 1.7.1, 1.8.10, 1.15.2, 1.167.7, 8.1.7-8, 10.71.11, 10.85.6, etc.

157.

2	3	1	2		3	1	2		3	2	3	1	2	
a	gna	ā	yā	hi	vī	ta	ye	gṛ	ṇā	no	ha	vya	dā	taye ।

1		2ra			3	1	2	
ni	ho	tā	sat	si	ba	rhi	ṣi	॥ — *SV* 1.1.1.1

Āraṇyasaṁhitā;[158] which is an appendage of *pūrvārcika*. Besides these, some more *ṛcs* from *pūrvārcika* have been included here. They were regarded as secret and hence fit to be studied in the solitude of forest.

Ūhagāna is actually an extension of *grāmageyagāna*. The difference is: *grāmageya* describes *sāmans* on single stanza in the same order in which they appear in the *pūrvārcika* whereas *ūhagāna* describes complete *sāman* based on two or three verses, shown in the *uttarārcika*.[159]

---

158. 2 3 1 2 3 1 2 3 1 2 3 1 2 3 1 2
in dra jye ṣṭham na ā bha ra o ji ṣṭhaṁ pu pu ri śra vaḥ ।

2ra 3 1 2 3 1ra
yaddi dhṛ kṣema vajra hasta ro da sī u bhe

2ra
su śipra paprāḥ ॥ — *SV (Ā Saṁ)*

159. 5 ra 4ra 5
om । u ccā tā S 3i jā ta ma ndha sāḥ ॥

2 1 2 2
di vā i sā S1 dbhū S2 । mi yā S 23 da dā i ॥

1 2 1 2
u graṁ śa rmā । ma hā S 23 i śra vā u । vā S 3 ॥ śrīḥ ॥

5 2 4ra 5
sa na ā S3 indra ya ya jya vā i ॥

2 2 2
va rū ṇā S1 yāS 2 । ma rū t 23 dbhi yāḥ ॥

1 2ra
va ri vo vā it ॥

5ra ra
pa rā S 23 i sra vā u । vā S3 ॥ e nā vā S3 i

śvā ni a rya ā ।

→

Ūhyagāna is an extension of *āraṇyageya gāna*.[160]

→

dyu mnā nā S1 i mā S2 ।

1 2 lra 2 1
nu ṣā S 23 ṇām ॥ si ṣā sa ntāḥ । va nā S 2 3

2 2ra 1 1 1
ma hā u । vā S 3 । stau ṣe S 3 4 5

— *SV Ūhagāna* (Daśarātra Parvan)1

160. 2ra ra ra 2
au ho i tvā mi ddhi ha vā ma hā S 3 e ॥

ra lra ra 2 3 5 1 2
ṣā tau vā jā । syā kā rā S 2 3 4 vā ḥ । tu vā S 3 4 ।

au ho vā । vṛ trā i ṣu vā i । dra sā S 31 t ।

pa ti nnā S 2 3 4 rāḥ ॥

lra ra 2 3ra 4ra 5 - - 1
tvām kā ṣṭhā S 3 4 । au ho vā ॥ su S2 ā rvā S 234 । tāḥ ।

5 5
u hu vā S 6 hā u । vā ॥ śrīḥ ॥

2ra ra 2 ra 1 2 3 -5
au ho i tu vā S 3 me ॥ kā ṣṭhā । sū a rvā S 234 taḥ

1 2 3ra 4ra 5 2 1
sa tvā S 3 4 । au ho vā । na scā i tra vā ।

2 2 5 2 1
jrā hā S 3 1 । sta dhṛ ṣṇu S 234 yā ॥ ma ha sta

2 3ra 4ra 5
vā S 2 3 4 । au ho vā ॥

1 5 5
na S 2 ā drā S 2 3 4 i । vāḥ । u hu vā S 6 hā u ।

vā ॥ śrīḥ ॥

→

As regards various details of *sāman* and its presentation, later texts, especially in Sāmavedic Brāhmaṇa and Upaniṣad (*CU*) and in some cases the *Puṣpa-Sūtra*, the *Nāradīya Śikṣā* and the *Lāṭyāyana Śrauta-Sūtra* provide us information. They have discussed on varieties of *sāmans*, their five/seven divisions[161] various *stomas* and their lauds[162] (*viṣṭuti*), six modifications of *sāman*[163] (*ṣaṭsāmavikāras*), etc.

Viṣṭuti is actually a special type of arrangement of singing *sāmans*. The *PB* has devoted two sections (2-3) on it entirely. Discussion of specific varieties of *viṣṭuti*, their intricate process of chanting and taking breaths in between, departure from which may cause harm (e.g., blindness, impotence[164]) to the

---

→ lra ra 2 1 2 3
au ho i ma hā S ta tra ll sta vā l no a drā S 2 3 4 i

lra 2 3ra 4ra 5
vāḥ gā mā S 3 4 au ho vā l

2 1 2 3 3
śu vā ◌̐ ra thā i l yā nā S 31 i l dra saṁ kā S 2 3 4 i

5 2 lra ra 2
vāḥ l sa trā vā jā S 3 4 l

3ra 4ra — 1 — 1
au ho vā ll nā S 2 jā i l nā S 2 ji gyū S 2 3 4 l

5 5 1
ṣā i l u hu vā S 6 hā u l vā ll has ll

— *SV Ūhyagāna* (Daśarātra Parvan) 5

161. *AB* 3.23, 5.23; *PB* 4.9.9; *JB* 1.292; *CU* 2.1.1-2.21.3, etc.

162. *PB* 2.1.1-3.13.3.

163. *Puṣpa-Sūtra* 8.5.1, 8.5.3, 10.6.7, etc.

164. Process of chanting: *PB* 2.9.1, 3.9.1, 3.1.1, 3.2.1, 7.1.2, 7.7.10-12; its harmful effect: *PB* 7.1.9-10, 7.7.15.

singer, bespeaks about the high standard of Indian music attained at that ancient period.

Five divisions of *sāman* (*pañcabhaktika sāman*), viz., *hiṁkāra*, *prastāva*, *udgītha*, *pratihāra* and *nidhana* have been mentioned in the Brāhmaṇa texts[165] (specially in the *AB*, *PB* and *JB*). The *CU*[166] adds two more names to this list, i.e., *ādi* and *upadrava*. These five/seven divisions have been explained here (*CU* 2.1.1-2.21-3) in terms of region, sun, rain, seasons, water, *prāṇa*s, animals, words, etc.

Definition and participants of these different parts (*bhakti*/*avayava*) have been discussed in the *LŚS*[167] (6.10.1ff). We know different portions of *sāman* were sung by different priests, chief among which was Udgātṛ assisted by the Prastotṛ and Pratihartṛ. In addition to these there were some more singers, who provided accompaniments. They were *upagāyaka*s, whose duty was to provide continuous vocal accompaniment with the syllable *oṁ* or *ho*. This *upagāna* continued from the beginning to the end. The peculiarity of *sāman* lay in the unbroken continuity of this basic note, without which recital of *sāman* would be regarded as broken or devoid of beauty[168] (*LŚS* 1.11.26-27).

---

165. *te vai pañcānyadbhūtvā pañcānyad-bhūtvā kalpetām-āhāvaśca, hiṁkāraśca prastāvaśca prathamā ca ṛgudgīthaśca madhyamā ca pratihāraścottamā ca nidhanaṁ ca vaṣaṭkāraśceti* I — *AB* 3.2.3, 5.23; *PB* 4.9.9; *JB* 1.292, etc.

166. *vāci saptavidhaṁ sāmopāsīta, yatkiñca vāco hum iti sa hiṅkāro* I *yat preti sa prastāvo, yad eti sa ādiḥ* I *yad uditi sa udgītho yat pratīti sa pratihāro yad upeti sa upadravo yannīti tannidhanam* I — *CU* 2.8.1-2

167. (i) *avasānaṁ prastāvānta lakṣaṇamavibhāgyānāma* I — *LŚS* 6.10.1
sarveṣām oṅkāreṇodgīthādānam I — *ibid.*, 6.10.13
padādiḥ pratihārasthānaṁ sarvatra I — *ibid.* 6.10.22
(ii) participants: *LŚS* 1.11.19-26.

168. *ta etenākṣareṇo pagāyeyur ho iti mandrasvareṇa santataṁ sahavācyeṣvārabhantaḥ* I — *LŚS* 1.11.26

The six modifications of *sāman* (*ṣaṭ sāmavikāra* — which were invariable at the time of converting *ṛc* into *sāman*) have been taught in the *Puṣpa-Sūtra*.[169] They are as follows:

1. *Vikāra* consists in the distortion of the text, e.g., *agne* changed into *ognāyi*.
2. *Viśleṣaṇa* means analysing a word or a syllable, e.g., *vītaye* analysed as *voyitoyā 2 yi*.
3. *Vikarṣaṇa* means substituting a long vowel for a short one or a prolated vowel for a long one, e.g., *ya 23 yi* changed into *ye*.
4. *Abhyāsa* is the repetition of a word *toyāyi-toyāyi*. Probably this repeated word was sung in a different tune.
5. *Virāma* is actually a short pause, occurred in the middle of a word for convenience of breathing.
6. *Stobha* means additional unmeaningful words/syllables occurred amidst the text. Thirteen varieties of *stobhas* have been mentioned in the *CU*[170] (1.13.1-3). It is interesting to note here that *avayavas* or *vikāras* of *sāman* (i.e., how *nidhanas, stobhas* should be applied) have been shown in the *ūha* texts of Sāma Saṁhitā though their names have not been specified there.

The concept of seven musical notes appears to have been indicated in the *ṚV*.[171] *Saptavāṇī* in some Ṛgvedic[172] passages

169. *Puṣpa-Sūtra* 8.5.1, 8.5.3, 10.6.7, etc.

170. *ayaṁ vāva loko hā ukāro vāyur hā ikāraś candramā athakāraḥ । ātmehakāro-'gnirīkāraḥ ॥ āditya ukāro nihava ekāro viśvadevā auhoyikāraḥ prajāpatir hiṅkāraḥ prāṇah svaro 'nnaṁ yā vāg virāṭ ॥ aniruktastrayodaśaḥ stobhaḥ sañcaro huṅkāraḥ ॥* — *CU* 1.13.1-3

171. *mātā yat santur yūthasya pūrvyābhir vāṇasya saptadhāturjjanaḥ ।* — *ṚV* 10.32.4

172. *ṚV* 3.1.6, 3.7.1, 9.103.3, etc.

in its application with *vāṇa* has been interpreted by some Western scholars as seven musical notes.[173] The *AB* in the context of ascertaining deity of morning litany referred to *saptadhā vāk*, without showing their names. The Hotṛ priest in the *AĀ*[174] has been described as playing with *audumbara vāṇa* and producing various notes in it, which makes it evident that by this time people had developed a clear idea about musical notes. That "notes are the essence of *sāman*" has been clearly declared in the *CU*[175] (1.8.4).

Composition of *svaramaṇḍala* consisting of seven notes (*sapta svarāh*), three scales (*trayo grāmāḥ*), twenty-one rise and fall of notes (*ekaviṁśati mūrchanāḥ*), and fortynine *tāna*s have been handled in the *Nāradīya Śikṣā*.[176] In course of discussing *svaramaṇḍala* Nārada has enumerated the list of seven musical notes of *sāman*, viz., *ṣaḍja, ṛṣabha, gāndhāra, madhyama, pañcama, dhaivata* and *niṣāda*,[177] though in a previous verse Nārada has given another set of seven notes followed by *sāma* chanters, viz., *kruṣṭa, prathama, dvitīya, tṛtīya, caturtha, mandra* and *atisvāra*.[178]

It is interesting to note the relationship of both sets of notes (i.e., *kruṣṭa*, etc., and *ṣaḍja*, etc.) which has been reflected in the verse *yaḥ sāmagānāṁ prathamaḥ sa veṇor madhyamaḥ*

173. Macdonell & Keith, VI, II, p. 283.

174. *niṣṭhite preṅkhe hotāvāṇaścaudumbaraṁ śatatantum ubhābhyāṁ parigṛhyottarataḥ upohate yathā vīṇām* । *saptaśchandobhiścaturuttaraiḥ sthānānyasyo 'rdhvam udgṛhṇīyād daśabhir vā* ॥ — *AĀ* 5.1.4

175. *kā sāmno gatir iti svara iti hovāca* . . . — *CU* 1.8.4

176. *saptasvarās-trayo grāmā mūrchanās tvekaviṁśatiḥ* ।
tānā ekona-pañcāśadityetat svara-maṇḍalam । — *NŚ* 1.2.4

177. *ṣaḍjaśca ṛṣabhaścaiva gāndhāro madhyamastathā* ।
pañcamo dhaivataścaiva niṣādaḥ saptamaḥ svaraḥ ॥ — *NŚ* 1.2.5

178. *prathamaśca dvitīyaśca tṛtīyo 'tha caturthakaḥ* ।
mandraḥ kruṣṭo hyatisvāra etān kurvanti sāmagāḥ ॥ — *NŚ* 1.1.12

svaraḥ[179] — *NŚ* 1.5.1). From Nārada's discussion, a remarkable difference between these two sets of notes has been noticed, specially regarding their ascending and descending order. From the verses of the *NŚ*[180] *aṅguṣṭhasyottame kruṣṭaḥ* (*NŚ* 1.7.3-4), etc., the purpose of showing both sets of notes has become distinct that *kruṣṭa*, etc., were used only as a way of indicating musical notation through the movement of hand, while *ṣaḍja*, etc., were used for chanting. In other Śikṣā texts[181] also *ṣaḍja*, etc., have been recorded as notes for chanting *sāmans*. Piṅgala in his *Chandaḥ-Sūtra*,[182] has tried to relate these seven notes with seven Vedic metres.

In this connection, we should mention the name of *CU*,[183] which through some narratives, informs us that chanting of *sāman* requires singer's detailed knowledge in this faculty (including the support of *sāman* and the deity associated with parts of *sāman*) violation of which may cause danger to the singer even up to death. Names of some experts of this science, e.g., Uṣasti Cākrāyaṇa, Pravahāṇa Jaivali, Dālbhya Caikitāyana, Śālāvatya Śilakya, etc., have been mentioned in the *CU*.

Some instances of the employment of music and dance in rituals have been recorded in the Yajurvedic Saṁhitā and

179. *yaḥ sāmagānāṁ prathamaḥ sa veṇor madhyamaḥ svaraḥ* ।
yo dvitīyaḥ sa gāndhārastṛtiyastvṛṣabhaḥ smṛtah ॥
caturthaḥ ṣaḍja ityāhuḥ pañcamo dhaivato bhavet ।
ṣaṣṭho niṣādo vijñeyaḥ saptamaḥ pañcamaḥ smṛtaḥ ॥ — *NŚ* 1.5.1-2

180. *aṅguṣṭhasyottame kruṣṭo 'ṅguṣṭhe tu prathamaḥ svaraḥ* ।
pradeśinyāṁ tu gāndhāra ṛṣabhastad anantaram ॥
anāmikāyāṁ ṣaḍjastu kaniṣṭhāyāṁ ca dhaivataḥ ।
tasyādhastācca yo 'nyastu niṣādaṁ tatra vinyaset ॥ — *NŚ* 1.7.3-4

181. *sapta sāmnām* । *ṣaḍjarṣabhagāndhāra-madhyamapañcamadhaivataniṣādāḥ* ।
— *Bhāṣika Sūtra* 3.16-17

182. *svarāḥ ṣaḍjarṣabha-gāndhāra-madhyamapañcamadhaivatanisādāh*
— *Chandaḥ Sūtra* 3.63

183. Narrative of *Uṣasti Cākrāyaṇa* — *CU* 1.10.9-1.11.9
Narrative of *Pravāhaṇa*, etc. — *CU* 1.8.4-1.9.1

Brāhmaṇas. In the context of *Vājapeya*, chanting of *sāman* accompanied by drum beatings along with chariot race has been mentioned in the *ŚB*,[184] which formed an important part of coronation ceremony. Further, in the Horse sacrifice singing of brāhmaṇa and a *rājanya* (*vīṇāgāthin*) in accompaniment to the lute has been prescribed in the *ŚB*,[185] for a whole year. It is interesting to note here that there was no compulsory rule that a person would have to sing traditional songs only. The singer was given an option to compose songs on his own and sing the same even on the sacrificial occasion.

> *brāhmaṇo vīṇāgāthī dakṣiṇata uttaramandrām udāghnaṁstisraḥ svayaṁ sambhṛtā gāthā gāyati . . .*
> — *ŚB* 13.4.2.8, 13.4.2.11, 13.4.2.14, 13.4.3.5.

Existence of *vīṇāgaṇaginas* (the masters conducting chorus of lutes) in the *ŚB*[186] indicates that lutes were played simultaneously in the Horse sacrifice to give rise to a chorus of lutes. In connection with *Mahāvrata* rite the Brāhmaṇa and Āraṇyaka texts[187] have described priests and the sacrificer's wives singing and playing with musical instruments, while *TS*[188] has recorded a short yet picturesque description of dancing and singing of slave girls round the *mārjālīya* fire on the same occasion.

In the context of *Sautrāmaṇī* the *VS*[189] refers to a ritual practice (where the performer identifies himself through the

---

184. (i) *atha saptadaśa dundubhīn anuvedyantaṁ* — *ŚB* 5.1.5.6
(ii) *dhāvanti ājimāghanti dundubhinābhisāma gāyati* — *ŚB* 5.1.5.17
185. *brāhmaṇau vīṇāgāthinau saṁvatsaraṁ gāyataḥ . . . brāhmaṇo 'nya gāyati . . . rājanyo 'nyo . . .* — *ŚB* 13.1.5.1, 13.1.5.3
186. *vīṇāgaṇagina upasametā bhavanti* ı *tān adhvaryuḥ sampreṣyati* ı *vīṇāgaṇagina ityāha . . .* — *ŚB* 13.4.3.3
187. *PB* 5.6.1-5.6.8; *JB* 2.406; *TB* 1.2.6.6; *AĀ* 5.1.5.
188. *parikumbhinyo dāsyo mārjālīyaṁ parinṛtyanti . . .* — *TS* 7.5.10.1
189. *VS* 30.5-8.

medium of dance), which may be considered as dance in its sanctified form. Here the performer touches all his members and bodily parts one by one in a rhythmic manner and recites the benedictory formula.

Apart from *Śrauta* rites, employment of singing and dancing was prevalent in domestic rites also. The *MS*[190] has mentioned the custom of singing *gāthā*s on the occasion of marriage ceremony. According to the Gṛhya-Sūtras,[191] singing and dancing of four/eight married girls (invariably not the widows) formed an important ritual in the marriage ceremony, which in later ages has been termed as Indrāṇī-pūjana/Indrāṇīkarma (Kane, *HDS,* vol. II, part 2, p. 536). According to the information of the *ĀGS*[192] and *GGS*[193] singing of Vāmadevya Sāman in accompaniment to the lutes was a part of the *Sīmantonnayana* rite.

PEOPLE'S ATTITUDE TOWARDS MUSIC AND DANCE

It is curious to note that though singing and dancing played a vital role in people's religious life and social activities as well, somewhere music and dance were looked upon as a contemptible practice. The *JB*[194] in a distinct language reproached the practice of dancing and singing for secular purpose and approved it only in connection with sacrifice.

---

190. *vivāhe gāthā gīyate* — *MS* 3.7.3

191. (i) *catasro 'ṣṭau vā 'vidhavāḥ śākapiṇḍībhiḥ sūrayā 'nnena ca tarpayitvā catur ānartanaṁ kuryaḥ* ॥ — *ŚGS* 1.11.5

(ii) *catasro 'ṣṭau vā 'vidhavāḥ śākapiṇḍībhiḥ striyo 'nnena ca brāhmaṇān bhojayitvā vīṇāgāthibhiḥ sāmgāyeyur apivā caturo nartanaṁ kuryāt . . .* — Lau*GS* 1.22.1

192. *vīṇāgāthinau saṁśāsti somaṁ rājānaṁ saṁgāyetāmiti* । — *ĀGS* 1.14.6

193. *GGS* 1.9.25, 2.4.4.

194. *tad yad yajñe stūyate yacchasyate yat pracaryate sā prajapateḥ senāsa* । *atha yad vīṇāyāṁ gīyate yannṛtyate, yatvṛthā caryate sā mṛtyos senāsa* ॥ — *JB* 2.70

In the context of *Vājapeya* sacrifice secular forms of music (*gāthā, nārāśaṁsī*) have been mentioned in the *TB*[195] as defiled portion of Brahmā on account of its being contaminated with human affairs. The text has declared the singing as a despicable practice. According to their opinion food/gift offered by professional singers is not permissible. In later ages the *sūtrakāras*[196] (esp., Āpastamba and Gautama) also have declared them (singers/dancers/actors) as forbidden professionals and prohibits one to use the food/gift offered by them. The *GB*[197] directly prohibits the brāhmaṇas and students to practise singing and dancing most probably on account of their being instruments of temptation and indiscipline. In this connection a sentence may be cited from the *CIDLA*[198] "this interdiction of students goes to show wide prevalence of these arts and their popularity."

---

195. *devā vai brahmaṇaścānnasya ca śamalam apāghnan* ।
yad brahmaṇaḥ śamalam āsīt sā gāthā nārāśaṁsī abhavat ।
yad annasya sā surā । *tasmād gāyataśca mattasya ca na pratigṛhṇīyat* ।
— *TB* 1.3.2.6-7

196. *ĀpDS* 1.6.18.18; *GDS* 2.1.52; *BDS* 1.5.10.25, etc.

197. (i) *noparīśāyī syāt na gāyano na nartano* . . . — *GB* 1.2.7
(ii) *tasmād brāhmaṇo naiva gāyet na nṛtyet* . . . — *GB* 1.2.21

198. Vatsyayan, *CIDLA*, p.32.

6

Education System

AS a matter of fact in the early Vedic period (specially in the *ṚV*), picture of education system is not distinct. Because the "system" was not developed in the early period, and it witnessed the beginning only, direct references to the education are very few in number. The Frog-hymn of *ṚV* (7.103) throws some light on this point, e.g.,

> *yad eṣām anyo anyasya vācaṁ śāktasyeva vadati śikṣamāṇaḥ*
> — *ṚV* 7.103.5

may be considered as a description of daily study. With the utterance of this verse one can easily visualize the picture of a classroom where students were being taught recitation of texts, their correct pronunciation and proper accentuation under a system of oral tradition. By constant practice they had to memorize the texts. But mere recitation of texts without comprehending its meaning would be useless. That is why after memorizing the text, each of the students had to employ his own effort for grasping the lesson which he was taught. From the description of frogs' sleeping in the seasons of slumber it appears that a period of contemplation has been prescribed here, so that by that time students could comprehend the meaning of learnt topics and after achieving the enlightenment they could burst into speech.[1]

1. *saṁvatsaraṁ śaśayānā brāhmaṇā vratacāriṇaḥ* ı
vācaṁ parjanya-jinvitāṁ pramaṇḍūka avādiṣuḥ ıı — *ṚV* 7.103.1

Students and teachers have been referred to for two or three times.[2] Names of some eminent scholars (both male and female seers) have been mentioned.[3] Apart from this, there are some more passages in the *R̥V*, which the modern scholar R.K. Mookerji (through the aid of Sāyaṇa's commentary) has tried to interpret as references to:

(1) the initiation of a student — Mookerji, *AIE*, p. 36,

taṁ dhīrāsaḥ kavaya unnayanti — *R̥V* 3.8.4

or

punanti dhīrā apaso manīṣā — *R̥V* 3.8.5

(2) students' approach to the teacher — *Ibid.*, p. 26

ratham ātasthur vacasaṁ na mantave — *R̥V* 1.112.2

(3) the picture of their being instructed — *Ibid.*, p. 26

śrutaṁ tacchāsur iva vadhrimatyā — *R̥V* 1.116.13

and

(4) students' classification according to their capacity — *Ibid.*, p. 25

It is to be remembered here that scarcity of direct references does not mean absence of study and teaching in the early Vedic age. Still so far as records are concerned, we must confess that various particulars of education, viz., *upanayana*, duties of a student, syllabus, tenure of studentship, etc., have been discussed mainly in the Brāhmaṇas and Upaniṣads texts, therefore, complete picture of Vedic Education has been reflected in the late Vedic literature.

---

2. *R̥V* 1.8.6, 1.112.2, 1.116.3, 7.103.1, 7.103.5, 10.109.5.
3. *R̥V* 1.11, 4.43, 9.98, 10.10, 10.14 (female seers); *R̥V* 1.126.7, 1.179.1-6, 8.91.1-7, 10.95, 10.125, etc.

Students: Brahmacārin

The technical name of a student is *brahmacārin*[4] somewhere called as *vratacārin*[5] or *dhiyaḥ*.[6] Upaniṣads have called him by the name *antevāsin*.[7]

Description of a long-bearded *brahmacārin* clad in black antelope-skin (*kṛṣṇājina*) and girdle (*mekhalā*) throws some light on the dress of a student, prevalent at the time.[8] (For details see under Students' Dress, in Dress Arrangement, Ch. 2).

In the *AV* an entire hymn (11.5) has been devoted to the glorification of *brahmacārin*. In another passage he has been described as the member of god's own limbs *sa devānāṁ bhavaty ekam aṅgam* (*ṚV* 10.109.8). The *ŚB* (11.5.4.7) also has recognized him as *divyaḥ prajāḥ*.

In the Vedas formal pupilage/studentship has been termed as *brahmacarya*. In the *AV* (11.5.16-17) it has been glorified in an exalted tone as a distinct stage of life. The *ŚB*[9] has compared *brahmacarya* as a long-term sacrifice.

The Brāhmaṇas and Upaniṣads have recorded names of some famous students, e.g., Nābhānediṣṭha, Śauceya Prācīnāyogya, Bhṛgu, Śvetaketu, Āruṇi, Nārada, Sanat Kumāra, and their pupilage, from which it has been evident that pupilage was almost compulsory for a student who sought

---

4. *ṚV* 10.109.5; *AV* 11.5.
5. *ṚV* 7.103.1.
6. *ṚV* 1.8.6, 1.112.2, etc.
7. *CU* 3.11.5, 4.10.1; *BU* 6.3.7-12.
8. *brahmacārī samidhā mekhalayā śrameṇa lokāṁstapasā piparti* ||

   ... ...

   brahmacāryeti samidhā samiddhaḥ kārṣṇaṁ vasāno dūkṣito dīrghaśmaśruḥ |

   — *AV* 11.5.4, 11.5.6
9. *dīrghasatraṁ vā eṣa 'upaiti yo brahmacaryam upaiti sa yām upayan samidham upadadhāti sā prāyaṇīyā yā snāsyant sodayanīyā* . . .

   — *SB* 11.3.3.2

knowledge, though in some special cases its exception also has been noticed. In the present thesis it will be discussed later on. (See View of Life, Ch. 8.)

UPANAYANA

Actually *upanayana,* was the admission of a student to a teacher's residential institution. Students on leaving their home went to the teacher and approached him. The teacher accepted him as a student through the ceremony of initiation (*upanayana*), i.e., formal inauguration of education.

Description of *upanayana* has been traced for the first time in the *AV*:

> *ācāryo upanayamāno brahmacāriṇaṁ kr̥ṇute garbhamantaḥ* ।
> *taṁ rātrīstisro udare vibharti taṁ jātaṁ draṣṭum abhisaṁyanti devāḥ* ॥ — *AV* 11.5.3.

A graphic picture of the initiated student's entrance into the teacher's residential institution has been recorded in the *ŚB* (11.5.4.1ff). At first the student approached the teacher by a formal declaration, "let me be a *brahmacārin,*" and the teacher received him by asking his name[10] (*ko nāmāsīti*).

Then the teacher by taking his student's right hand committed him to Prajāpati and Sāvitrī so that the student may escape any suffering or harm.[11] The *ŚB*[12] says "by laying his right hand on the pupil the teacher becomes pregnant and on the third night being taught Sāvitrī the embryo issues forth out of the teacher."

---

10. *brahmacaryam āgāmityāha* । *brahmacaryasānītyāha* । . . . *ko nāmāsīti*. . . — *ŚB* 11.5.4.1
11. *athāsya hastaṁ gr̥hṇāti* । *indrasya brahmacāryasyagnir ācāryas tavāham ācāryastavāsāviti* । *ete vai śreṣṭhe baliṣṭhe devate* । *etābhyām evainaṁ śreṣṭhābhyāṁ baliṣṭhābhyāṁ devatābhyāṁ paridadāti tathā hāsya brahmacāri na kāñcanārtim ārcchati* । — *ŚB* 11.5.4.2-4
12. *ācāryo garbhī bhavati hastam ādhāya dakṣiṇam* ।
tr̥tīyasyāṁ sa jāyate sāvitryā saha brāhmaṇaḥ ॥ — *ŚB* 11.5.4.12

The entrance on a term of studentship has been recognized as the spiritual rebirth of a fellow.[13] This initiation has given the admission a spiritual character and made it distinct from the modern mechanical process of enrolment of a student in the institution. Normally, initiation was compulsory before instruction.

TENURE OF STUDENTSHIP

As regards the tenure of studentship it appears from the *CU*[14] (the narrative of Upakosala, Śvetaketu, etc.) that its normal span was twelve years. But it is to be remembered here that there was no hard and fast regulation on this point. Most probably the tenure varied according to the necessity and adaptability of the student. The *AB*[15] has mentioned the name of one Nābhānediṣṭha, who while practising celibacy was absent from his home for such a long period that his father distributed his property among his other sons. Further, terms of thirty-two years or hundred and one years' studentship also have been recorded in the Upaniṣads.[16] (For details, see View of Life, Ch. 8.)

DUTIES OF A STUDENT

While discussing *brahmacarya* and *upanayana*, the *ŚB*[17] has prescribed some primary injunctions for the student in the

---

13. . . . *divyaḥ prajāstāni mukhato janayate* । — *ŚB* 11.5.4.17.

14. (i) *upakasalo ha vai kāmalāyanaḥ satyakāme jābāle brahmacaryam uvāsa* । *tasya ha dvādaśavarṣāṇyagnīn paricacāra* । — *CU* 4.10.1

    (ii) *sa ha dvādaśa varṣa upetya caturviṁśativarṣaḥ sarvān vedān adhītya mahāmanā anūcānamānī stabdha eyāya* । — *CU* 6.2.1

15. *nābhānediṣṭhaṁ vai mānavaṁ brahmacaryaṁ vasantaṁ bhrātaro nirabhajan* . . . — *AB* 5.14

16. *CU* 8.7.3 – 8.8.3.

17. *brahmacaryasītyāha* । *brāhmaṇa evainaṁ tat paridadāti* । *apo 'śāna iti* । *amṛtaṁ vā 'paḥ . . . karma kuru iti, vīryaṁ vai karma . . . samidham ādhehi* । *samitsvam ātmānaṁ tejasā brahmavarcasenetyevainaṁ tad āha* । *mā suṣupthāḥ* . . . — *ŚB* 11.5.4.5

form of instructions to the newly initiated student by the teacher. Actually, some external duties have been allotted here for the student which were to be done regularly and almost compulsorily. Apart from these duties, some disciplines and restrictions also have been imposed on his behaviour. Those are as follows. (1) hard work, (2) non-sleepiness during day time, (3) service to the teacher in the form of tending his fire, cattle and other works (as they were required), (4) begging alms, (5) study, and (6) development of inner disciplines.

[Details discussed under *brahmacārin* and *brahmacarya*, see Social Life, Ch. 7.]

STUDY

Beside the acts of service, in the time left with — the student, they practised their own lesson daily.[18] Study has been technically termed as *svādhyāya* in the Brāhmaṇa texts. It was one of the compulsory duties of a student.[19] The *AV*[20] has recorded the prayer of a *brahmacārin* to the Lord of Might for the non-interruption of his studies. Because study has been considered as the *ṛṣis*' treasure-warden (*ṛṣīṇāṁ nidhigopaḥ* — *ŚB* 1.7.2.3.)

Subjects of Study

As regards the course of study, we find that an exhaustive syllabus has been given in the late Vedic literature (specially in the Brāhmaṇas and Upaniṣads). In the shape of a formulated syllabus it has been recorded for the first time in the *ŚB* (11.5.6.8).

---

18. *ācārya kulād vedam adhītya yathavidhānaṁ guroḥ karmātiśeṣeṇa . . .* — *CU* 8.15.1

19. *yāvantaṁ ha vā imāṁ pṛthivīṁ vittena pūrṇāṁ dadallokaṁ jayati । tristāvantaṁ jayati bhūyāṁsaṁ cākṣayyaṁ ya evaṁ vidvān aharahaḥ svādhyāyam adhīte । tasmāt svādhyāyo 'dhyetavyaḥ ।* — *ŚB* 11.5.6.3

20. *eṣa tasmān mā hiṁsīt vedaḥ pṛṣṭaḥ śacīpate ।* — *AV* 7.54.2

svādhyāyo vai brahmayajñaḥ . . . paya āhutayo ha vā etā devānāṁ yadṛcaḥ । . . . *ājyāhutayo ha vā devānaṁ yadyajūṁṣi . . . somāhutayo ha vā etā devānāṁ yat sāmāni . . . meda āhutayo ha vā etā devānāṁ yad atharvāṅgirasaḥ* । . . . *madhvāhutayo ha vā etā devānāṁ yad anuśāsanāni vidyā vākovākyam itihāsapurāṇaṁ gāthā nārāśaṁsītyaharahaḥ svādhyāyam adhīte* ॥

Apart from the study of Vedic texts, other subjects which were taught, are precepts (*anuśāsanāni*), sciences (*vidyāḥ*), theological discourses (*vākovākyam*), cosmological myths and legends (*itihāsa purāṇāni*) and *gāthānārāśaṁsī*.

Sāyaṇa while commenting on this passage has explained *anuśāsanāni* as *vyākaraṇa-niruktādīni ṣaḍaṅgāni*, i.e., six *vedāṅgas*, *vidyāḥ* as *nyāyamīmāṁsādayaḥ*, i.e., six systems of philosophy, *vākovākyam* as theological discourses, *itihāsapurāṇaṁ* as cosmological myths, *sṛṣṭi pratipādakaṁ brāhmaṇam itihāsaḥ purātanapuruṣa vṛttānta pratipādakāni purāṇaṁ* and *nārāśaṁsī* as laudatory stanzas, *manuṣya praśaṁsā parāḥ mantrāḥ*.

It is interesting to note that Eggelling[21] has rendered the term *vidyā* (in a wider sense) as a special science like science of snakes or venoms (*sarpavidyā* or *viṣavidyā*). The *ŚB*[22] (13.4.3.9ff) mentions science of snakes (*sarpavidyā*), demonology (*rakṣo-vidyā*), magic trick (*asuravidyā*), *devajanavidyā*, etc., as science. In the same place the teachers and pupils of the said subjects have been mentioned. The myth of Indra and Vṛtra (narrated in the *TS* 6.5.1.2 in which Indra learned magic tricks from

---

21. J. Eggeling. (tr.), *The Śatapatha Brāhmaṇa* SBE, V, p. 96.

22. *arvudaḥ kādraveyo rājā bhavati* । *tasya sarpāḥ viśaḥ, ta ima āsata iti* । *sarpāśca sarpavidaś 'copasametā bhavanti* । *tān upadiśati, sarpavidyā veda so 'yam iti* । *rakṣāṁsi viśaḥ* । *tān imānyāsata iti* । *selagāḥ pāpakṛta upasametā bhavanti* । *tan upadiśati* । *devajanavidyā so 'yam iti* । . . . *tasyāsurā viśasta ima āsate iti* । *kusīdina upasametā bhavanti* । *tān upadiśati māyāvedaḥ so 'yam iti* ।
— *ŚB* 13.4.3.9-11

Vṛtra) indicates that witchcraft was taught as a separate subject.[23]

In course of time with the inclusion of new subjects, the bulk of syllabus swelled gradually. A larger list of subjects has been recorded in the narrative of Nārada and Sanat Kumāra,[24] where Nārada stated the names of subjects which he had studied already, e.g., four Vedas, Itihāsa-Purāṇa, the Veda of Vedas (*vedānāṁ vedam*), rituals concerning worship of manes (*pitṛyam*), Arithmatic (*rāśim*), the science of portents (*daivam*), science of divination (*nidhim*), art of debate (*vākovākyam*), codes of conduct or polity (*ekāyanam*), knowledge relating to gods (*devavidyā*), *brahmavidyā*, the political science (*kṣatravidyā*), astronomy (*nakṣatravidyā*), physical science, biology, etc., (*bhūtavidyā*), the science of snakes and toxication (*sarpavidyā*), and *devajanavidyā*.

Time and Place of Study

The *TĀ*,[25] while discussing rules and regulations for study, has prescribed its proper place and time. From this we come to know that students facing eastward started to practise their lesson before sunrise in a lonely place and they had to complete it before evening. In the mid-noon they could read aloud.[26]

---

23. *indro vṛtrāya vajram udayacchat* I *sa vṛtro vajrād udyatād abibhet so 'bravīn mā me prahārasti vā idaṁ mayi vīryaṁ tat te pradāsyāmīti tasmā ukthyaṁ prāyacchat* I . . . *taṁ nirmāyaṁ bhūtam ahan* I *yajño hi tasya māyā* . . . I
— *TS* 6.5.1.1-2

24. *ṛgvedaṁ bhagavo 'dhyemi, yajurvedaṁ sāmavedam ātharvaṇaṁ caturtham, itihāsa purāṇaṁ pañcamaṁ vedānāṁ vedaṁ, pitryaṁ, rāśiṁ, nidhiṁ, vākovākyam ekāyanam, devavidyāṁ, brahmavidyāṁ bhūtavidyāṁ, kṣatravidyāṁ, nakṣatravidyāṁ, sarpa-deva-janavidyāmetad bhagavo-'adhyemi* I — *CU* 7.1.2

25. *brahmayajñena yakṣyamāṇaḥ prācyaṁ grāmād achadirdarśa udīcyāṁ prāg vdīcyāṁ vo 'dita āditye dakṣiṇata upavīyopaviśya* . . . *prāṇāsīnaḥ svādhyāyam adhīyīta* I . . . *tasya prāk sāyam avabhṛthaḥ* . . .
— *TĀ* 2.11-13

26. . . . *madhyadine prabalam adhīyīta* . . . — *TĀ* 2.13

Alternative place and hour of study also have been mentioned here for emergency period. Then one could study even in the village, any time in the day or night but then he had to read silently.[27] If anyone became physically unfit he could practise his lesson silently even in the forest.[28] In case of a sick person rules and regulations could be relaxed to some extent but by any means he (student) was not allowed to discontinue his regular routine.

Holidays

How the holidays were observed in Vedic schools, have been recorded in the *AV*.[29] According to this information, cloudy or windy weather (*yadi vāntarikṣe yadi vāta āsa*) was considered improper for the study of sacred texts; similarly under the shade of tree (*yadi vr̥kṣeṣu — vr̥kṣacchāyāyām*), in the sight of green barley (*yadivolapeṣu*) or within the hearing of cattle, study of Vedic texts was not permitted. From this it becomes evident that under the said circumstances, pupils enjoyed holidays. From the *AĀ* and *TĀ*, some more holidays have been traced. According to the *AĀ*[30] raining out of season was an occasion for three days' vacation. Telling stories (even at night) also was not permissible during this time. Again, in the forenoon or afternoon when shades meet or when old water about the roots were dried, students had to refrain themselves from

---

27. *grāme manaṣā svādhyāyam adhīyīta divā naktaṁ veti ha smāha śauceya āhreyaḥ . . .* — *TĀ* 2.12

28. *iti ha smāha śauca āhreyaḥ utāraṇye 'bala uta vācota tiṣṭhannuta vrajannutāsīna uta śayāno 'dhīyītaiva . . .* — *TĀ* 2.12

29. *yady antarikṣe yadi vāta āsa yadivr̥kṣeṣu yadi voḷapeṣu* ।
yadaśravan paśava udyamānaṁ tad brāhmaṇaṁ punarasmān upaitu ॥
— *AV* 7.66.1

30. *meghe 'partau varṣe trirātraṁ vaidikenādhyāyenāntarīyānnāsmin kathāṁ badeta nāsya rātraucana cikīrtayiṣet* । *. . . upa purāṇenāpīte kakṣodake pūrvāhṇe na saṁbhinnāsu chāyāsvaparāhṇe nādhyūḍha . . .* — *AĀ* 5.3.3

study. The *TĀ*[31] has prohibited the student to study if he was impure/contaminated (in contact with dead body or something likewise) or when the place was unclean.

ELIGIBILITY OF BEING A STUDENT

In the late Vedic literature, we come across some prohibitions regarding the teaching of lessons. Sacred and secret doctrines were not to be disclosed to everybody. Therefore, some terms and conditions were set up. The students had to fulfil those criteria which would qualify them for being taught.

From the *ŚB*[32] we find that only the son or a competent student residing with the teacher since a year, were entitled to inherit the mysterious lesson of the ceremony of *Pravargya* rite. More or less same instruction has been traced in the *BU* (6.3.12). According to the injunction of the *AĀ*[33] and the *SĀ* the mystical meaning of euphonic combination could not be communicated to one who was not a pupil, not pupil for a whole year, who did not propose himself to be a teacher.

That Vedic education was preserved for limited persons only, has been supported by Yāska[34] also. In this view, non-grammarian, non-residential pupil, one incapable of understanding — were not eligible for Vedic education. Only the residential, intelligent and diligent students were entitled

---

31. *tasya vā etasya yajñasya dvāvanadhyāyau yadā 'tmāśucir yad deśaḥ . . .* — *TĀ* 2.15

32. *tanna sarvasmā anubrūyāt । . . . yo 'nveva vrātaḥ । tasmaibrūyāt । atha yo 'nūcānaḥ । atha yo 'sya priyaḥ syāt । na tveva sarvasmā eva । saṁvatsaravāsine 'nubrūyāt । . . .* — *ŚB* 14.1.1.26-27

33. *tā etāḥ saṁhitāḥ nānantevāsine prabrūyānnāsaṁvatsaravāsine nā pravaktṛ ityācāryā cāryāḥ ।* — *AĀ* 3.2.6; cf. *ŚĀ* 8

34. *naika padāni nirbrūyāt । nāvaiyākaraṇāya । nānupasannāya । anidaṁvide vā । nityaṁ hyavijñāturvijñāne 'sūyā । upasannāya tu nirbrūyāt । yo vālaṁ vijñātuṁ syāt । medhāvine tapasvine vā ।* — *Nirukta* 2.3

for being a student. With citations from the Smṛti texts Yāska[35] has put forth his opinion.

STUDENTS' MANNERS

During the time of study the students had to maintain some manners. Instructions on the same have been furnished in the late Vedic texts (from the Brāhmaṇas onwards).

In course of describing *upanayana* ceremony the *ŚB*[36] has prescribed proper place of student's seat. At the time of study, students were not allowed to stand or sit on teacher's right side but they had to sit in front of the teacher facing him towards the west, while the teacher faces east. But at the time of practising lesson on his own, the student used to sit facing eastwards.[37] According to the *GB*[38] students had to be modest enough. They were to sit down, lie down on the gound, walk and move about with humility.

The *AĀ*[39] has prohibited the teacher to instruct in standing, lying or walking condition (of both the teacher and student). According to this text, at that time they were not allowed to sit on the couch. Then both of them had to sit on the ground.

---

35. *vidyā ha vai brāhmaṇamājagāma gopāya mā śevadhiṣṭe 'hamasmi* ।
asūyakārjave 'yatāya na mā brūyā vīryavatī tathā syām ॥
yameva vidyā śucimapramattaṁ medhāvinaṁ brahmacaryo papannam ।
yaste na druhyet katamaccanāha tasmai sa brūyā nidhipāya brahman ॥
— *Manu* 2.114-15

36. *atha haike dakṣṇitastiṣṭhatevā 'sīnāya vā 'nvāhuḥ* । *na tathā kuryāt* । *yo hainaṁ tatra brūyāt bulvaṁ nvā ayam imam ajījanata* । *bulvo bhaviṣyatīti* । *iśvaro ha tathaiva syāt* । *tasmāt purastād eva practīce samīkṣamāṇāyānu brūyāt . . .* — *ŚB* 11.5.4.14

37. *. . . prāṇāsīnaḥ svādhyāyam adhīyīta . . .* — *TĀ* 2.13

38. *adhaḥ śayītādhastiṣṭhed adho brajet . . .* — *GB* 1.2.4

39. *na tiṣṭhaṁstiṣṭhate* । *na brajan brajate* । *na śayānaḥ śayānāya noparyāsīna uparyāsīnāya, adha evāsīno 'dha āsīnāya* । — *AĀ* 5.3.3

According to the *Ṛgvedaprātiśākhya,*[40] the students embraced teacher's feet everyday at the beginning and end of study.

In case of one or two students, right side of the teacher was fixed as their seat.[41] In case of many students, they could sit according as there was room.[42] Before starting the lesson they approached their teacher for the same. They could not leave the class without the permission of the teacher, even at the end of study (*ṚP* 15.27-31).

It is interesting to observe that just as the students, the teacher also had to maintain some restrictions regarding his behaviour at the time of instruction (especially when he had initiated a student). The *ŚB*[43] (in the context of *upanayana vidhi*), has cited ancient teachers' saying, "as to they say when one has admitted a brāhmaṇa to a term of studentship he should not carry on sexual intercourse."

Teachers

In the vast range of Vedic literature (from the *ṚV* onwards), the teachers have been met with very often.

From the study of Vedic literature, we find that the main part of education was that of the student, still that cannot preclude the necessity of a teacher. That the pupil can achieve the right path only through the proper guidance and instruction of the teacher, has been indicated in the *Ṛgveda*.

akṣetravit kṣetravidaṁ hyaprāṭ sa praiti kṣetravidānuśiṣṭaḥ ।
etad vai bhadram anuśāsanasyota śruti vindatyañjasīnām ॥
— 10.32.7.

---

40. *te adhīhi bho 'ityabhicodayanti guruṁ śiṣya upasaṁgṛhya sarve* । — *ṚP* 15.4

41. *ekaḥ śrotā dakṣiṇato niṣīded dvau vā* । — *ṚP* 15.2

42. *bhūyāṁsastu yathāvakāśam* । — *ṚP* 15.3

43. *na brāhmaṇaṁ brahmacaryam upanīya mithunaṁ caret garbha vā eṣa bhavati* । — *ŚB* 11.5.4.16

Necessity of a teacher has been explicitly mentioned by a student, the knowledge acquired from the teacher alone becomes best for student.[44] Uddālaka Āruṇi, in course of teaching his son, explained to him that the teacher alone can remove the ignorance of student and enkindle his consciousness. It is evidently expressed in the *CU*,[45] where it says, "just as a person who has been brought blindfolded from the country of Gāndhāra and set at liberty in a solitary place, goes to various directions shouting "I have been brought blindfolded and left blindfolded," then if somebody having removed the bandage set him forth in the proper direction then only he can reach Gāndhāra. In this way a man having a teacher acquires knowledge in this earth."

Actually in the realm of Vedic education, teachers occupied a central position. As already mentioned, students on reaching the age of initiation (*upanayana**), went to the teacher's place, approached him for their education and the teacher admitted them through initiation, to his institution. The students had to stay with him and learn lessons. These residential teachers served the purpose of a type of educational institution.

---

44. *ācāryāddhaiva viditā vidyā sādhiṣṭhaṁ prāpatīti* . . . — *CU* 4.9.3

45. *yathāsomya puruṣaṁ gandhārebhyo 'bhinaddhākṣam ānīya taṁ tato 'jine visṛjet* । *sa yathā tatra prāṅ vodaṅ vādharāṅ vā pratyaṅ vā pradhmāyītābhinaddhākṣa ānīto 'bhinaddhākṣo visṛṣṭaḥ* । *tasya yathābhinahanaṁ pramucya prabrūyād etāṁ diśaṁ gandhārā etāṁ diśaṁ brajeti* । *sa grāmād grāmaṁ pṛcchan paṇḍito medhāvī gandhārān evopasampadyeta* । *evam evācāryavān puruṣo veda* । — *CU* 6.14.1-2

* It is to be remembered here that the age of *upanayana* has not been mentioned in early Vedic texts. It has been recorded for the first time in the Sūtra texts, according to which eighth, eleventh and twelfth year (counting from the conception of the child) have been prescribed for the initiation of brāhmaṇa, kṣatriya and vaiśya respectively (*ĀGS* 1.19.2-4; *ĀpDS* 4.10.2-4).

Sometimes, father himself taught his son. The *ŚB*[46] says in a clear tone that a brāhmaṇa was supposed to instruct his son both subjects, i.e., study of Vedas and performing sacrifices. The story of Varuṇa has been illustrated in the *Br*[47] texts, which describes that the father (Varuṇa) taught his son (Bhṛgu) by sending him to various regions. Further, the *Taitt* (Bhṛguvallī) tells us how Bhṛgu was taught Supreme *Brahman* through the graded instruction by his father. The incident of Śvetaketu has been recorded in the 6th Prapāṭhaka of *CU* from which we find that Śvetaketu managed to furnish his knowledge from both the teachers (the preceptor and father himself).

From this it is clear that students received their lessons from the residential teachers and (sometimes) father as well.

Besides these, Dr. J. Basu[48] in his work has informed us of another type of teachers. They were *caraka*s, the peripatetic scholars, who served as another agency for the cultivation and campaign of education. The name *caraka* being derived from *car*, to move, indicates their mobile nature. Like mobile schools they visited various places and imparted lessons to the students seeking after it. From this discussion, it appears that probably Dr. Basu through the term peripatetic scholars wanted to mean *carakādhvaryu*s (mentioned in the Brāhmaṇas[49]) who visited sacrificial spots and taught how to perform sacrifices/rites perfectly. In this connection we may mention the story of Mṛgavu Rāma who taught king Viśvāntara about proper food of kṣatriya during sacrifice and specified prohibited items also.[50]

---

46. *tato ebhyo yajñaṁ prārocata, tam asṛjanta, tam atanvata so 'yaṁ paro 'varaṁ yajño 'nūcyate pitaiva putrāya brahmacāriṇe* । — *ŚB* 1.6.2.4
47. *ŚB* 11.6.1.1; cf. *JB* 1.42-44.
48. J. Basu, *India of the Age of the Brāhmaṇas*, p. 48.
49. *AB* 7.34; *ŚB* 3.8.2.24, 4.1.2.19, 4.2.4.1, 6.2.2.1, 8.1.3.7, etc.
50. *tam evam etaṁ bhakṣaṁ provāca rāmo mārgaveyo viśvantarāya sauṣadmanāya* । — *AB* 7.34

A band of wandering scholars have been mentioned in the *BU*[51] (3.3.1) who while wandering travelled as far north up to the land of Madras and involved in discussion and disputation.

DUTIES OF A TEACHER

According to the *ŚB*'s injunction, the teacher was duty bound to explain everything to a disciple who has dwelt with him for a whole year —

saṁvatsaravāsine 'nu brūyāt — *ŚB* 14.1.1.26

The *TĀ*[52] has advised the teacher to teach the student with utmost effort. Almost similar sound has been echoed in the Upaniṣadic passages which suggests the teacher to teach worthy student invariably who has approached him in a due manner.[53] In the *Praśna*,[54] the teacher (Paippalāda) confessed that the teacher's duty is to impart the knowledge to a student without concealing anything, otherwise he would be ruined. The sentence *yathākāmaṁ praśnaṁ pṛcchata yadi vijñāsyāma sarvaṁ ha vo vakṣyāmaḥ* (*Praśna* 1.2) clearly indicates that it was the duty of a teacher to satisfy the student's query according to his capacity. Uddālaka Āruṇi had confessed in a clear tone against the complaint of his son that he did not expound the subject to him because it (the topic) was unknown to himself. Right then he went to King Pravāhaṇa and learnt the subject from him like a student.[55] From this, it has been evident that

51. *atha hainaṁ bhujyur lāhyāyaniḥ papraccha yājñavalkyeti hovāca madreṣu vayaṁ carakā paryavrajāma* । *te patañcalasya kāpyasya gṛhān aima* ।
— *BU* 3.3.1

52. *TĀ* 7.4.

53. *tasmai savidvān upasannāya samyak praśāntacittāya śamānvitāya* ।
yenākṣaraṁ puruṣaṁ veda satyaṁ provāca tāṁ tattvato brahmavidyām ॥
— *Muṇḍ* 1.2.13

54. *yadyaham imam avediṣaṁ kathaṁ te nāvakṣāma iti* ।
samūlo vā eṣa pariśuṣyati yo 'nṛtam abhibadati ॥ — *Praśna* 6.1

55. *CU* 5.3.1ff; cf. *BU* 6.2.1ff.

the teacher did not hesitate to take another lesson, if it was necessary to meet his student's requirement.

Sometimes the teacher sent his student to consult other teachers, if the particular student required specialized knowledge in any topic. The *TB*[56] has narrated the story of one Āruṇi, who sent his student to consult Plakṣa Dayyāmpāti in order to solve the problem regarding twenty-four sources and twelve joints of *sāvitrī*.

The same story has been narrated in the *GB*[57] with a slight variation where two teachers Maudgalya and Maitreya, while they were engaged in a discussion, Maitreya found his friend to be more competent and have a keen knowledge in that subject. Maitreya was so conscientious that right at that moment he stopped his own class and consulted the topic with him. Similar incidents have been noticed in the Upaniṣads[58] also.

TEACHER'S DESIRE FOR STUDENTS

In the late Vedic literature (specially in Upaniṣads) there are some passages which indicate that teachers also had a desire for students most probably to maintain the line of succession through the students. For example, the *Taitt*'s[59] prayer may be cited here where the teacher says

---

56. *sa hovāca plakṣo dayyāmpātiḥ* । *yad vai brahmacārin prāṇamatya-prākṣyaḥ* । *mūrdhā te vyapatiṣyat* । *ahamuta ācaryācchreyān bhaviṣyāmi yo mā sāvitre samavādiṣṭeti* । *tasmāt na sāvitre saṁvadeta* । — *TB* 3.10.9.5

57. *sa ha maudgalyaḥ svām antevāsinam uvāca-parehi saumya glāvaṁ maitreyam upasīda* । *adhīhi bhoḥ sāvitrīṁ gāyatrīṁ caturviṁśati-yoniṁ dvādaśa-mithunām* — *GB* 1.1.31

58. *CU* 5.11.1; *BU* 2.1.1, etc.

59. *ā mā yantu brahmacāriṇaḥ svāhā* । *vi mā yantu brahmacāriṇaḥ svāhā* । *pra mā yantu brahmacāriṇaḥ svāhā* । . . . *yathāpaḥ pravatā yanti yathā māsā aharjaram* । *evaṁ mā brahmacāriṇo dhātarāyantu sarvataḥ* ॥ — *Taitt* 1.4.2-3

> may the *brahmacārins* come to me from all sides. May the *brahmacārins* come to me in various ways. May the *brahmacārins* come to me in the proper way. . . . As the water flows down a slope, as months roll into a year similarly O Lord, may the students come to me from all quarters.

It is a remarkable point that teachers liked to have qualified and competent students; Yama's desire *tvādr̥ṅg no bhūyān naciketāḥ praṣṭā* (*Kaṭha* 1.2.9) proves the reality of the fact. In the *Taitt*,[60] the teacher prays to the Lord that his students be physically and mentally prepared.

CONVOCATION

On the completion of study, the students put sacrificial faggots on the fire for the last time which has been mentioned as the concluding rite (*udayanīyeṣṭi*) of a prolonged sacrifice.[61] After that, before leaving the teacher's residence he took his final ablution and hence he has got the name *snātaka* the graduate (which is applicable till today) and returned back.

The ceremony of his returning back to his home has been termed as *samāvartana* which was conducted by the teacher himself. In this ceremony the preceptor certified his students and affirmed their graduation. He used to give them some post instructions as guiding principle in their future life.

The convocational address of that period has been recorded in the *Taitt*.[62] In this address emphasis has been laid on some important points, e.g., to enter a householder's life and fatherhood has been considered compulsory (better to say almost religious) duty in the interest of race and society. Next

---

60. *pra mā yantu brahmacāriṇaḥ svāhā* ।
damāyantu brahmacāriṇaḥ svāhā । — *Taitt* 1.4.2

61. *dīrghasatraṁ vā eṣa 'upaiti yo brahmacaryam upaiti . . . yā snāsyant sodayanīyā . . .* — *ŚB* 11.3.3.2

62. *Taitt* 1.11.

importance has been attached to the study and teaching of Vedas for the sake of continuity of culture. The *Taitt* has instructed the student repeatedly to practise study and teaching along with other activities of life. Domestic and social duties also were not to be neglected, e.g., to honour parents and guests as gods; to honour superiors, to give in proper manner and spirit, to perform rites regularly and to follow the judgement of approved authorities in doubtful cases. His advice to take care of personal health and wealth proves that the teacher was fully aware of practical life. In another passage the student has been repeatedly advised to carry on study and teaching along with all the pursuits of life. This valedictory address may be compared with the Chancellor's Convocational address to the students of any modern University.

Description of "*samāvartana*" ceremony (with full details) has been recorded in the Sūtra[63] literature.

RELATION BETWEEN TEACHER AND STUDENTS

The relation between the teacher and students as it appears from the above-mentioned convocational address delivered by the teacher at the time of students' departure from the forest-school, was almost pleasant and happy. Students looked upon their preceptor as good as their father. Similarly the teacher also was equally affectionate towards his students. Six sages (mentioned in the *Praśna*[64]) after having been taught by Paippalāda, had expressed their respect and gratitude by addressing him as father.

Again from the propitiatory passage (*Taitt, Śāntipāṭha*) beginning with *sahanāvavatu* probably which was uttered at the beginning of their daily study, it indicates that the teacher

---

63. *ĀGS* 3.8.1-21; *SGS* 3.1.1-8; *PGS* 2.6.1-32; *GGS* 3.4.9-34; *GSH* 1.3.9-11; *ĀpDS* 1.13.9.

64. *tvaṁ hi naḥ pitā yo 'smākam avidyāyāḥ paraṁ pāraṁ tārayasīti namaḥ* ।
— *Praśna* 6.8

and student both were united with a common aim of preserving and propagating sacred thoughts.

The *Nirukta*[65] with citations from Smṛti texts has advised the student to regard the teacher as good as his parents; otherwise his knowledge would become ineffective.

System of Free Education

While going through the passages of Brāhmaṇas and Upaniṣads, we find that the teachers did not accept any tuition fee from their students. They have been called by the name *apratigrāhakā*.[66] From this it becomes clear that education was rendered free of cost. Parents had not to spend a single penny for their children's education, because students had to beg alms (as a compulsory duty) for their subsistence.

Though there was no system of paying regular fees to the teacher, still at the end of their education to give some kind of honorarium (may be in the form of some token) was not out of convention. In this connection we may mention the *BU*'s[67] passage which says repeatedly it is improper to take any wealth from the student before instructing him fully. From this it becomes evident that at the end of imparting lessons some kind of remuneration could be accepted from the disciples (which they offered at their own will).

---

65. *ya āvṛṇattyavitathena karṇāvaduḥkham kurvannamṛtaṁ samprayacchan* ।
ta manyeta pitaraṁ mātaraṁ ca tasmai na druhyet katamaccanāha ॥
— *Manu* 2.14

adhyāpitā ye guruṁ nādriyante viprā vācā manasā karmaṇā vā ।
yathaiva te ha guror bhājanīyās tathaiva tān na bhunakti śrutaṁ tat ॥
— *SRV* cited in *Nir* 2.4

66. *śrotriyā apratigrāhakā upasametā bhavanti* ॥ — *ŚB* 13.4.3.14

67. *so hovāca yājñavalkya pitā me 'manyata nānanuśiṣya hareteti* ।
— *BU* 4.1.2-4.1.7

King Janaśruti's offering gifts to Raikva[68] and that of Ajātaśatru[69] to Gārgya Bālāki may be mentioned here as exceptional cases who offered remuneration to the teacher before instruction.

Method of Study and Teaching

In the early Vedic period direct method was followed for study and teaching, because primarily education was a matter of learning and memorization of texts by constant practice in a prescribed manner.

But direct references to the method of study and teaching under a system of direct instruction are scanty in number. Its earliest (and most probably only) example has been recorded in the Frog-hymn of *R̥V* (7.103.5), which appears to describe students' recitation of texts following the teacher's pronunciation. That proper understanding of the text along with its recitation was equally important, has been indicated in the same hymn *R̥V* (7.103.1). Description of practising lesson with immediate understanding, has been traced once again in the *Kaṭha*,[70] where Yama imparted to Naciketās lessons on sacrificial fire (*agnividyā*) which leads to Heaven and Naciketās also repeated verbatim with understanding as those were spoken to him.

Actual description of teaching in a Vedic school has been reflected in the *R̥gveda-Prātiśākhya* (XV). The text furnishes not only all the methods of oral instruction but to some external manners also, to be maintained by students during their

---

68. *tad u ha jānaśrutiḥ pautrāyaṇaḥ ṣaṭśatāni gavāṁ niṣkam aśvatarī-rathaṁ tad ādāya praticakrame . . .* — *CU* 4.2.1-4

69. *sa hovācājātaśatruḥ sahasram etasyāṁ vāci dadmaḥ . . .* — *BU* 2.1.1

70. *lokādim agniṁ tam uvāca tasmai yā iṣṭakā yāvatī vā yathāvā* ।
sā cāpi tat pratyabadat yathoktam athasya mr̥tyuḥ punar evāha tuṣṭaḥ . . .
— *Kaṭha* 1.1.15

studies. Even proper position of sitting (of both the student and teacher) has been instructed (that is in the opening verse).

East or north or north-east has been mentioned as the proper place of teacher's seat[71] and student's position has been fixed at the right side of teacher[72] (if they were one or two in number), but in case of many students they were allowed to sit anywhere in the class room.[73]

The picture of daily study (as it has been reflected in the *ṚP*) is as follows: At first students embraced their teacher's feet and approached him to start their lesson.[74] With the utterance of the syllable *oṁ* the lesson started.[75] The method, used by the teacher was, he used to pronounce all the words with *udātta* accent in a slow pace and repeat some words twice.[76] Detailed discussion on the peculiarities of *sandhi* proves that the main difficulty for the students in the pronunciation of Vedas, were changes (due to *sandhi*) of final and initial letters.[77]

Normally students were instructed independently but if there was any case of difficulty the teacher examined his

71. *pārāyaṇaṁ bartayet brahmacārī guruḥ śiṣyebhyastad anuvratebhyaḥ* ।
adhyāsīno diśam ekāṁ praśastāṁ prācīm udīcim aparājitāṁ vā ॥
— *ṚP* 15.1

72. *ekaḥ śrotā dakṣiṇato niṣīded dvau vā* । — *ṚP* 15.2

73. *bhūyāṁsastu yathāvakāśam* — *ṚP* 15.3

74. *te 'dhīhi bho ityabhicodyanti guruṁ śiṣya 'upasamgṛhya sarve . . .*
— *ṚP* 15.4

75. *sa omiti prasvarati trimātraḥ prasvārasthāne sa bhavaty udāttaḥ . . .*
— *ṚP* 15.5

76. *sarvodāttaṁ tviha tasminnapṛktam akṣaiprayuktaṁ dvir upasthitaṁ vā . . .*
— *ṚP* 15.9

77. *paripannaṁ prākṛtam ūṣma-sandhiṁ nakārasya loparephoṣmabhāvam* ।
asaṁyuktam ṛparaṁ rephasandhiṁ vivṛttim ityatra nidarśanāni ।
— *ṚP* 15.12

students and explained the difficulty. The sentence *abhikrānte dvaipade vādhike vā pūrvaṁ padaṁ prathamaḥ prāha śiṣyaḥ* (*ṚP* 15.10) may be considered as a focus on the method which the teacher followed at the time of explaining difficult points.

After the teacher's utterance of a group of words consisting of two or more words (probably in long compounds) the student repeated the first word. If any explanation was required the teacher stopped him and asked him to clarify the point. After it has been explained by the student the permission to continue was given with (the utterance) *oṁ bhoḥ* (i.e., well). After the teacher's word has been repeated by one student, the next one was asked to try the same.[78] If there was no difficulty probably the rule was that the teacher uttered two words at a time which was to be repeated by the student. If it was a compound, the teacher uttered only one word followed by the student's repeat.[79]

After the completion of a section, all the students practised it repeatedly.[80] When they acquired mastery over it they had to recite the whole without any break, with an even voice observing all the rules of *sandhi*, making slight division in the middle of compounds and pronouncing every syllable in *udātta* accent.[81] Students were not allowed to work out their lessons in group, as it has been distinctly mentioned that the tutor first told the verses (*praśna* — constituting three verses) to his student on the right side and every pupil after having finished

---

78. *abhikrānte dvaipade vādhike vā pūrvaṁ padaṁ prathamaḥ prāha śiṣyaḥ* ı *nirvācyetu bho iti codanā syān nirukta oṁ bho iti cābhyanujñā* ı — *ṚP* 15.10-11

79. *guru śiṣyasya padam āha mukhyaṁ samāsaśced asamāso yadi dve,* — *ṚP* 15.14

80. *etena kalpena samāpya praśnaṁ nāyustaṁ punar eva sarve* ı — *ṚP* 15.15

81. *ṚP* 15-16-20.

his work used to turn right and walked round the teacher.[82] From this, it becomes clear that whole day the students had to pay full attention never allowing their mind to wander away during the period of study. The sentences, e.g., *samayāstvagaṇyāḥ parāvarārdhāḥ* (*ṚP* 15.27) or *te ṣaṣṭiradhyāyā upādhikā vā sūkte 'samāpte yadi te samāptāḥ* (*ṚP* 15.31), etc., suggest that everyday the class continued for long hours, considering a day's lecture comprised sixty or more *praśnas*, i.e., near about 180 or more verses. The students were not allowed to leave the classroom till the study was over.

At the end of imparting lesson, after the last half verse was uttered the teacher addressed his students with *bhoḥ* and the students used to respond *oṁ bhoḥ*. After that the students uttered proper formulas to be repeated everyday at the end of reading and then left the classroom with due permission.[83]

It is interesting to observe that with the passage of time (as the students became advanced) some other methods (obviously developed) were adapted for imparting lessons. But so far as the study of Vedic texts (specially recitation and pronunciation) were concerned, down to the ages the technique of oral transmission continued with same accuracy from generation to generation.

The style of teaching in ancient period has been accurately observed by a modern scholar also:

> Each day the *guru* gathered his pupils around him to teach the Vedas. . . . The method he used consisted of making them repeat correctly after him word by word, whole passages of the sacred script. To ensure that their memory

---

82. *dakṣiṇāya prathamaṁ praśnam āha pradakṣiṇaṁ tata ūrdhvaṁ parīyuḥ* ı
evaṁ sarve praśnaśo 'dhyāyam uktvo prasaṁgṛhyātisṛṣṭā yathārtham ı
— *ṚP* 15.20-21

83. *bho 'ityardharce guruṇokta āha śiṣya oṁ bho ityucitāṁ ṛcaṁ ca* ı
— *ṚP* 15.23

> remained perfect he used mnemonic techniques. Each word was repeated independently, then together with the word preceding it, then in the reverse order and each was repeated once again before the following was tackled.
>
> — Auboyer, *DLAI*, II, p. 171

In the late Vedic literature (specially in the Brāhmaṇa and Upaniṣads) very often we find the teachers to instruct their students through dialogues/discourses, i.e., by way of discussing the topic through a series of questions and answers. In these discourses/discussions all the familiar devices of oral teaching have been used, viz. :

(1) ***Illustrations***: In the *Praśnopaniṣad*[84] the sage Paippalāda taught his students various topics (e.g., theory of creation, deities, etc.) by using illustrations. Similarly, Uddālaka Āruṇi has been found in the *CU*[85] (VI) to teach his son *ekavijñānena sarvavijñānam* by using illustration of lump of clay, gold, iron, etc.

(2) ***Stories/Narratives***: In the *Kaṭhopaniṣad*,[86] theory of Fire (*agnividyā*) has been taught through the narrative of Yama and Naciketās.

(3) ***Parables***: In the *Kenopaniṣad*[87] (III) the parable of the Yakṣa and Haimavatī Umā has been presented in order to propagate inability of other gods before Supreme Self.

After this discussion, students had to think over the problem on their own. Study of Upaniṣads suggests that

---

84. *Praśna* 1.3-1.16, 2.2-2.13, etc.

85. *yathā somyaikena mṛtpiṇḍena sarvaṁ mṛṇmayaṁ vijñātaṁ syāt vācārambhaṇaṁ vikāro nāmadheyaṁ mṛttiketyeva satyam iti* । *yathā somyaikena lohamaṇinā sarvaṁ lohamayaṁ vijñātaṁ syāt . . . yathā somyaikena nakhanikṛntanena sarvaṁ kārṣṇāyasaṁ . . .* — *CU* 6.1.4-6

86. *Kaṭha* 1.1.14-18, 1.2.16ff.

87. *Kena* 3.1-12.

introspection/contemplation on part of the student was very much essential. The *BU* sentence *ātmā vā 're draṣṭavyaḥ śrotavyo mantavyo nidhidhyāsitavyaḥ* (*BU* 2.4.5) has prescribed to practise *śravaṇa* (listening), *manana* (contemplation) and *nididhyāsana* (meditation) for the attainment of Highest Knowledge.

In some cases, the preceptor furnished broad hints only and instructed the student to realize the truth on his own.[88] Varuṇa instructed his son only on *anna, prāṇa, cakṣus, śrotra, vāc* and *manas* — as the sources of attaining self and asked him (Bhṛgu) to meditate on these things.

Sometimes the teacher sets forth his student through some kind of practical courses so that the student may achieve a direct perception of that truth by his own experience.[89] In short, the main part of education was that of the student and not of the teacher.

Variety of Institutions

From the references to the method of teaching at that period, we find that there were at least three types of institutions, which were evolved for the sake of imparting lessons and expansion of learning as well. They were (1) teacher (himself), (2) debates or literary contests, and (3) large gathering of scholars (which may be compared with modern congress/conference).

1. Homes of teachers, better to say the teacher himself was the first type of institution. From the texts it has been clear that Vedic education was teacher-centred education. The *ṚV* (specially the Frog-hymn) appears to present before us the picture of a residential school, where students were being taught.

---

88. *adhīhi bhagavo brahmeti । tasmā etat provāca annaṁ prāṇaṁ cakṣuḥ śrotraṁ mano vācam iti . . . tad vijiñāsasva ।* — *Taitt* 3.1

89. *CU* 6.7.1-6.

In the Upaniṣads[90] so many examples of this type of institutions have been traced. On reaching the age of learning, it was compulsory for every upper caste boys to join this institution, violations of which stamped a person as *brahmabandhu*. In the *CU*[91] (Ch. VI) we find the story of Śvetaketu, a brāhmaṇa boy who was sent to school by his father under the fear, lest he would be marked with such a worse stamp.

2. Debates/literary contests which are held in the *sabhā*/*pariṣads* may be mentioned as another type of educational institution. Actually these debates/disputations ministered the never-to-be-satisfied needs of advanced scholars whose quest of truth and knowledge did not cease with the elementary education of formal course but continued afterwards. In these debating circles advanced students improved their knowledge by mutual discussion with renowned scholars. Specimens of these debates have been recorded in the Brāhmaṇa and Upaniṣad texts. In this connection we may mention here a custom of that period, i.e., to flinge a gold coin as a token of challenge for debate. With reference to this context, the *ŚB*[92] narrates the story of Āruṇi, a Kurupāñcāla boy, who, while wandering reached the country of Madras and flung a coin to the brāhmaṇas of that place. But ultimately he was over-powered by Svaidāyana, a northern boy and having offered the coin as his remuneration sought his disciplehood.

---

90. *Praśna* 1.1; *CU* 4.4.1, 4.10.1, 6.1.2, 8.11; *BU* 2.1.1, etc.

91. *śvetaketur hāruṇeya āsa* । *taṁ ha pitovāca-śvetaketo vasa brahmacāryaṁ na vai somyāsmat kulīno 'nanūcya brahmabandhur iva bhavati . . .*

— *CU* 6.1.1-2

92. *ŚB* 11.4.1.1.ff.

The story of Aśvapati Kekaya also may be taken in this account. The *BU* has recorded description of several meetings of king Janaka and Yājñavalkya, in which the king quenched his thirst of knowledge by raising different question to Brahmarṣi Yājñavalkya (*BU* 4.1.2-4.4.24). The *CU*[93] informs us of Nārada, an advanced scholar, who had mastered all the arts and sciences prevalent at that time and extended his knowledge by further discussion with Sanatkumāra. The story of king Pravāhaṇa, Citra Gāṅgyāyaṇi, etc., also may be mentioned here as other examples of debate.[94]

The *Kauṣ*[95] has flourished the narrative of Dṛpta Bālāki, who was famous for his scholarship in several countries was beaten at a discourse with King Ajātaśatru and was taught the same by the king.

3. Large gathering of scholars, where representatives of various countries attended to exchange their views, may be considered as the third type of educational institution which was developed for the spread of knowledge. It may not be wrong to consider this type of gathering as an ancient form of national congress or conference (which are prevalent in recent times).

From the *BU*,[96] we have been reported about one of such congress organized by King Janaka, where the king offered a handsome prize for *brahmiṣṭha* the best scholar. At once the prize was appropriated by Yājñavalkya. Other scholars became furious and challenged Yājñavalkya's assumed superiority by

93. *CU* 7.1.3, 7.26.2.
94. *CU* 5.3.1ff; *BU* 6.2 ff.
95. *Kauṣ* 4.1.
96. *BU* 3.1.1, 3.9.28.

throwing series of perplexing problems regarding rituals, deities, self, etc. Yājñavalkya answered all those one by one very calmly and his supremacy which was once challenged, now won a country-wide fame for him.

Women's Education

As regards women's education in the Vedic age at first we are to confess that there is hardly any direct reference to imparting lessons to the girls (specially in the early Vedic age). But there are some references from which it may not be wrong to suppose that there may not be any system of institution-based training for girls, still education was not denied to them.

Names of female scholars/seers recorded in the *R̥V*[97] is an indirect proof that at least girls were not deprived of education. Besides, references to women's participation in sacrificial rites also may be considered as indication of imparting lessons to the girls. The *ŚB*[98] declares wife as a regular participant in the sacrifice.

Again *brahmacaryeṇa kanyā yuvānaṁ bindate patim* (*AV* 11.5.18) suggests the system of girls' marriage (at that time) only after the completion of their pupilage (*brahmacarya*).

Names of some female savants have been mentioned in the Brāhmaṇa and Upaniṣads. A learned maiden under the obsession of *gandharva* has been mentioned in the *AB*[99] (5.29) who could instruct the people (regarding the performance of rituals) in cases of doubt.

The Upaniṣad (*BU* 4.5.1) has called Maitreyī as *brahma-vādinī, tayor ha maitreyī brahmavādinī babhūva*. Yājñavalkya's

---

97. *R̥V* 1.126.7, 1.179.1-6, 8.91.1-7, 10.10, 10.39-40, 10.125, 10.151, etc.
98. *jaghanārdho ha vā yajñasya yat patnīḥ* — *ŚB* 5.2.1.8
99. *etad u haivovāca kumārī gandharvagr̥hītā vaktāsmo vā idaṁ pitr̥bhyo yad vaitad agnihotram ubhayedyur ahūyatānyedyur vāva tad etarhi hūyata iti* — *AB* 5.29

instruction to his wife Maitreyī may be mentioned as an instance of women's keen interest for learning.[100]

The story of Yājñavalkya's discourse with Gārgī informs us that girls were not only allowed education but they had the right to share intellectual interests also by joining public lectures, held in king's court (*BU* 3.6; 3.8). In this connection we may mention here the custom of performing an interesting ritual with a desire to have a daughter who would be a learned lady.[101]

Apart from lessons on the Vedic studies some vocational training also were given to women. Existence of some female vocations (mentioned in the *VS* and *TB*[102] in the context of human sacrifice) proves the validity of the fact. From the *ŚB tad vā etat strīṇāṁ karma yad ūrṇāsūtraṁ karma* (*ŚB* 12.7.2.11) or *nṛtyaṁ gītaṁ strīṇaṁ karma* (*ŚB* 3.2.4.6) it appears that at the time cultivation of crafts like sewing, knitting or that of fine arts, e.g., singing, dancing were mainly fixed for women though it is true that practice of dancing and singing by men also have been traced in the range of Vedic literature.

Education for Common People

References to famous brāhmaṇa and kṣatriya scholars, narratives on their names (as they have been recorded in the Vedas), suggest that education was open, better to say, compulsory for the three upper castes and at the same time forbidden for śūdras and other outcastes. That Vedic education was preserved for limited and eligible persons (specially for brāhmaṇas) and not meant for common mass has been

100. *sa hovāca maitreyī yenāhaṁ nāmṛtā syām tenāhaṁ kiṁ kuryām* ।
yad eva bhagavān veda tad eva me brūhīti — *BU* 2.4.3ff, 4.5.4ff

101. *atha ya icched duhitā me paṇḍitā jāyeta sarvam āyur iyāditi tilaudanaṁ pācayitvā sarpiṣmantam aśnīyātām iśvarau janayitavai* । — *BU* 6.4.17

102. *VS* 30.8-14; *TB* 3.4.

established in the *Nirukta*[103] also. Yāska with a citation from the *ṚV*[104] (probably belonging to the Śākala school) has established this theory.

Having observed this ancient convention of our country, a modern scholar has opined in a similar language:

> the Ṛgvedic education, being purely religious and literary in character was for the few, who were fit and eager for a dedicated life in quest of Highest Truth and Supreme Knowledge. It was thus not meant for many or mass.
>
> — Mookerji, *AIE*, p. 54

We are to mention here that prohibition was there, still there are some other references, on the basis of which it can be safely assumed that those people were not totally deprived of education.

Existence of some śūdra scholars/seers like Aitareya Mahidāsa or Kavaṣa Ailūṣa indicates that śūdras' prohibition for Vedic studies was not maintained very hard and fast.[105]

The *KS*'s[106] reference to a non-brāhmaṇa fellow's study of Vedas lends support to the fact. Further, it is interesting to note *Vrātyas*' behaviour (who, in spite of not being initiated used to instruct others) which suggests that even teaching the people by members of lower castes was prevalent (though such cases were rare).

Besides this traditional Vedic education, there must have been a considerable amount of non-religious education which was open to common people, e.g., medical science, cultivation of which was almost necessary for people's protection against disease and development of general health as well.

---

103. *Nirukta* 2.3-4.
104. *vidyā ha vai brāhmaṇam ājagāma* . . . — *SṚV* cited in *Nir* 2.4
105. *KB* 12.1; *AĀ* 2.1.8, 2.3.7; *CU* 3.16.7.

Since the time of *ṚV*[107] repeatedly physicians, specially divine physicians — the Aśvins, have been met with. So many wonderful deeds have been ascribed to their credit, e.g., they restored the eye-sight to blind Ṛjrāśva (*ṚV* 1.116.16) and revived the youth of the old Cyavana (*ṚV* 1.117.13) — all these bespeak of the high standard of ancient Indian medical science.

The story of Viśpalā may be referred to here as an example of well developed surgery prevalent at that time.[108] The *AV* may be regarded as the repository of medical science. Names of various diseases[109] and medicinal herbs[110] prove that doctors of that period were aware of the treatment of so many types of diseases. Study of this text makes it clear that details of toxicology, hydropathy, osteology, embryology were known to the people of that period. Brāhmaṇa literature also provide some information regarding this subject.

But as regards the details of (1) training in Medical Science, and (2) eligibility of students (i.e., who could be the practitioner of this science) Vedic texts have hardly furnished any direct evidence. Only the *TS* may be cited here *tasmād brāhmaṇena bheṣajaṁ na kuryāt* (6.4.2.9) as an opposite example of śūdras' prohibition for Vedic studies, which makes us suppose that training of Medical Science was open to other castes. It is stated in a distinct language in the medical texts (which are

---

106. *yo 'brāhmano vidyām anūcya naiva roceta . . .* — *KS* 9.16

107. *ṚV* 1.116.16, 1.117.4, 1.117.13, 1.117.17, 1.117.19, 1.117.22, 1.117.24, 1.157.6, 2.33.4, 2.9.3, 2.9.5, 10.39.3-5, etc.

108. *caritraṁ hi beribāccchedi parṇamājā khelasya parityaktāyām* ।
sadyo jaṅghām āyasīṁ viśpalāyai dhane hite sartave pratyadhattam ॥
— *ṚV* 1.116.15

109. jaundice : *AV* 1.22; *kṣetriya* : 2.8; *yakṣma* : 2.33; *viṣkondha* : 3.9; *takman*, i.e., fever 5.22-23.

110. Medicinal herbs : *AV* 1.34, 2.3, 2.8, 4.12, 4. 17-19.

considered as Upavedas). According to the *Suśruta Saṁhitā*,[111] not only three upper castes but śūdras also were allowed to be initiated and admitted in the mysteries of *Āyurveda*, if they were qualified by the purity of lineage and possession of virtues.

From this text, we have been informed that training in medical science required performance of a separate initiation (*upanayana*) of the student, though as a *dvija* he was already initiated according to the rule of his own caste.[112]

As regards prerequisite qualifications of a medical student the *Suśruta Saṁhitā*[113] has laid stress on the physical and moral qualities, on properly formed bodily organs (viz., tongue, lips, teeth, eye, etc.) and on cleanliness, good manners and morals, courage, humility, intelligence, patience, retentive-ness and zeal, purity of body, mind and capacity of taking pains. A student lacking these qualities would not be eligible for this *upanayana*. Rites of this *upanayana* ceremony have been discussed in the *Suśruta Saṁhitā*.[114]

A similar system (of *upanayana*) was prevalent for the study

---

111. *brāhmaṇa kṣatriya vaiśyānām anyatamam . . bhiṣak śiṣyam upanyet* । *brāhmaṇastrayāṇāṁ varṇānām upanayanaṁ kartum arhati . . . śūdram api kulaguṇa-sampannaṁ mantrabarjam upanītam adhyāpayed . . .*
— *SuS* 1.2.3; 1.2.5 (Sūtrasthāna)

112. *yadyapi brāhmaṇādaya prāg upanītāḥ tathāpyāyurvedapaṭhanārmbhe punar upanayanaṁ bhavati . . .* — Ḍalhaṇa on *SuS* 1.2.1

113. *brāhmaṇa kṣatriya vaiśyānām anyatamam anvayavayaḥśīla śaurya-śaucācāra-vinayaśakti-bala-medhā-dhṛti-smṛti-matipratipattiyuktaṁ tanujihvāsusthadantāgram ṛju vakrākṣināsaṁ prasannacitta vāk-ceṣṭaṁ kleśasahaṁ ca bhiṣak śiṣyam upanayet* । *ato viparītaguṇam nopanayet . . .*
— *SuS* 1.2.3

114. *SuS* 1.2.4.

of military education. According to the *Dhanurveda Saṁhitā*,[115] ascribed to one Vaśiṣṭha, on an auspicious day the preceptor after having performed the prescribed rites should give the student a weapon according to his caste —

> *brāhmaṇāya dhanurdeyaṁ khaḍgaṁ vai kṣatriyāya ca* ।
> *vaiśyāya dāpayet kuntaṁ gadāṁ sūdrāya dāpayet* ॥
> — *Dhanurveda Saṁhitā*, 1.8

A bow should be given to a brāhmaṇa, a sword to a kṣatriya, in case of vaiśya the weapon should be lance and for śūdra it should be mace. From this, it is evident that śūdras had access in the field of military education also.

The study of Kṣātra Kośa, Vyākaraṇa, seventh and eighth chapters of the *Manu Saṁhitā*, the Vyavahārādhyaya (of *Yājñavalkya Saṁhitā*) with Mitākṣarā (*ṭīkā*), the Jayārṇava, the Viṣṇuyāmala, the Vijayākhyatantra and science of notes (musical notes — *svaraśāstra*) would make a student eligible for the training in the military science.[116]

Similarly practice of vocal music and dance for non-religious purpose has been condemned in the *TB* and the *JB*.[117] In the Sūtra literature[118] (specially in the *Dharma-Sūtras*)

---

115. *ravivāraḥ śukravāro guruvārastathaiva ca* ।
etad vāra-trayaṁ dhanyaṁ prārambhe śastrakarmaṇām ॥
ebhir dinaistu śiṣyāya guru śastrāṇi dāpayet ।
santarpya dāna-homābhyāṁ śurān svāhā vidhānataḥ ॥
— *Dhanurveda Saṁhitā* 1.14-15

116. *Dhanurveda Saṁhitā* 68.

117. (i) *tad yad yajñe stūyate yacchasyate yat paricaryate sā prajāpateḥ senāsa* । *atha yad vīṇāyāṁ gīyate* । *yannṛtyate, yat bṛthā caryate sā mṛtyos senāsa* । — *JB* 2.10
(ii) *devā vai brahmaṇścānnasya ca śamalam apāghnan* ।
yad brahmaṇaḥ śamalam āsīt sa gāthā nārāśaṁsī abhavat ।
yad annasya sā surā, tasmād gāyataśca mattasya ca na pratigṛhṇīyāt ॥
— *TB* 1.3.2.6-7

118. *ĀpDS* 2.7.17.21; *GDS* 15.15-16; *BDS* 1.5.10.25.

professions of physician, the singer, the dancer, etc., have been stamped as despicable and declared not to be followed by brāhmaṇas. If any brāhmaṇa does so he would lose his status. From this it can be assumed safely that śūdras and other lower caste people had access to the cultivation of these subjects.

Moreover, some other subjects should be mentioned here, which made up the economic life of our country. Since long India is well known to other nations for its progress in all the departments of political, religious, economic development, and various arts and crafts (which were mainly built up on the basis of cottage industries). Undoubtedly, this progress required the foundation of appropriate technical, industrial and commercial education, which found its outlet in a corresponding diversity of occupations. In the Vedic literature there is hardly any direct evidence of such education. But a glimpse of the *R̥V*[119] (9.112) may focus some light indirectly on this point. Beside this, references to some other vocations also have been traced in various places of the Vedic literature, viz., weaving (*R̥V* 10.71.9), wood-wright (*R̥V* 9.112.2; *AB* 6.27), glass work (*AB* 6.27; *JB* 1/263), metal work (*R̥V* 1.58.8, 2.20.8; *AB* 6.27), cane work (*VS* 30.8; *TB* 3.4.5.1), leather work (*R̥V* 1.191.10, 4.51.1; *AV* 7.18.1; *VS* 16.18-19), pottery (*VS* 30.7; *MS* 1.8.3, 2.1.5).

Again existence of stone buildings, iron cities/fortifications proves cultivation of engineering of architecture. Further, the *VS* (30th ch.) in the context of Human Sacrifice provides a long list of vocations some of which were allotted to various outcastes.

All these economic progress was built up by the talents and it required methodical training by the schools of craftsmanship, existence of which can only be supposed in the absence of direct evidence from the Vedas.

---

119. *R̥V* 9.112.1-3.

7

Social Life

In course of our discussion on the social life of Vedic people, at first we have to think of the structure of social organization which they belonged to. In fact, everyday life of the people was mainly determined by two factors, i.e., (1) four castes (*varṇas*) and (2) four orders of life (*āśramas*), because the daily activities were fixed according to the particular caste and stage of life to which one belonged (at that time). Jeanine Auboyer in her work has remarked:

> From the time that he was conceived, an Indian belonged to a caste, corresponding to a religious social structure.
>
> — *DLAI*, II, p. 143

Classification of Society Based on Four Classes

Though traditionally the Vedic society was divided into four groups, it is to be remembered here that this situation has not been fixed at the early stage (i.e., in the *ṚV*), there are some stray references only to the brāhmaṇas and kṣatriyas which formed the priesthood and ruling noble classes. Other two classes, i.e., vaiśyas and śūdras have been mentioned repeatedly in the late Vedic texts. However, division of the society into four classes has been recorded for the first time in the Creation Hymn of *ṚV* (10.90.12). The class division in the Vedas based on four castes has been noticed not only among men and gods, but also in case of the *sāmans*, *stomas*, metres, seasons (even in the animal world and vegetables also), which indicate their social status and relationship (in case of men and gods) and importance in the ritual (applicable in case of *sāmans*, *stomas*, metres, seasons, animals and trees).

Though by tradition there were four castes, from the ethnic viewpoint there were two groups only, i.e., *traivarṇika* Aryans (i.e., three upper castes) and other lower caste peoples (i.e., śūdras).

Now, as regards the daily life of these people (divided in the said two groups) at first we must confess that as because Vedic texts were not daily register books of that period, it is difficult to get the actual picture therefrom. It has been portrayed in the later texts.* Still on the basis of references to the origin of four castes, their status and privileges (scattered mainly in the late Vedic Saṁhitā and *Brs*) we may form a rough idea of the same.

Origin of Four Castes

The Creation Hymn of *R̥V* (10.90.12) has described not only the origin of four castes but at the same time thrown some light on their status:

> *brāhmaṇo 'sya mukham āsīd bāhū rājanyaḥ kr̥taḥ* ।
> *urū tad asya yad vaiśyaḥ padbhyāṁ śūdro 'jāyata* ॥
> — *R̥V* 10.90.12

Brāhmaṇas sprang forth from his mouth, kṣatriyas were originated from his arms, vaiśyas came out from his thighs while śūdras were born from his feet. Here brāhmaṇas have been mentioned as *mukha*. Just as in the human organism *mukha*, being the seat of intelligence and learning, is considered the

* Detailed routine of king's daily life has been described in the *Manu-Saṁhitā* (7.145-225). Similarly, the daily routine of a fashionable young man (belonging to Gupta period) has been depicted in the *Kāma-Sūtra* of Vātsyāyana (1.4.8) and the *Suśruta Saṁhitā* (Cikitsāsthāna, 24th ch.).

best limb and is towering over the body, similarly brāhmaṇas having been created from the mouth of Primordial Man enjoyed a supreme position. As regards the origin of brāhmaṇas some other views have been traced in different texts, e.g., some say gods created brāhmaṇas by uttering three *stomas*,[1] while another text has recorded his origin from the sacrifice performed by Prajāpati.[2] According to the *ŚB*[3] with the utterance of first *vyāhṛti 'bhūḥ'* by Prajāpati, brāhmaṇas were created. However, whatever may be their origin, having been created at first of all the castes, they occupied the upper most position in the social hierarchy.

Kṣatriyas being born from the arms (of the Primordial Man), i.e., the seat of power, were symbolizing vigour and strength. Vaiśyas, on account of their birth from His thighs, the seat of production, symbolized chief support, while śūdras being born from His feet, the emblem of activity, indicated that the whole society depended on their toil for survival and development, just as in the human organism the whole body depends on feet for its movement. The *TS*[4] has remarked about them as the foundation of society (*bhūtasaṅkrāmin*). According to Sri Aurobindo:

> The ancient Indian idea was that man falls by his nature into four types. There are first and highest, the man of learning and thought and knowledge; next the man of power and action, i.e., ruler, warrior, leader, administrator; third in the scale the economic man, producer and wealth getter, the merchant,

---

1. *tisṛbhir astuvata brahmāsṛjyata* — *MS* 2.8.6; *KS* 17.5; *KapKS* 26.4; *TS* 4.3.10.1; *VS* 14.28.

2. *prajāpatir yajñam asṛjata* | *yajñaṁ sṛṣṭam anu brahmakṣatre asṛjyetām* | — *AB* 7.19

3. *bhūr iti prajāpatiḥ brahma ajanayata* — *ŚB* 2.1.4.12

4. *patta ekaviṁśatiṁ niramimīta, tam anuṣṭup chando 'nvasṛjyata* | *vairājaṁ sāma śūdro manuṣyāṇām* | *aśva paśūnāṁ tasmāt tau bhūtasaṅkrāmiṇāvaśvaśca śūdraśca* . . . — *TS* 7.1.1.6

> artisan, cultivator: these were the twice-born who received the initiation, i.e., Brāhmin, Kshatriya and Vaiśya. Last came the more undeveloped human type not yet fit for these steps of the scale, unitellectual, without force, incapable of creation or intelligent production, the man fit only for unskilled labour and menial service, the Śūdra.
>
> — *Foundation of Indian Culture*, II, p. 111

Characteristic Features and Occupations

Characteristic features and occupations of these four castes have been hinted at in the *AB*[5]. It has described (1) brāhmaṇas as recipient of gifts (*ādāyī*), drinker of Soma (*āpāyī*), moving at will (*āvasāyī*), smart and optionally submissive to the king. (2) vaiśyas have been portrayed as tributary to the others (*anyasya balikṛt*), to be lived upon by others (*anyasyādyaḥ*) and to be oppressed at will (*yathā kāmajjeyaḥ*), and (3) śūdras have been mentioned as servant of others (*anyasya preṣyaḥ*) evicted at will (*kāmotthāpyaḥ*) and to be slain at will (*yathākāmabadhyaḥ*). The compliments applied to brāhmaṇas *ādāyyāpayyāvasāyī* suggest that chief occupations of brāhmaṇas were mainly performing sacrifices and receiving gifts. Study and teaching were also included within their duties.

The phrases like *ojaḥ kṣatraṁ vīryaṁ vai rājanyaḥ* (*AB* 8.37) or *yuddaṁ vai rājanyasya vīryam* (*ŚB* 13.1.5.6) indicate that kṣatriyas formed an administrative ruling class whose noble duty was to fight against the enemies, punish the miscreants and render help and protection to the needy. In the *AB* (8.12) king has been called guardian of the law (*dharmasya goptā 'jani*), lord of all the beings (*viśvasya bhūtasyādhipatiḥ*) and a terror to the enemies (*asurāṇāṁ hantā*) which prove validity of this statement. On account of their birth from the thighs of the

---

5. (*brāhmaṇaḥ*) *ādayyāpāyyāvasāyi yathākāma-paryāpyaḥ* । (*vaiśyaḥ*) *anyasya balikṛd anyāsyādyaḥ yathākāmajjeyaḥ* । (*śūdraḥ*) *anyasya preṣyaḥ kāmotthāpyo yathākāmavadhyaḥ* — *AB* 7.29

Supreme Person, vaiśyas symbolized the chief support of the society. By practising agriculture and trade they provided support to the society. The adjectives *anyasya balikṛt anyasyādyaḥ* applicable to the vaiśyas have made it evident that they had to pay taxes and render service and support (mainly financial) to the members of the upper classes. Lastly the śūdras, on account of their birth from the Creator's feet indicated the foundation of society (*bhūta-saṅkrāmin*). The sentence *anyasya preṣyaḥ kāmotthāpya yathākāmabadhyaḥ* (*AB* 7.29) indicates that they were servants of upper classes, they could be evicted from their lands and dispossessed of their belongings and even might be killed at will.

Right to the Vedic Studies

Now, the people of the three upper castes, on account of their belonging to the same community (*traivarṇika*s), had some common features (though specific peculiarity and points of distinction among themselves were always there). As for example, all these people were entitled to be initiated to receive Vedic education and perform sacrifices. In the *TB* (1.1.2.7) proper seasons of establishing fire have been prescribed for brāhmaṇas, kṣatriyas and vaiśyas which clearly indicate that in the matter of performing sacrifices there was no special discrimination against any of these three castes.

But as regards further details concerned with sacrifices, distinctions and differences were there. First of all different seasons of establishing fire have been prescribed for the members of the three castes.[6] Hence, spring was fixed for brāhmaṇas, summer for kṣatriyas and autumn for vaiśyas.

---

6. *vasantā brāhmaṇo 'gnim ādadhīta, vasanta vai brāhmaṇasyartuḥ* I . . . *grīṣme rājanya ādadhīta grīṣmo vai rājanyasyartuḥ* I . . . *śaradi vaiśya ādadhīta* I *śarad vai vaiśyasyartuḥ* I — *TB* 1.1.2.6-7

Further, in the Brāhmaṇa texts[7] (and the Sūtra texts[8] as well) caste distinctions have been recognized on basis of which different metres, trees, foods, dresses (to be used in sacrificial purpose) were prescribed for the people belonging to various castes. As because the objects to be achieved by brāhmaṇas, kṣatriyas and vaiśyas were holy lustre (*brahmavarcas*), physical strength (*vīryam/ojas*) and cattle or wealth (*paśavaḥ*[9]) therefore metres prescribed for them (in the coronation ceremony) were *gāyatrī, triṣṭubh* and *jagatī*[10] conducive to the holy lustre, strength and wealth. Moreover, they were connected with Agni, Indra and Maruts, the presiding deities of the said things.[11] Other differences (e.g., food, dress, prescribed according to the caste) have already been discussed in the first two chapers (see under (1) Food, prescribed on ritual occasions in the Food Habits, Ch. 1 and (2) Students'/Brahmacārins' Dress in Dress Arrangement, Ch. 2).

As already mentioned, brāhmaṇas on account of their sacred birth acquired the topmost position in the society. They became teachers, priests, administrative consultants (of the kings), spiritual guides, etc. Quite normally these people (brāhmaṇas) in their everyday life enjoyed some special and extra advantages for which members of other castes were not

---

7. *AB* 1.28, 8.6; *PB* 6.3.5, 18.4.6; *ŚB* 13.2.6.10; *TB* 3.8.13.1.
8. *ĀGS* 1.19.8-13; *SGS* 2.1.2-5; *GGS* 2.10.8ff; *PGS* 2.5.17-19; *BGS* 2.5.16; *GSH* 1.1.5; *BhGS* 1.1, etc.
9. (i) *kṣatraṁ rājanyaḥ kṣatreṇaiva kṣatraṁ samardhayati . . .* — *AB* 8.6
   (ii) *sarvā̆ agnir apsuṣado huve mayi varco balam ojo nidhatteti* — *AB* 8.6
   (iii) *PB* 18.4.3-6.
10. *gāyatrīṁ brāhmaṇasyānu brūyāt . . . gāyatro vai brāhmaṇaḥ . . . triṣṭubhaṁ rājanyasyānu brūyāt . . . traiṣṭubho vai rājanyaḥ . . . jāgatīṁ vaiśyasyānubrūyāt . . . jāgato vai vaiśyaḥ* । — *AB* a1.28
11. *agniṣṭvā gayatryā sayuk chandasā 'rohatu . . . indrastriṣṭubhā . . . viśvedevā jagatyā . . .* — *AB* 8.6

entitled at all. According to the *ŚB*.[12] "People should protect brāhmaṇas in four ways by showing respect and liberality, acknowledging his invincibility and by granting him security against capital punishment. "Not only they were performers of sacrifice, they were the guardians of sacrifice."[13] In the divine society brāhmaṇa Bṛhaspati was the spiritual guide and prime minister of Indra. According to this example in the mortal world also brāhmaṇas played double roles of spiritual guide and administrative consultant to the king.

Next to brāhmaṇas were kṣatriyas. But as a kingly class they were at the top of administration. Real power rested with them, hence they were entrusted with administration and protection of people. They had the right to dominate everybody except brāhmaṇas. According to theory brāhmaṇas were in a higher position than kṣatriyas; but kṣatriyas by virtue of their sovereign power enjoyed superiority over all. The story of Janaka and Yājñavalkya (*ŚB* 11.6.1.1ff) is a clear proof that nobody (even the brāhmaṇas) could dare to challenge kṣatriyas. The king could subjugate even the brāhmaṇas, whenever he liked so, though he would have to fare worse for doing so.[14] No offensive act would smite sin on them. Even after they have committed serious offences like falsehood, illicit relation with sisters, oppressing brāhmaṇas, etc., they could be released of their guilt by performing an expiatory rite to Varuṇa and a gift of gold to the brāhmaṇas.[15] Means of purification were always open for them.

---

12. *caturbhir dharmaiḥ brāhmaṇam arcayā ca dānena cājeyatayā cāvadhyatayā* — *ŚB* 11.5.7.1

13. *ete vai yajñasya śrāvitāro ye 'nūcānāḥ* I — *ŚB* 1.5.1.12

14. *yadā vai rājā kāmayate brāhmaṇaṁ jināti, pāpīyāṁstu bhavati* — *ŚB* 13.1.5.4

15. *hiraṇyaṁ dakṣiṇā* I *pavitraṁ vai hiraṇyam* I *punāty evainaṁ bahu vai rājanyo 'nṛtaṁ karoti* I *upajāmyai harate* I *jināti vai brāhmaṇam* I *badaty anṛtam* I . . . *vāruṇaṁ yavamayaṁ caruṁ nirvapati varuṇapāśād evainaṁ muñcati* I — *TB* 1.7.2.5-6

The position of Vaiśyas was inferior to that of brāhmaṇas and kṣatriyas and superior to that of the śūdras. They practised agriculture, trade, controlled other modes of production, produced wealth and thus rendered support to the upper class. But in spite of that, they were unquestionably taxed by the ruling people. They had to pay taxes and remain under the rule of kingly class. In return the king protected them. But it is clear that they were not slaves.

Lastly, there were śūdras. They were not fit for any type of intellectual production. According to the description of *AB* (7.29), their only duty was to serve the three upper classes. In words of Sri Aurobindo:

> The economic order of society was cast in the form and gradation of these four types. The Brāhmin class was called upon to give the community its priests, thinkers, men of letters, legislators, scholars, religious leaders and guides. The Kṣatriya school gave it its kings, warriors, governors and administrators. The Vaiśyas order supplied it with its producers, agriculturists, craftsmen, artisans, merchants and traders. The Śūdra class ministered to its need of menials and servants. — *Foundations of Indian Culture*, II, p. 111

Four Orders of Life

As the social body was divided into four stages according to people's intellectual capacity and activities, the total tenure of human life was divided into four periods and each of them marked out a stage in the working out of this cultural idea of living. There was the period of a student (*brahmacarya*), the period of a householder (*gārhasthya*), the period of a recluse or forest-dweller (*vānaprastha*), and the period of a super-social man the *parivrājaka* (i.e., *saṁnyāsa*) (Sri Aurobindo, *Foundation of Indian Culture*, II, p. 115).

In every stage people had fixed duties. The student life was framed to lay the ground work of what the man had to know, do and be. The householder's stage was meant for earning, to satisfy the first three human objects (*dharma*, *artha* and *kāma*), i.e., rendering duties to the society and to take the joy of life. In the third stage the man retired to the forest and worked out in a certain seclusion the truth of his spirit. In the last stage he became free from all the ties of social life, then he could wander over the world in an extreme spiritual detachment, satisfying only the barest necessities, communing with the universal spirit, making his soul ready for eternity. It is interesting to observe that one's duty in a certain period was considered prohibited in another, e.g., begging was a compulsory duty of a student but the same was prohibited on the completion of studenthood.[16] Similarly earning or enjoying pleasure which were allowed in domestic stage, were not permissible in the forest-order.

Studenthood

Among these four stages, first one was studenthood (i.e., *brahmacarya*), which was formally inaugurated by the ceremony of initiation, i.e., *upanayana*. We have already discussed it in the previous chapter (see: Initiation under Education System, Ch. 6).

The initiated student was called by the name *brahmacārin*, who has been described as the member of god's limbs, *sa devānāṁ bhavatyekam aṅgam* (*R̥V* 10.109.5). His divinity has been recognized in the *ŚB*[17] also. The *AV* has devoted an entire hymn (11.5) to the glorification of *brahmacārin* (11.5.1-13, 11.5.16-21) and *brahmacarya* (11.5.16-19). The names of celibate-cum-students and their practice of celibacy (as recorded in the *Br*[18] and Up. texts) imply that it was obligatory for every candidate

16. *na ha vai snātvā bhikṣeta* — *ŚB* 11.3.3.7
17. *divyaḥ prajās tāni mukhato janayate* — *ŚB* 11.5.4.7
18. *AB* 5.14; *ŚB* 11.5.3.13; *GB* 1.2.31; *Praśna* 1.1; *CU* 4.4.1ff, 4.10.1ff, 7.1.1-7, 8.7.1-8.12.6, etc.

who sought knowledge. Benefits of *brahmacarya* have been discussed in the *CU*.[19] People could attain results of performing (i) sacrifice (*yajña*), (ii) worship (*iṣṭa*), (iii) keeping silence (*mauna*), (iv) *sattrāyaṇa*, (v) fasting (*anāśākāyana*), and (vi) living in the forest (*araṇyāyana*), etc. People believed that celibacy could lead them even up to *brahmaloka*.[20] The purpose of practising *brahmacarya* (i.e., to attain Supreme Reality) has been indicated in the *Kaṭhopaniṣad*[21] also.

DAILY ROUTINE OF A STUDENT

At the time of discussing *brahmacarya* and *upanayana*, the *ŚB*[22] has prescribed some primary injunctions for the student in the form of instructions to the newly initiated student by his teacher. Actually some duties have been allotted here for the student, which he had to do everyday almost compulsorily. Those are as follows: (1) Hard work, (2) non-sleepiness during day time, (3) service for the teacher in the form of tending his fire, cattle and other work (as they were required), (4) study, and (5) development of inner discipline. From these instructions we may form an idea about the daily life of a student.

---

19. *atha yad yajña ity ācakṣate brahmacaryam eva tat . . .*
atha yad iṣṭam ity ācakṣate brahmacaryam eva tat . . .
atha yad sattrāyaṇam ity ācakṣante brahmacaryam eva tat . . .
atha yad maunam ity ācakṣate brahmacaryam eva tat . . .
atha yad anāśakāyanam ity ācakṣate brahmacaryam eva tat . . .
atha yad araṇyāyanam ity ācakṣate brahmacaryam eva tat . . .
— *CU* 8.5.1.4

20. *tad ya evaitāvaraṁ ca ṇyaṁ cārṇavau brahmaloke* ।
brahmacaryeṇā nubindanti teṣām evaiṣa brahmalokaḥ ॥
— *CU* 8.5.4

21. *yad icchanto brahmacaryaṁ caranti tat te padaṁ saṁgraheṇa brabīmi*
— *Kaṭha* 1.2.15

22. *brahmacāry asī tyāha* । *brahmaṇa evainaṁ tat paridadāti* । *apo 'śāna* । *amṛtaṁ vā 'paḥ . . . karma kuru iti* । *vīryaṁ vai karma samidham ādhehi iti* । *samitsvam ātmānam tejasā brahmavarcasenety evainaṁ tad āha . . . mā suṣupthāḥ* । *. . .* — *ŚB* 11.5.4.5

Begging was one of the compulsory daily duties of a student which has been mentioned time and again from the *AV* onwards. The *ŚB* and the *GB*[23] have described how the student being devoid of shame and vanity begged alms. The text has instructed him to beg at first from the wife of his teacher and then from his mother,[24] most probably to avoid the sorrow and despair of refusal at the first chance. To pass seven nights without begging was considered a serious offence for a student. On doing so his candidature was to be renewed by another initiation[25] — this injunction suggests that the student had to beg daily as much as it was necessary for his subsistence. To collect in excess and make any saving was forbidden for him.

Another compulsory duty of a student was to tend the teacher's fire by bringing sacrificial faggots daily. Otherwise death cuts off a day from the span of his life tenute.[26] The *ŚB*[27] says "by putting fuel on the fire the student enkindled his mind with holy lusture." Description of a religious student approaching his teacher by carrying sacrificial faggots in hands — is a common picture in the Brāhmaṇa[28] and the Upaniṣads.

---

23. *atha yad ātmānam daridrīkṛtyeva ahrīr bhūtvā bhikṣate* । . . .
— *ŚB* 11.3.3.5; cf. *GB* 1.2.3

24. *sa yady anyām bhikṣitavyānna binded api svāmevācāryajāyāṁ bhikṣet ātho svāṁ mātaraṁ* . . . — *ŚB* 11.3.3.5

25. *saptamīṁ nātinayet* । *saptamīm atinayan na brahmacārī bhavati* । *samid bhaikṣe saptarātram acaritavān brahmacārī punar upaneya bhavati* ।
— *GB* 1.2.6

26. *yāṁ rātriṁ brahmacārī samidhaṁ nāharaty āyuṣa eva tam avadāya vasati* । *tasmād brahmacārī samidham āharannāyuṣo 'vadāya vasānīti* ।
— *GB* 1.2.6 cf. *ŚB* 11.3.3.1

27. *samidham ādhehi iti* । *samitsvam ātmānaṁ tejasā brahmavarcasenety evainam tad āha* । — *ŚB* 11.5.4.5

28. *ŚB* 11.5.3.13; *Muṇḍ* 1.2.12-13; *CU* 4.10.1-2, 5.11.7, 8.7.2; *BU* 2.1.7, etc.

The *CU*[29] has recorded how Upakośala tended his teacher's fire for long twelve years.

That looking after the house of a teacher and tending his cattle also formed an important part of a student's compulsory duties, has been recorded in the *ŚB* for the first time. The *ŚB*[30] has declared "the student guards his teacher, his house and cattle." From the *AĀ*[31] we have been informed of a Tārukṣya who guarded his teacher's cattle for a whole year to get a tough lesson on the euphonic combination. The story of Satyakāma has been narrated in the *CU*[32] who after initiation departed from his teacher's institution with four hundred cows and promised not to return until their number would increase upto one thousand.

Daily study technically called *svādhyāya* also has been included in the compulsory duties (probably most important, in comparison to others) of the religious student.[33] In this stage mainly they learnt Vedic texts and memorized the same from the teacher under a system of oral transmission. Rules and regulations regarding the time, place and manner of the study could be relaxed to some extent if it was necessary, but continuity of study was never to be broken.[34] Other details of

---

29. *upakosalo ha vai kāmalāyanaḥ satyakāme jābāle brahmacaryam uvāsa* ৷ *tasya ha dvādaśa varṣāṇy agnīn paricacāra* — *CU* 4.10.1
30. *brahmacāriṇa ācāryaṁ gopāyanti gr̥hān paśūn nennopaharāṇīti* ৷ — *ŚB* 3.6.2.15
31. *etasyāṁ ha smopaniṣadi saṁvatsaraṁ gā rakṣayate tārukṣyaḥ* ৷ — *AĀ* 3.1.6
32. *iti tam upanīya kr̥śānām abalānāṁ catuḥśatā gā nirākr̥tyovācemāḥ somyānuvrajeti* ৷ *tā abhiprasthāpayannuvāca nāsahasreṇāvartayeti sa ha varṣagaṇaṁ provāsa tā yadā sahasraṁ sampeduḥ* ৷ — *CU* 4.4.5
33. *ācārya kulād vedam adhītya yathāvidhānaṁ guroḥ karmātiśeṣeṇa . . .* — *CU* 8.15.1
34. *iti ha smāha śauca āhreya utāraṇye 'bala utavācota tiṣṭhan nuta vrajannutāsīna utaśayāno 'dhīyītaiva . . .* — *TĀ* 2.12

study have already been discussed. (See: Study — its time and place, syllabus under Education System, Ch. 6.)

Apart from these duties, some restrictions were imposed on the students' daily routine so that he could develop some mental or moral attributes, which would make him internally disciplined and qualified for the subsequent stages of life. They are as follows:

The student had to forsake his addiction to drowsiness during day time. By practising *brahmacarya* he had to overcome some passions, e.g., caste pride, lethargy, hankering after name and fame, anger, greed, bragging, vanity, cultivation of personal beauty, avoidance of perfumery goods, any type of luxury, company of women, addiction for music, dance, etc., which stand as a bar to his intellectual and spiritual progress.[35]

In the Dharma-Sūtras (esp. *ĀpDS, GDS, BDS*) we find some further details regarding the daily routine of a celibate/student. The time of his waking up and going to bed, morning and evening prayer, everything has been recorded in a specific language. According to the *ĀpDS*[36] the student had to wake up before his teacher and before sunrise. Then he took a bath and purified himself. After that he performed his morning prayer silently in a pure place in the eastern or northern direction.[37] He used to begin murmuring Sāvitrī (hymn) at a time when stars were still visible in the sky and complete it

---

35. *jāyamāno ha vai brāhmaṇo saptendriyāṇyabhi jāyate । brahmavarcasaṁ ca yaśaśca svapnaṁ ca । krodhañca ślāghāñca rūpañca — puṇyam eva gandhaṁ saptamam । tāni ha vā asyaitāni brahmacaryam upetasyopa krāmanti ।*
— *GB* 1.2.2

36. (i) *svapnaṁ varjayet* — *ĀpDS* 1.1.4.22.
(ii) *abhyudiyācched akarmaśrāntam anabhirūpeṇa karmaṇā vāgyata . . .*
— *ĀGS* 3.7.1

37. *yajñopavītī nityodakaḥ sandhyām upāsīta vāgyataḥ । . . . evaṁ prātaḥ prāṅ mukham . . .* — *ĀGS* 3.7.5-6; cf *ŚGS* 2.9.3

after sunrise.[38] As already mentioned, everyday twice he had to tend his teacher's fire. The time of collecting fuels also was fixed. He could not go out to fetch wood after sunset.[39] Begging alms also was a compulsory duty and whatever he had collected, he had to announce to his teacher and take it only after his permission.[40] He was not allowed to take pungent condiments, salt, honey, meat,[41] etc. He could go to sleep after his teacher. Any type of enjoyment was forbidden for him. The *ĀpDS* states that a student's only duty was to please the teacher by performing prescribed acts and working hard for his studies.[42]

Domestic Life (Gārhasthya)

Vedic Indians considered the whole life process as a journey towards ultimate perfection and at the beginning of each of the order of life they performed a sacrament which gave that particular order a sanctified form. As already mentioned, the first stage of life, the studenthood, was opened with the ceremony of initiation (*upanayana*), similarly, the second stage or domestic order was inaugurated with the marriage ceremony.*

NECESSITY OF DOMESTIC LIFE

This second stage of life was equally important for each and every person. From the convocational address of the teacher,

38. *prāṅmukhaṣṭiṣṭhannāmaṇḍala-darśanāt* । — *ĀGS* 3.7.6
39. *nāstamite samiddhāro gacchet* — *ĀpDS* 1.1.4.15
40. *ĀGS* 1.22.9-10; *SGS* 2.6.7; *PGS* 2.5.8; *GGS* 2.10.40
41. *GSH* 1.8.9; *BGS* 2.5.7; *PGS* 2.5.10.
42. *GDS* 2.19; *PGS* 2.5.12.

* Details of marriage rituals have been discussed in the Gṛhya-Sūtras and by some eminent scholars as well. For example we, may cite here *History of Dharmaśāstra* by P.V. Kane, *India of the Vedic Kalpa-Sūtras* by Ram Gopal and *Hindu Saṁskāras* by R.B. Pandey. As because it is beyond the scope of our discussion, it has been left in the present study.

which he used to give at the end of a student's education, it becomes evident that on the completion of studentship, to enter a householder's life and fatherhood was almost compulsory.[43] Better to say, to enter this stage (by getting married) was a religious duty in order to fulfil the interest of race and society.

Advantages of having a wife and thereby a son have proved the necessity of this order.[44] First of all marriage was necessary for the completion of one's own self.

> *tasmāt puruṣo jāyāṁ vittvā kṛtsnataram ivātmānaṁ manyate* ।
> — *AĀ* 1.3.5

The *ŚB* has clearly stated that so long as a person remains unmarried he cannot be regenerated, hence remains incomplete and he becomes complete only after getting a wife. Therefore, for the continuation of lineage, it was necessary to get married. Again for the repayment of the debts to the Manes this order (*gārhasthya*) only can help a man, because by way of marriage and begetting children people could be released of their debt to the Fathers.[46] In the legend of King Hariścandra, the *AB*[47] has considered the delight of having a son to be greater than any earthly enjoyment. By getting a son a father could

---

43. *ācāryāya priyaṁ dhanam āhṛtya prajātantuṁ mā vyavacchetsīḥ*
— *Taitt* 1.11

44. *AB* 7.13.3-12.

45. *yāvajjāyāṁ na bindate naiva tāvat prajāyate* ।
sarvo hi tāvat bhavatyatho yāvadaiva jāyāṁ bindate ॥
—*ŚB*5.2.1.10

46. *ṛṇam asmin saṁnayaty anṛtaṁ ca gacchati* ।
pitā putrasya jātasya paśyecchejjīvato mukham ॥
— *AB* 7.13.3

47. *yāvantaḥ pṛthivyāṁ bhogāḥ yāvantojātavedasi* ।
yāvanto 'psu prāṇināṁ bhūtān putre pitustataḥ ॥
— *AB* 7.13.4

overcome the darkness of this world.[48] Therefore, marriage was necessary for his own pleasure and that of his predecessors. Further, for the performance of religious rites also existence of a wife was very much important. Wife has been declared in the *ŚB*[49] as the integral part of the sacrifice. The person without a wife was not at all eligible to perform a sacrifice.[50] Gods do not accept oblations from such a person. Again, wives' participation in the performance of rituals in the Horse Sacrifice, is also another proof of wife's importance.[51] Therefore, to get married and accept a householder's life was necessary for a person in order to attain eligibility of performing religious rites.

A PEN-PICTURE OF DOMESTIC LIFE

While going through Vedic texts, so many passages have been met with, which make us visualize different scenes of domestic life. Sweet and affectionate domestic relations have become prominent sometimes through similes or (sometimes) prayers or passing remarks.

Children were brought up under parent's care and affection. Always they provide their babies sure and firm protection, *pātām avadyād duritād abhīke pitā mātā ca rakṣatam avobhiḥ* (*R̥V* 1.185.10). Sometimes a mother is found offering breast to her son *yathā kumārāya vā jātāya vatsāya vā stanamapidadhyāt* (*ŚB* 2.2.1.1) or trying to protect her baby by wrapping it with the end of her garment: *mātā putraṁ yathā sicābhyenaṁ bhūma ūrṇuhi* (*R̥V* 10.18.11). In the morning she awakens her children and sets them to their duty: *admasanna*

---

48. *śaśvat putreṇa pitaro 'tyatāyan bahulaṁ tapaḥ* ।
ātmā hi yajña ātmanaḥ irāvatyatitāriṇīḥ ॥
— *AB* 7.13.5

49. *jaghanārdho ha vā yajñasya yat patnīḥ* । — *ŚB* 5.2.1.8

50. *ayajño vā eṣaḥ yo 'patnīkaḥ* । — *TB* 3.3.3.1

51. *ŚB* 13.4.1.8-10.

sasato bodhayantī śaśvattam āgāt punareyuṣīṇām (*ṚV* 1.124.4). Father is always kind and generous to his children and approve their demand similingly, *yathā pitā putrāya syonaḥ suśevaḥ* (*ŚB* 8.2.1.6) or *atha yat putrāh pitari . . . tathā ityevāha* (*ŚB* 8.4.1.4). Even sometimes he is found to rebuke his son, who is defaulter in his studies.

> *adhīṣva svādhyāyam* । *kasmānnu svādhyāyaṁ nādhīṣa iti* ।
> — *ŚB*, 11.6.1.7

Similarly, children depend on their parents for their subsistence. Sometimes the baby son is found trying to attract his father's attention by clutching the end of his garment: *rājeva yudhvā nayasi tvam it sicau yad āsām agraṁ pravatām inakṣasi* (*ṚV* 10.75.4), or the hungry boy is looking for his mother: *yatheha kṣudhitā bālā mātaraṁ paryupāsate* (*CU* 5.24.5), even sometimes the boy is found complaining something to his father: *sa hāyastaḥ pitur ardham eyāya taṁ hovācānanuśiṣya vāva kila mā bhagavān abravīd anu tvā 'śiṣam iti* (*CU* 5.3.4). They (children) receive their father warmly on his return from abroad; *yathā putrāḥ pitaraṁ proṣuṣam āgataṁ śivam upaspṛśanti* (*ŚB* 12.5.2.8). Similarly, the father accepts them with affectionate blessings:

> *atha yat proṣyā 'yan putrasya mūrdhānam abhijighret* ।
> *aṅgādaṅgāt sambhavasi hṛdayād adhijāyase* ।
> *ātmā vai putra nāmāsi sa jīvaḥ śaradaḥ śatam* ॥
> — *ŚĀ* 11.4

The *AV* has given a beautiful picture of an ideal family where children are obedient to their parents, wife is calm and gentle and speaking sweet words, brothers and sisters are ungrudging and unanimous in opinion:

> *anuvrataḥpituḥ putro mātrā bhavatu saṁmanāḥ* ।
> *jāyā patye madhumatīṁ vācaṁ vadatu śantivām* ॥
> *mā bhrātā bhrātaraṁ dvikṣan mā svasāram uta svasā* ।
> *samyañcaḥ savratā bhūtvā vācaṁ vadata bhadrayā* ॥
> —*AV* 3.30.2-3

Sweet and inseparable relation between husband and wife has been expressed beautifully at various places. Sometimes the wife appears before her husband in an excellent dress:

uta tvasmai tanvaṁ visasre jāyeva patya uśatī suvāsā ।
— *Ṛ̥V*, 10.71.4

or approaching him in a sweet manner, *vadhūr iyaṁ patim icchanti* (*Ṛ̥V* 5.37.3). Sometimes they are engaged in exchanging gentle talks and coaxing each other:

(i) *jāyā patiṁ vahati vagnunā* — *Ṛ̥V* 10.32.3;

(ii) *haye jāye manasā tiṣṭha ghore vacāṁsi miśrā kṛ̥ṇavāmahai nu* — *Ṛ̥V* 10.95.1

Sometimes the wife is serving food to her husband:

katarat āharāṇi dadhi manthaṁ parisrutam ।
jāyā patiṁ vipṛ̥cchati . . . — *AV* 20.127.9

Again, in another place they (the couple) are found quarreling together *yad agne adya mithunā śapāto* (*Ṛ̥V* 10.87.13) or overwhelmed with grief at the time of another's departure:

sudevo adya prapatedanāvṛ̥t parāvataṁ paramāṇgantavā u ।
adhā śayīta nirṛ̥tir upasthe 'dhainaṁ vṛ̥kā rabhasāso adyaḥ ॥
— *Ṛ̥V* 10.95.14

Thus, through the expressions of love or quarrel or pangs of separation their sweet and inseparable relation has been hinted at.

The Brāhmaṇa texts also throw some light on this point. However, the wife was not considered within one's personal belongings or slave-like person. She was rather a confident friend *sakhā ha jāyā* (*AB* 7.29). Her dignified status has been reflected in the *ŚB*[52] where she has been declared as the incarnation of the goddess of Grace. In another passage she

52. *strī vā eṣā yacchrīḥ* । — *ŚB* 11.4.3.2

has been mentioned as one-half of one's own self.[53] Their inseparable relationship is more prominently expressed in: "truth is male, faith is female; mind is husband, speech is wife; wherever the husband is, there is wife, too."[54] Just as truth and faith go together or mind and speech are inseparable from each other, similarly relation between the married couple was indissoluble. In this connection, we may mention here the story of Sukanyā, the daughter of King Śaryāta, who was given in marriage by her father to the old sage Cyavana who was almost ghostly in appearance. It is interesting to note that Sukanyā in spite of being allured by Aśvins was not agreeable to repudiate her husband. On the contrary she expressed everything to him and according to his advice she played a trick with Aśvins and revived the youth of her husband. This story proves that the chastity of women was regarded a priceless treasure.[55]

EXCEPTIONS

In spite of that, some exceptions have been traced. There are some passages in the *Yajurveda Saṁhitā*[56] and Brāhmaṇas, wherein out of lawful marriages, practice of maintaining illicit relationship between men of higher caste and śūdra women and vice versa have been recorded.

From the *ŚB*'s[57] remark, "it is disgraceful for a person, if his wife consorts with another person," it appears though such relationship was considered disgraceful, still it was practised. As another example, it may not be irrelevant to mention the rite in the Varuṇapraghāsa sacrifice, where the priest Pratiprasthātṛ, in order to remove sinful act from the sacrifice,

53. *ardho ha va eṣa ātmanaḥ yajjāyā* — *ŚB* 5.2.1.10
54. *vṛṣā satyaṁ yoṣā śraddhā* । *vṛṣā mano yoṣā vāk* । *yatraiva patistatra jāyā* । — *ŚB* 12.8.2.6
55. *ŚB* 4.1.5.8-9.
56. *VS* 23.30-31; *MS* 3.12.
57. *kastad ādriyeta yat paraḥ-puṁsā syāt . . .* — *ŚB* 1.3.1.21

publicy asked the sacrificer's wife to utter her paramour's name (*kena saha carasi* — *ŚB* 2.5.2.20; cf. *TB* 1.6.5.2).

But all these are stray references rather as exceptions to the general rule that normally the standard of sexual morality was high. The story of Sukanyā proves the validity of this statement. But after all society was human and most probably such isolated cases can be traced in all the ages. Therefore, unnecessary importance need not be attached to this point.

DUTIES OF A HOUSEHOLDER

As regards daily duties of a householder we find there were mainly three or four types of activities: (1) earning livelihood, (2) sustaining family and society, i.e., other orders of life, (3) performance of some daily rites (which were obligatory), and (4) repaying the debts (which people incurred since their birth). In order to do these works people required wealth, therefore the principal duty of this stage was to practise the second *puruṣārtha* (*artha*), i.e., to earn. That is because they followed different vocations (details of which have already been discussed. See Modes of Production, Ch. 4). It is to be remembered here that one's course of life was governed mainly by the vocation, which he followed.

Practice of daily rites (of Vedic people) also may be divided under two headings: (1) *śrauta* (Vedic) and (2) *gṛhya* (domestic). Performance of daily fire-rite (*Agnihotra*) and five great sacrifices (*Pañca Mahāyajña*s) fall under the first category.

AGNIHOTRA

After having installed sacrificial fires and on the completion of Pavamāneṣṭi, the householder started *Agnihotra* from that evening, performance of which became compulsory for him, (i.e., each of the members of three upper castes) since that time. A Ṛgvedic passage may be cited here as a specimen of a householder's daily performance of *Agnihotra* since the early Vedic period, e.g.,

yamī dvā savayasā saparyataḥ samāne yonā mithunā samokasā ।
divā na naktaṁ palito yuvājani purū carannajaro mānuṣā yugā ॥
— *R̥V* 1.144.4

Even gods performed this rite (*R̥V* 1.84.18, 3.4.2).

As regards the details of *Agnihotra*, the *Br* texts provide us information. The sentence *brāhmaṇo 'harahar agnihotraṁ juhuyāt* — instructs a brāhmaṇa to perform the fire-rite daily. As because the term "brāhmaṇa" has been mentioned separately, are we to suppose here that members of other two castes (i.e., kṣatriya and vaiśya) who were entitled to perform *Agnihotra* could appoint a priest to perform it on their behalf?

In the *ŚB* (12.4.1.1) this fire rite has been called *jarāmaryaṁ sattram*, i.e., a compulsory rite from which one could be exempted only on the ground of excessive senility or death. If anyone became physically unable to perform it, only then he could perform it through his son or grandson.[58] But on the new moon or full moon day no proxy was allowed. On these two days he had to do it on his own. With a view to praise this agnihotra the *ŚB* has remarked "Agnihotra is unlimited, never does it come to an end" (*ŚB* 2.3.1.13).

It was performed twice daily in the morning and in the evening to the Sun god and Fire god as its main deities. The name Agnihotra has been justified in the *TB*[59] through a story. As because Prajāpati bestowed this sacrifice to Agni, the whole sacrifice goes by the name of *Agnihotra*. Therefore, people

---

58. *putrān pautrān naptr̥̄nityāhur asmiṁśca loke 'muṣmiṁścāsmi͘lloke 'yaṁ svargo svargeṇa svargaṁ lokam ārurohety amuṣyaiva lokasya santatiṁ dhārayati* । —*AB* 7.10

59. *so 'gnir abibhet/āhutibhir vā mā 'pnotīti* । *sa prajāpatiṁ punaḥ prāviśat* । *tam prajāpatir abrabīt jāyasveti* । *so 'abrabīt kiṁ bhāgadheyam ajaniṣya iti* । *tubhyam evedam huyatā ityabrabīt* । *sa etad bhāgadheyam abhyajāyata yad agnihotraṁ* । *tasmād agnihotram ucyate* । — *TB* 2.1.2.5

offered this rite first to Agni in the evening and then to the Sun god in the morning.[60]

In the morning, oblation was offered to the Sun god accompanied by the hymn *sūryaḥ jyotir jyotiḥ sūryaḥ svāhā* (*VS* 3.9; *TB* 2.1.2.10). The same formula was uttered for the evening oblation with a slight variation *agniṛ jyotiṛ jyotir agniḥ svāhā* (*VS* 3.9; *TB* 2.1.2.10). As regards proper time of *Agnihotra* there was a controversy, whether the morning sacrifice should be performed before sunrise or after sunrise and the same problem was there regarding the time of evening rite. Scholars could not solve it unanimously. Some say, morning rite should be performed before sunrise[61] while others opine, it should be offered after sunrise.[62] Reasons and arguments are there in favour of both the views.[63] The solution is given in the Śrauta-Sūtras. They have reasoned that this difference arose due to the difference of schools. According to the Vahvṛca and the Chandoma School, morning rite was offered before sunrise, they were *anudita homin*s whereas the followers of the Kaṭha, the Taittirīya and Maitrāyaṇīya School offered it after sunrise, they were *udita homins*. But in both the cases they had to cull the fire from *gārhapatya agni* before sunrise[64] and place it on the sacrificial pit. In case of evening rite also the same method

---

60. *taddhūya-mānam ādityo 'brabīt . . . sāyam eva tubhyaṁ juhvan prātar mahyam ityabrabīt* । *tasmād agnaye sāyaṁ hūyate* । *sūryāya prātaḥ* ।
— *TB* 2.1.2.6

61. *yad udite sūrye prātar juhuyāt, yathā 'tithaye pradrutāya śūnyayā-'vasathāyā 'hāryaṁ baranti, tādṛg eva tat . . . tasmād yad auṣasam juhoti tad eva samprati* । — *TB* 2.1.2.12; cf. *ŚB* 2.3.1.5

62. (i) *āgneyī vai rātriḥ* । *aindram ahaḥ* । *yad anudite sūrye prātar juhuyāt* । *ubhayam evā 'gneyaṁ syāt* । *udite sūrye prātar juhoti* ।
— *TB* 2.1.2.7

(ii) *tasmād udite hotavyam* — *AB* 5.29

63. *AB* 5.29; *ŚB* 2.3.1.15; *TB* 2.1.2.7, 2.1.2.12, etc.

64. *uddharāhavanīyam iti prātar āha yad eva rātryā sādhu karoti tad eva tat* । *prāñ uddhṛtya tad abhaye nidhatte* । — *AB* 5.26

was applied, i.e., whether they performed it before sunset or after sunset, they culled the fire before sunset.[65] Another controversy was there (regarding tenure of *Agnihotra*) whether it would be considered as one-day or two-day sacrifice. As because *Agnihotra* starts from the evening, the time should be counted from the evening and in that case the time schedule (as mentioned above, i.e., covering from previous evening to the following dawn) should be considered as one day only.

Regular oblation of *Agnihotra* consisted of milk,[66] that is because a separate milch-cow called *Agnihotrī gābhī*[67] was reared. Milk was boiled in the earthen pot and offered to the deity[68] (*ŚB* 2.3.1.16). A little water was mixed with the milk.[69] An alternative oblation of barley-gruel has been prescribed for the new moon evening *atha yavāgvaitāṁ rātrimagnihotraṁ juhoti* (*ŚB* 1.7.1.10). When people performed *Agnihotra* as an optional rite (*kāmyeṣṭi*) they used some other things, e.g., curd, milk, ghee, rice, etc., according to their desire. Each of the ingredients was conducive to the particular result. According to the *TB* (2.1.5.5-6) people, who desired brilliance used ghee as oblation *ājyena juhuyāttejaskāmasya.* Similarly milk indicated sacrificer's desire for cattle *payasā paśukāmasya.* To attain virile power people offered curd, *dadhnendriyakāmasya.* Barely offering was meant for those who desired village *yavāgvā grāmakāmasya.*

The number of offering and its proper manner have been recorded in the *ŚB* (2.3.1.23) and the *TB* (2.1.2.8). From these texts we find two oblations were offered at a time. In the

65. *uddharāhavanīyam ityaparāhṇa āha, yad evāhnā sādhu karoti tat prāṅ uddhṛtya tad abhaye nidhatte* | — *AB* 5.26
66. *AB* 5.26-27; *ŚB* 2.3.1.14-16; *TB* 2.1.3.2, etc.
67. *yasyāgnihotry upāvasṛṣṭā duhyomānopaviśet* — *AB* 5.27
68. *adhiśrityaiva juhuyāt . . . tad avaijyotayati śṛtaṁ vedānīti, athāpaḥ pratyānayati . . .* — *ŚB* 2.3.1.15-16
69. *gharmo vā eṣo 'śāntaḥ aharahaḥ pravṛjyate yad agnihotraṁ, pratisiñcet* |. . . — *TB* 2.1.3.2

morning first oblation was offered to the Sun god, next one to Prajāpati. In the same manner in the evening two oblations were offered to the Fire god and Prajāpati.[70] Usually the first oblation was offered comparatively little in amount (*kanīyastasya pūrvaṁ hutvā* — *TB* 2.1.4.1) and it was accompanied by the utterance of Yajus *mantra* (*yajuṣā 'ṅyat-*) whereas the latter one was a bigger oblation (*uttaraṁ bhūyo juhuyāt*) — *TB* 2.1.4.1), and it was offered silently (*tūṣṇīm uttarāhutiṁ juhoti* — *TB* 2.1.2.12). At the time of second offering, the sacrificer had to change the former place, and oblation was offered in the eastern direction on the sacrificial faggots (*atihāya pūrvamāhutiṁ juhoti* — *TB* 2.1.4.4). Further, these oblations were to be offered, after the fire was kindled brightly (*ādīptāyaṁ juhoti* — *TB* 2.1.4.9).

From the *AB*[71] (3.40) we have been informed, after having performed the rite in the evening and morning, sacrificer should partake of the remnant milk. According to the *ŚB*[72] this remainder of oblation served as the sacrificer's midday and evening meal. After having performed the rite and distributed the oblative portions all around he could partake the remaining portion only. According to the *TB* this partaking of the remnant of the oblation just after the completion of rite, was a part of the sacrifice (*yat tato 'śnāti hutameva tat* — *TB* 2.1.5.4).

With a view to praise this sacrifice the *ŚB*[73] has stated that in the other world regular performer of *Agnihotra* would be

70. *agneḥ pūrvāhutiḥ, prajāpater uttarā* — *TB* 2.1.7.1; cf. *AB* 5.26

71. *sāyaṁ prātar agnihotraṁ juhvati sāyaṁ prātar vrataṁ prayacchanti* ।
— *AB*. 3.40

72. *sa yat tato rātryā 'śnāti hutocchiṣṭam eva tanniravattabalyaśnāti* । *hutocchiṣṭasya hyevāgnihotraṁ juhvad aśitā* । *sa yat tato ahnā 'śnāti hutocchiṣṭam eva tanniravattabalyaśnāti* । *hutocchiṣṭasya hyevāgnihotraṁ juhvad aśitā* ।
— *ŚB* 2.3.1.11-12

73. *sāyaṁ prātar ha vā amuṣm̐illokehud aśnāti* । — *ŚB* 10.1.5.4

rewarded with good regularly. On the contrary, to abstain from its performance was a serious offence.[74] In that case the sacrificer would be called a mock man.[75] Both the regions (this earth and heaven) would be secluded for him. The sentence *'tasmād apatnīko 'pyagnihotram āharet* (*AB* 7.9) indicates even widowers were not allowed to interrupt or stop its performance.* In order to continue this performance the *AB* has given the widower some alternative suggestions: either he could marry once again and continue performing rites. In case, if he was not willing to remarry, he could perform it through his son or grandson,[76] or having taken Śraddhā as his wife he could perform it mentally.[77] As because this performance was totally mental, it had nothing to do with external ceremonies and ingredients.[78] Hence, it was called *mānasa* or *āntara Agnihotra*. The *ŚĀ*[79] (Ch. Xth) has handled this in detail. Even at the time of staying abroad the sacrificer could not stop it. The *ŚB*[80] has instructed him to continue the

---

74. *tam eṣa devatā 'paruddhā 'paruṇaddhyasmācca lokād amuṣmāccobhābhyāṁ yo'lam agnihotrāya san nāgnihotraṁ juhoti . . . .* — *AB* 5.30
75. *yadi nāhared anaddhā puruṣaḥ* — *AB* 7.9
* In this connection we should remember that bacnelors were not entitled to perform *Agnihotra*.
76. *niviṣṭe mṛtā patnī naṣṭā vā 'gnihotraṁ katham agnihotraṁ juhoti? putrān pautrān naptṝn ityāhu . . .* — *AB* 7.10
77. *yasyaiṣāṁ patnīṁ naicchet . . . śraddhā patnī satyaṁ yajamānaḥ . . . śraddhayā satyena mithunena svagållokāñjayatīti* — *AB* 7.10
78. *yadyu vai sarvaṁ riktaṁ syād . . . ātveva śraddhāyai hotavyam* । — *AB* 5.27; cf. 7.3
79. *athāta ādhyātmikam āntaram agnihotram ityācakṣate* । *. . . daśavidham agnihotraṁ bhavati tasya prāṇa evāhavanīyo 'pāno gārhapatyo vyāno 'nvāhārya-pacano manodhūmo manyur arcayitā aṅgārāḥ, śraddhā payo vāk samit, satyam āhutiḥ prajñātmā sa rasaḥ . .* — *ŚĀ* 10.1, 10.10
80. *yat sa dūraṁ paretyātho tatra pramādyati kasmin sā 'sya hutā 'hutiḥ . . . prāṇam evaitad āha* । *tasmād āhuḥ* । *prāṇa evāgnihotram* । — *ŚB* 11.3.1.7

performance of *Agnihotra* (while staying abroad) by his breath. On his return he showed reverence to the Fire in proper manner.[81]

In the context of *Agnihotra*, various expiatory rites have been prescribed in the Brāhmaṇa[82] texts, which indicates that during the sacrifice, all the shastric injunctions (regarding ritual particulars) were to be followed religiously on violation of which people required these expiations.

PAÑCA-MAHĀYAJÑA

Besides *Agnihotra* people had to perform everyday five great sacrifices (*Pañca-Mahāyajña*) as they have been enunciated in the *ŚB*.[83] According to the Yajurvedic texts people incur some debts from the time of their birth (i.e., to the gods, sages, fathers and men), and for the repayment of these debts Vedic people performed these five types of rites daily. They are: (i) *bhūtayajña*, (ii) *nr̥yajña*, (iii) *pitr̥yajña*, (iv) *devayajña*, and (v) *brahmayajña*.

Actually services of beings have been called *bhūtayajña*. By offering an oblation to the beings the sacrificer performed it.[84]

Nr̥yajña was nothing but to render hospitality to men/guests. The easiest way of performing this rite has been directed in the *ŚB*.[85] By offering a cupful of water to the guests people could perform this rite.

---

81. *tad āhuḥ katham agnīn prāvasannupatiṣṭheta proṣya vā . . . tūṣṇīm ityāhuḥ, tūṣṇīṁ vai śreyasā ākaṅkṣante . . .* — *AB* 7.12

82. *AB* 5.27-28, 7.2-12; *TB* 1.4.4.1-10, etc.

83. *pañcaiva mahāyajñāḥ* । *tāny eva mahāsatrāni bhūtayajño manuṣya-yajñaḥ pitr̥yajño devayajño-brahmayajña iti* । — *ŚB* 11.5.6.1

84. *aharahar bhūtebhyo baliṁ haret* । *tathaitaṁ bhūtayajñaṁ samāpnoti* । — *ŚB* 11.5.6.2

85. *aharahar dadyād odapātrāt* । *tathaitaṁ manuṣyyajñaṁ samāpnoti* । — *ŚB* 11.5.6.2

Other texts also have discussed on this hospitality from which it becomes evident that people rendered hospitality to guests as one of the noble virtues of a householder.[86] The *AV* (9.6) has instructed how to honour and treat the guest in a proper manner. Hospitable reception of the guest has been compared with various rituals (*AV* 9.6.48-54). The *AB* (5.30) sentence *na sāyam atithir aparudhya* has clearly directed that guest should never be repulsed under any circumstances, specially in the evening. In this text, this principle of courtesy and hospitality has been applied to *Agnihotra*, which has stated in the evening the Sun god comes as a guest to the sacrificer, therefore, if the sacrificer fails to offer evening rite he thereby repulses the divine guest.[87] Hence, the *nṛyajña* came to mean as rendering hospitality to the guests. In the *Soma*-sacrifice king Soma was hailed as a guest and rites of hospitality were offered to him, which has been named as *Ātithyeṣṭi* in the *Br* texts. From the description of this *Ātithyeṣṭi*, we have been informed that cooking a great goat or ox in the honour of a king or a brāhmaṇa, was the convention of that period: *tasmād rājñe brāhmaṇāya vā mahokṣaṁ mahājaṁ vā pacet* (*ŚB* 3.4.1.2). In the later ages we find that the teacher in the convocational address advised his students to honour and treat the guest as veritable gods.[88]

The word *pitṛyajña* meant offering oblations to the Fathers. The *ŚB*[89] has advised to perform it by offering a cupful of water with the word *svadhā*. *Devayajña* stood for daily

---

86. *AV* 9.6; *AB* 1.17; *KB* 8.1; *ŚB* 3.4.1.1-2.

87. *eṣa haiva sa ekātithiḥ, sa eṣa juhvatsu vasatyetāṁ vāva sa devatāṁ aparuṇaddhi yo 'lam agnihotrāya san nāgnihotraṁ juhoti . . .*
— AB 5.30

88. *atithi devo bhava . . .* — *Taitt* 1.11.2

89. *aharahaḥ svadhā kuryād odapātrāt* । *tathaitaṁ pitṛyajñaṁ samāpnoti* ।
— *ŚB* 11.5.6.2

performance of Fire-rite. People could perform it even by placing a single log of wood on the fire accompanied with the word *svāhā*.[90]

Lastly there was *brahmayajña*, which was nothing but to continue one's study regularly.[91] The *ŚB*[92] has declared in a distinct language how regular study becomes beneficial to a person. They are source of pleasure to a brāhmaṇa, he becomes ready-minded, independent of others and day by day, he acquires wealth. He sleeps peacefully, he is the best physician for himself and peculiar to him are self-restraint, delight in one thing, growth of intelligence, fame and the task of perfecting the people. Even practice of daily study provides a man with the result of performing religious rites.[93] Therefore, study is compulsory, interruption of which makes a man inactive and immobile.[94] With reference to this context the *ŚB* (11.5.6.8) has furnished a list of the subjects of study (for details see Education, Ch. 6). It is interesting to note here that evey item of study has been compared with sacrificial implements

90. *aharahaḥ svāhā kuryād ākāṣṭhāt* । *tathaitaṁ devayajñaṁ samāpnoti* । — *ŚB* 11.5.6.2

91. *atha brahmayajñaḥ* । *svādhyāyo vai brahmayajñaḥ* । — *ŚB* 11.5.6.3

92. *atha svādhyāyapraśaṁsā* । *priye svādhyāya-pravacane bhavataḥ* । *yuktamanā bhavati* । *aparādhīno 'harahar arthān sādhayate* । *sukhaṁ svapiti* । *parama-cikitsaka ātmano bhavati* ।*indriyasaṁyamaśca* । *ekārāmatā ca* । *prajñāvṛddhiḥ* । *yaśolokapaktiḥ* । *prajñā vardhamānā caturo dharmān brāhmaṇam abhi-niṣpādayati brāhmaṇyaṁ* । *pratirūpa-caryā yaśolokapaktim* । — *ŚB* 11.5.7.1

93. *paya-āhutayo-ha vā etā devānaṁ yad ṛcaḥ* । . . . *ājyāhutayo ha vā etā devānāṁ yad yajūṁṣi* . . . *somāhutayo ha vā etā devānāṁ yad ātharvāṅgirasaḥ* . . . *madhvāhutayo ha vā etā devānāṁ yad anuśāsanāni vidyā* . . . — *ŚB* 11.5.6.4-8

94. *yathā hā vā etā devatā neyur na kuryuḥ evaṁ haiva tad ahar brāhmaṇo bhavati* । *yadahaḥ svādhyāyaṁ nādhīte* । *tasmāt svādhyāyo 'dhyetavyaḥ* । — *ŚB* 11.5.7.10

and rites.[95] According to the prescription of the *ŚB*,[96] if it was not possible for anyone to go through all the texts they could perform this *brahmayajña* only by uttering a single *ṛc* or *sāman* or *yajus* or *kuṁbyā* or a *gāthā*, i.e., just by maintaining regular continuity. And this much only helped a man to get released from his debts to sages which he has incurred at the time of his birth.[97] In order to glorify this *svādhyāya* the *ŚB* has declared, "even if a man studies his lesson though lying on couch, anointed, adorned and completely satisfied (which are normally prohibited for a student) he is burned with the tips of his nails."[98] The *Taitt* (1.9) also has instructed to carry on *svādhyāya* at every stage of life along with other duties. All this proves the importance of daily study.

As a counterpart of these Śrauta sacrifices there were some *gṛhya* rites also. In the everyday life of common people probably these *gṛhya* rites were more important than these *Śrauta* sacrifices which were more expensive and complicated by nature. Not only that, the sacrifices, enjoyed by the Śrauta-Sūtras were meant for an *āhitāgni* only, while *gṛhya* rites were obligatory upon all the householders. Some of them were offered daily, while some others periodically.

BALIKARMA

Among them *bali* offerings were daily rites, which were enunciated in the Sūtra texts. Actually these *bali* offerings are re-oriented forms of *bhūta-yajña* or *bhūta-bali* "offerings to

---

95. *etasya brahma-yajñasya vāgeva juhūr mana upabhṛt, cakṣur dhruvā medhā sruvaḥ satyam avabhṛthah . . .* — *ŚB* 11.5.6.3

96. *tasmādapi ṛcam vā yajurvā sāma vā gāthāṁ vā kuṁbyāṁ vā 'bhivyāharet vratasyā 'vyavacchedāya* । — *ŚB* 11.5.7.10

97. *atha yad evānu-brubīta tenarṣibhya 'ṛṇaṁ jāyate* । *tad dhyebhya etat karoti-ṛṣīṇāṁ nidhigopaḥ-iti hyanūcānam āhuḥ* । — *ŚB* 1.7.2.3

98. *yadi ha vā apy abhyaktaḥ alaṁkṛtaḥ suhitaḥ sukhe śayane śayānaḥ svādhyāyam adhīta 'āhaiva sa nakhāgrebhyas-tapate* । . . . — *ŚB* 11.5.7.4

beings," which is the first one of five great sacrifices, recorded in the *ŚB* (11.5.6.2). According to Sūtra[99] texts it consisted of several offerings on the ground, meant for all sorts of beings. Among them the first one was sacred to the mother Earth, second one was meant for Vāyu, third and fourth were offered for all gods and Prajāpati.[100] Fifth one was offered at the water pitcher meant for the God of Water, the sixth offering was given at the middle post sacred to the herbs, plants and trees, the seventh one was offered at the entrance of door sacred to the Ether, next one was offered in the bed or in the privy, which was meant for God of Love or Wrath and the last one was offered in the dustbin, meant for evil-spirits.[101] The *GGS*[102] continues to say that both the husband and wife were entitled to offer *bali* rites. Husband offered in the morning, and evening was fixed for wife's rite.[103]

Apart from these sacrificial rites people had to perform some other duties and cherish moral values throughout their life. In the *Taitt* (1.11) we find at the end of imparting lessons the teacher used to give his students, some post-instructions for creating proper tendencies in a man, i.e., to follow the duties, inculcated in the Vedas and Smṛti texts religiously.

Truthfulness, righteousness, regular study, copulation and procreation in proper time, performance of rituals for Manes and gods, propitious activities, service for parents, rendering

---

99. *ĀGS* 1.1.3-10; *GGS* 1.4.8-20; *PGS* 2.9.3-7.

100. *sa yat prathamaṁ nidadhāti sa pārthivo balir bhavaty atha yad dvitīyaṁ sa vāyavyo, yat tṛtīyam sa vaiśvadevo yaccaturthaṁ, sa prājā-patyaḥ* ।
— *GGS* 1.4.8

101. *athāparān balīn haret udadhānasya madhyamasya dvārasyabdaivataḥ prathamo balir bhavaty oṣadhivanaspatibhyo dvitīya ākāśāya tṛtīyaḥ* । *atha parān balīn harecchayyāyāṁ vā 'dhivarcaṁ vā sa kāmāya vā balir bhavati manyave vā* । *atha saṁstūpam sa rakṣojanebhyaḥ* । — *GGS* 1.4.9-11

102. *dampatī eva* । — *GGS* 1.4.17

103. *strī ha vā śāyaṁ prātaḥ pumān iti* । — *GGS* 1.4.19

hospitality to the guests, good conduct, charity in modest and friendly way, etc., have been considered as proper duties of a householder.

Vānaprastha and Saṁnyāsa

Though, first two stages of life (i.e., studenthood and domestic life) are frequently spoken of in the Vedic literature, there is hardly any discussion on the other two (i.e., anchorite and renunciation). Therefore, it may not be wrong to presume that these last two stages were not obligatory for all.

Still, occurrence of some terms, scattered in the Brāhmaṇa and Upaniṣads help us infer about these stages. In the famous legend of Śunaḥśepa, we find a verse uttered by the sage Nārada, where he has stressed on the importance of having a son.

> *kiṁ nu khalu malaṁ kim ajinaṁ kiṁ śmaśrūṇi kiṁ tapaḥ* ।
> *putraṁ brāhmaṇa icchadhvaṁ sa vai lokaḥ avadāvadaḥ* ॥

On the basis of Sāyaṇa's[104] commentary the terms *mala, ajina, śmaśru* and *tapaḥ* have been explained by a modern scholar as *caturāśramas* (Basu, *IAB*, p. 223). A point should be noted here that domestic order has been mentioned here at first instead of studentship. This stage has been termed as *mala* the filth, on account of its being connected with impurities and imperfections in comparison to the other stages of life. By the word *ajina* the antelope skin, studenthood has been meant, on account of its being normal dress of students. The word *śmaśru* (beard) signifies *vānaprastha* as because a person

---

104. *atra malājinaśmaśrutapaḥ śabdair āśramacatuṣṭayaṁ vivakṣitam* । *mala-rūpābhyāṁ śukraśoṇitābhyāṁ saṁyogāt malaśabdena gārhasthyaṁ vivakṣitam* । *kṛṣṇājina saṁyogādajinaśabdena brahmacaryaṁ vivakṣitam* । *kṣaura-karmarāhityācchmaśruśabdena vānaprasthaṁ vivakṣitam* । *indriyaniyamanasadbhāvāt tapaḥ śabdena pārivrājyaṁ vivakṣitam* ।
— Sā on *AB* 7.13.4

(following that order) was not allowed to shave and *tapaḥ* the penance bespeaks of the final stage of life. In the *Muṇḍ*[105] (1.2.11) also existence of forest-dwellers and their subsistence on begging only have been hinted at. In the minor Upaniṣads[106] the followers of this third stage have been called *vanī*; but there is least discussion on their (hermits') lifestyle and daily duties. Only the Jābāla sentence *brahmacaryaṁ samāpya gṛhī bhavet, gṛhī bhūtvā vanī bhavet, vanī bhūtvā pravrajet* (4.2) suggests that after having completed the duties and responsibilities of domestic life the person retired to the forest along with his wife leaving the household and property to his children.

However, the Dharma-Sūtras[107] have thrown some light on the lifestyle and regular duties of a forest-dweller. According to the *ĀpDS*[108] (2.9.21.18, 2.9.22.6), people could embrace this life directly after the completion of studenthood or in due order (i.e., after following domestic order). The boy, who went to follow the forest life directly from studenthood, he subsisted on the roots, fruits, leaves and grass collected from the forest and wore garments of forest materials[109] (i.e., bark). He was allowed to keep a fire, but he had no house, enjoyed no pleasure, had no protector.[110] He had to observe silence normally but could speak at the time of

105. *tapaḥśraddhe ye hyupavasantyaraṇye* ।
śāntā vidvāṁso bhaikṣa-caryāṁ carantaḥ ॥ — *Muṇḍ* 1.2.11

106. Jābāla-4; *Bhikṣukopaniṣat*; *Āruṇikopaniṣat*.

107. *ĀpDS* 2.9.21.18-2.9.23.2; *GDS* 3.26-35.

108. (i) *ata eva brahmacaryavān pravrajati* । — *ĀpDS* 2.9.21.19
(ii) *atha vānaprasthasyanupūrvyam eka upadiśanti* । *vidyāṁ samāpya dāraṁ kṛtvā 'gnīn ādhāya karmāṇy ārabhate* । *bahir grāmād vaset* ।
— *ĀpDS* 2.9.22.6-8

109. (i) *tato mūlaiḥ phalaiḥ parṇaistṛṇair iti vartayaṁścaret* । — *ĀpDS* 2.9.22.2
(ii) *tasyāraṇyam ācchādanam vihitaṁ,* — *ĀpDS* 2.9.22.1

110. *tasyopadiśanty ekāgnir aniketas syād aśarmā 'śaraṇo* . . . — *ĀpDS* 2.9.21.20

practising his daily lesson.[111] At the beginning of this stage he was allowed to sustain his life by fruits, etc., collected from forest but in the end he could live on the fruits which has become detached spontaneously and he decreased its limit gradually and then he lived on water, air and ether.[112]

But if he retired to the forest in proper order (after the completion of duties of domestic life) he could live in a hut outside the village along with his family members or he might live there alone. He supported his life by gleaning corns only and did not take any gift from anybody.[113]

Āpastamba in his work quoted others' opinion and stated that the person before leaving the house, prepared two sets of utensils, gave one set to his family and having taken the rest (minimum required implements) for himself retired to the forest. There he performed (daily) burnt oblations with wild corns or fruits (which he collected from the forest) feed the guests and ate himself the rest. According to the *BDS*[114] (3.3.6) he could use the flesh also, killed by carnivorus animals. Besides, he practised his daily study and used bark as his garment. He built a hut for his fire but himself lived under the open sky.[115] If the person who wanted to perform hard austerities he did not make any saving.[116] He collected his

---

111. *tasyopadiśanty . . . muniḥ svādhyāya evotsṛjamāno vācam* ।
— *ĀpDS* 2.9.21.20

112. *tato mūlaiḥ phalaiḥ parṇaistṛṇair iti vartayaṁścaret* । *antataḥ pravṛttāni* । *tato 'po vāyum ākāśam ityabhiniśrayet* । — *ĀpDS* 2.9.22.2-4

113. *gṛhān kṛtvā sadāras saprajas sahāgnibhir bahirgrāmād vaset* । *eko vā* । *siloñchena vartayet* । *na cā 'ta ūrdhvaṁ prati gṛhṇīyat* ।
— *ĀpDS* 2.9.22.8-10

114. *reto 'vasiktā nāma māṁsa-vyāghravṛkaśyenādibhiranyatamena vā hatamānayitvā srapayitvā sāyaṁ prātar agnihotraṁ hutvā yatyatithibhyaśca dattvā 'thetaraccheṣa bhakṣāḥ* । — *BDS* 3.3.6

115. *agnyarthaṁ śaraṇam* । *ākāśe svayam* । — *ĀpDS* 2.9.22.21-22

116. *bhūyāṁsaṁ vā niyamam icchannanvaham eva pātrena sāyaṁ prātar artham āharet* । — *ĀpDS* 2.9.23.1

food everyday by begging and took only as much as was necessary for the day. Gradually he left this practice and started to live on water or air.[117]

The *Baudhāyana Dharma-Sūtra*[118] (3.3.1-14) has recorded names of various schools of forest-dwellers. Some of them cooked their own food, they were *pacamānakā*s; while some (were there who) did not, they were *apacamānakā*s. Those who cooked their food, were divided into five groups, they were (1) *sarvāraṇyakā*s, those who ate everything which the forest contains (even flesh of animals, slain by ferocious animals), (2) *vaitūṣikā*s, those who lived on unhusked grain, (3) *kandamūlabhakṣā*s, those who ate bulbs and roots, (4) *phala-bhakṣā*s, those who ate fruits, and (5) *śākabhakṣā*s, those who ate pot herbs. The members of these schools performed their fire rite (*Agnihotra*) and five great sacrifices everyday, with the articles on which they subsisted.

Those who did not cook their food, they also belonged to five separate schools,[119] viz.: (i) *unmajjakā*s, (ii) *pravṛttāśina*s, (iii) *mukhenādāyinas*, (iv) *toyāhārā*s (subsisting on water only), and (v) *vāyubhakṣā*s (fasting). The first three groups were named after the mode of their taking food.

From this stage he entered the fourth and last stage of life. The story of Yājñavalkya's renouncing has been narrated in the *BU* (4.5.15). Before leaving, Yājñavalkya sought permission from his wife, which proves that renouncing (from

---

117. *tato mūlaiḥ phaliaḥ parṇaistṛṇair iti vartayaṁścaredantataḥ pravṛttāni tato 'po vāyum ākāśamityabhiniśrayet* । — *ĀpDS* 2.9.23.2

118. *atha vānaprasthasya dvaividhyam* । *pacamānakā apacamānakāśceti* । *tatra pacamānakāḥ pañcavidhāḥ* । *sarvāraṇyakā vaitūṣikāḥ kandamūlabhakṣāḥ phalabhakṣā śākabhakṣāśceti* । — *BDS* 3.3.1-3

119. *pañcaiva 'pacamānakāh-unmajjakāḥ pravṛttāśino mukhenādāyinas toyāhārā vāyubhakṣāśceti* । — *BDS* 3.3.9

family life) required prior permission of one's wife.[120] From that time he started to lead a life of austerity and complete resignation to God.

Detailed discussion on *saṁnyāsa*, its (everyday) rites and practises, various schools of ascetics have been traced in the Dharma-Sūtras[121] and minor Upaniṣads[122] as well. From the *ĀpDS*[123] (2.9.21.7-13; cf. *GDS* 3.26-36) we find that they lived without fire, house, pleasure and protection. Remaining silent and uttering speech only to practise daily Vedic studies (*svādhyāya*), begging in village, only as much to sustain his life, they wandered neither caring for this world nor for heaven. Acording to minor Upaniṣads,[124] they were not allowed to live more than one night in a village, five nights in a town and never more than seven nights in an open field. However, the *GDS*[125] (3.13) allowed him to stay in a place during rainy season, but out of that season he did not dwell a second night more in the same village (*GDS* 3.21). Use of clothes was optional for them. They could use clothes thrown away by others or old rags or go naked.[126] They subsisted on begging in village or could eat in any pious man's house but in any case he was not allowed to take more than eight

---

120. *maitreyīti hovāca yājñavalkya pravrajiṣan vā are 'smāt sthānād asmi* । *hanta te 'nayā kātyāyanyā 'ntaṁ karavāṇīti* । — *BU* 4.5.2

121. *GDS* 1.3.10-24; *ĀpDS* 2.9.21.7-13; *BDS* 2.10.17-18.

122. Jābāla 4-5; *Bhikṣukopaniṣat*; *Āruṇikopaniṣat*; Sannyāsopaniṣat 2.18-23; *Nāradaparivrājakopaniṣat*-5;

123. *anagnir aniketas syād aśarmā 'śaraṇo muniḥ svādhyāya evotsṛjamāno vācaṁ grāme prāṇavṛttiṁ pratilabhya 'nihinamūtraścaret* ।
— *ĀpDS* 2.9.21.10

124. *atha haṁsā nāma grāma ekarātraṁ nagare pañcarātraṁ kṣetre saptarātraṁ tad upari na vaseyuḥ* । — *Bhikṣukopaniṣat* 5

125. *dhruvaśīlo varṣāśu* । . . . *na dvitīyām apartuṁ rātriṁ grāme vaset* ।
— *GDS* 1.3.12, 1.3.20

126. *tasya muktam ācchādanaṁ vihitam* । *sarvataḥ parimokṣam eke* ।
— *ĀpDS* 2.9.21.11-12

mouthfuls of rice[127] (or any food). They were beyond virtue and vice, gain or loss, purities or impurities. To them, clods or stone or gold, everything was of equal value. The characteristic feature of an ascetic has been reflected in the last sentence of the *Bhikṣukopaniṣat*[128] (8). Naked as he was born, above the pairs of opposites, without any belongings, wholly devoted to meditation, begging alms in due times only for sustaining his life, staying homeless either in a deserted house, in a temple, on a heap of grass or an ant-hill, at the roots of tree, potter's workshop, fire sanctuary, on a river bank, cave, hollow of tree, at a water fall or on the bare ground firmly rooted in the Supreme Self and pure mind becomes released of this body, by following the manners of *paramahaṁsa* — (he) should be called a *paramahaṁsa*.

Names of different schools of ascetics have been recorded in the *Nāradaparivrājakopaniṣat*.[129] They were *kuṭīcaka, bahūdaka, haṁsa, paramahaṁsa, turīya* and *avadhūta*. Regarding their characteristics all the texts are more or less unanimous. From this discussion we may have a rough idea about *saṁnyāsins* belonging to different categories and their various activities according to their school.

---

127. *aṣṭau grāsā muner bhakṣyāḥ . . .* — *BDS* 2.10.18.15

128. *atha jātarūpa-dhara nirdvandva-niṣparigraḥ, śukla dhyānaparāyaṇa ātmaniṣṭhitah prāṇa saṁ-dhāraṇārthaṁ yathokta kāle bhaikṣam ācarntaḥ śūnyāgāra-devagṛhatṛṇakūṭabalmīka vṛkṣamūla kulālaśālā-gnihotraśālānadī-pulina-giri-kandara-kuhara-koṭara-nirjhara-sthaṇḍile tatra brahmamārge samyaksaṁpannaḥ śuddhamānasaḥ paramahaṁsācaraṇena saṁnyāsena dehatyāgaṁ kurvantīte paramahaṁsā nāmety upaniṣat* ।

— *Bhikṣukopaniṣat* 8

129. *saṁnyāsaḥ ṣaḍvidho bhavati* । *kuṭīcako bahūdako haṁsaḥ parama-haṁsaḥ turīyātīto 'vadhūtaśceti* । — *Nāradaparivrājakopaniṣat* 5.14

8

View of Life

FROM the study of Vedic literature, it appears that people's attitude towards this life (as it has been reflected in the things and practices connected with their everyday life) was not at all pessimistic. On the contrary, it was thoroughly optimistic. The prayer *paśyema śaradaḥ śataṁ, jīvema śaradaḥ śatam* (*R̥V* 7.66.16) clearly reflects people's appreciation of this worldly life. The *AV* (XII) has described this earth as full of treasures and "a nice place to live in."

Long life[1] was one of their desired objects, and to make this life smooth, rich and enjoyable they required ample food,[2] rain,[3] cattle,[4] furnished dwelling,[5] strength,[6] heroic offspring,[7] safe delivery of pregnant ladies,[8] etc. With a desire to attain worldly prosperity they practised different modes of production (details of which have already been discussed under Mode of Production and Other Occupations, Ch. 4).

---

1. *R̥V* 6.2.5, 6.3.6, 7.66.16, etc.
2. *R̥V* 1.48.14-16, 1.49.4, 1.71.6-7, 2.9.5, 6.1.12, 7.32.23, etc.
3. *R̥V* 1.129.3, 6.31, 6.44.18, 7.103, 10.98.8-10; *AV* 3.24, 6.129.2-3, 7.39.1, etc.
4. *R̥V* 1.42.1-20, 5.20.4, 6.1.12, 7.32.23, 7.92.3-4, 7.97.9, 8.76.1-3, 8.76.9.
5. *R̥V* 7.1.7, 7.1.19, etc.
6. *R̥V* 1.58.7-9, 1.71.6-7, 1.79.11, 1.151.1.
7. *R̥V* 1.58.8, 1.149.5, 2.9.5, 5.20.4, 7.96.4-6.
8. *R̥V* 5.78.7-9, 10. *AV* 1.11.1; *BU* 6.4.23, etc.

With the same intention they also invoked gods and uttered prayers to them. Practice of varieties of vocations and utterance of prayer to the deities for the same purpose makes it clear that people attached so much importance to the attainment of worldly prosperity. Equal stress has been laid for its enjoyment (*kāma*). In majority of the ritual performances (recorded in the *Br* texts especially in the *ŚB*) concept of sexual behaviour has been suggested,[9] which makes us believe that enjoyment of sexual pleasures was no less important to the people. Through the performance of these rites they wanted to achieve success in this aspect in their practical life. From the *Taitt*[10] we find that copulation and procreation in proper time were considered within compulsory duties of a householder. Otherwise he would become a defaulter in his duties.

People's belief in supernatural agents and objects (both the auspicious and inauspicious) and their (these objects/ things) impact on their practical life have been reflected in their utterance of prayer and performance of rites. They believed in both the gods and demons.[12] Similarly, they had belief in the power of hymns (uttered to the gods[13]) and charms/spells[14] as well. That is why by the aid of prayer, worship and sacrifice they attempted to propitiate gods for their welfare[15] and by the employment of charms, magic rites, amulets, etc., they tried to remove evil effects of trouble-creating demons and goblins and to overcome misfortune

9. *MS* 4.7.4; *KS* 28.8; *KapKS* 44.8; *TS* 6.5.8.5-6; *AB* 2.35, 2.38-39, 6.3; *ŚB* 1.1.1.20-22, 1.8.3.11, 1.2.5.15, 1.9.2.1-11, 1.9.2.21-24, 4.6.7.9-12, 6.3.1.10, 13.2.8.1-5, 13.5.10.2-3, etc.

10. *ācāryāya priyaṁ dhanam āhṛtya prajātantuṁ mā vyavacchetsīḥ* ।
— *Taitt* 1.11.1

11. *ṚV* 1.1.1-1.1.9, 1.19.9, 1.115.1-6, 1.159.1-2, etc.

12. *AV* 5.29, 5.31, 8.3, 8.4, 8.6, etc.

13. *ṚV* 1.42.1-10, 1.7.6, 1.29.5-7, 1.58.8, etc.

14. *AV* 1.11.1, 1.2.4, 3.24, 5.4.1-2, 6.42.1-2, 6.56, 6.106.2.

15. *MS* 2.1.10, 2.2.2, 4.11.4; *TS* 1.3.14, 2.2.3, etc.

and calamities.[16] Thus, at every step of life (be it for the acquisition of *dharma* or *artha* or for their enjoyment, i.e., *kāma*) they followed a joint process of employing human endeavour and seeking divine intervention.

From the study of Vedic texts we find that religion (*dharma*) covered different aspects of their life. Actually religion was not any institution to the Vedic Indians, better to say it was their way of life. From birth to death their entire life was subordinated to the religious concepts. That is why at every juncture of life, they performed sacraments,* i.e., *jātakarma, annaprāśana, upanayana, vivāha,* etc., which attached sanctity to the particular stage.

People considered their whole life as a collection of debts (to the gods, sages, fathers and men[17]) and they tried to get released of these debts through the pursuit of *artha* and *kāma* restrained by the employment of *dharma*, i.e., sense of duty. Some obligatory rites were to be performed as daily duties, without having any expectation of results. Daily fire rite (*Agnihotra*) and five great sacrifices (*Pañca-Mahāyajña*) fall under this group. We have already discussed it in the previous chapter. (See under Daily duties of Householder in Social Life, Ch. 7.)

---

16. *AV* 2.2.5.5.29.8-10, 5.31.3-4, 8.6.23, etc.

* All these sacraments have been discussed in detail by the eminent scholars like P.V. Kane in the *History of Dharma-Śāstras*, vol. II, Part I-II; R.B. Pandey in the *Hindu Saṁskāras* and Ram Gopal in the *India of the Vedic Kalpasūtras*, Ch. XI-XVI. As we have nothing new to contribute in this aspect, I have abstained from its discussion.

17. (i) *jāyamāno vai brāhmaṇastribhir ṝṇavā̐ jāyate* । *brahmacaryeṇa ṛṣibhyo yajñena devebhyaḥ prajayā pitṛbhya* । *eṣa vā anṛṇo yaḥ putrī yajvā brahmacarīvāsi . . .* — *TS* 6.3.10.5

    (ii) *ṛṇaṁ ha vai jāyate yo 'sti* । *sa jāyamana eva devebhya ṛṣibhyaḥ 'pitṛbhyo manuṣyebhyaḥ* । — *ŚB* 1.7.2.1

Śrauta Sacrifices

The sacrifice occupies a very important position in the Vedic literature. It was through the sacrifices that the Vedic people tried to enter into communion with the gods. Though these sacrifices are not daily rites, they are significant for understanding their view of life. These sacrifices were of three types, viz.: (A) compulsory *nitya,* (B) occasional *naimittika,* and (C) optional *kāmya.*

COMPULSORY

The compulsory sacrifices were not performed for the fulfilment of desires; they were performed as a duty in discharge of one's debt to the gods.

Among them at first we should mention the name of the *Darśapūrṇamāsa* rite which people practised on every fortnight. The word *Darśa* means confluence of the Sun and the Moon, i.e., the new moon day called *amāvasyā* and *Pūrṇamāsī* stands for the full moon day. The names indicate that Darśayāga was performed on the new moon day and Paurṇamāsīyāga was performed on the full moon day. The members of the three upper castes who were neither bachelors nor widowers were entitled to perform this rite. The ceremony lasted two days. In case of full moon rite, it started from the morning of full moon day and lasted up to the next forenoon (i.e., *pratipadā*). It was the same with the new moon rite, which continued from the morning of new moon up to the next forenoon.[18] Obviously when people started to perform this rite for the first time they started from the full moon rite. All the details of this sacrifice have been discussed in the *TS* (1st Prapāṭhaka) and the *ŚB* (1st Kāṇḍa). Some people performed it life-long (on every new moon and full moon) as obligatory rite, while others performed it optionally/

18. *TS* 1.1.2ff; *ŚB* 1.1.1.11ff.

occasionally, i.e., for the fulfilment of their desire (i.e., *kāmyeṣṭi*).

In the list of their religious rites/activities there were seasonal sacrifices also (*cāturmāsya*), which were performed on every fourth month, viz., Vaiśvadeva, Varuṇapraghāsa, Śākamedha/Śunāsīrīya. Actually on the commencement of every season (i.e., the Spring, the Rainy Season and the Autumn) people performed these rites as forms of seasonal festival.[19] The Vaiśvadeva[20] (*ŚB* 2.6.3.13) was performed on the full moon of Phālguna, the Varuṇapraghāsa coincided with the Aṣāḍhā full moon,[21] and the Śākamedha was celebrated on that of Kārttika.[22] In the *ŚŚS* (3.13.1, 3.14.1-2, 3.15.1) the Caitrī, the Śrāvaṇī, and the Mārgaśīrṣī full moon have been prescribed as alternative dates for the performance of these rites.

Further, there was an annual sacrifice called the *Agniṣṭoma* literally meaning the praise of Agni. It was considered as model for all the *Soma* sacrifices,[23] and closely related to *Jyotiṣṭoma*. This sacrifice was named so, as because it ended with the chanting of *Agniṣṭoma stotra*. Every year the sacrificer performed it in the Spring.[24] The main oblation constituted of *Soma* juice. The rare creeper Soma was to be procured from distant places and preserved with care. As because it was not

19. *bhaiṣajya yajña vā ete yaccāturmāsyāni tasmād ṛtusandhiṣu prayujyante* ।
— *KB* 5.1

20. *tad yat phālgunyāṁ paurṇamāsyāṁ yat vaiśva devena yajate* ।
— *ŚB* 2.6.3.13

21. *atha yad eṣa etaiścaturthe māsi yajate . . . tā ubhayor varuṇapāśāt muñcate* ।
— *ŚB* 2.5.2.4

22. *athaitaiḥ śākamedhaiḥ . . . tasmād vā eṣa etaiścaturthe māsi yajate* ।
— *ŚB* 2.5.3.1

23. *agniṣṭomaḥ prathamaḥ yajñaḥ* । — *ĀpDS* 10.2.3

24. *vasante vasante jyotiṣṭomena yajeta* । — *ĀpDS* 10.2.5

easily available some alternative names have been prescribed in the *ŚB*,[25] as its substitutes. All the sixteen priests were required for the performance of *Agniṣṭoma*. According to the Kauṣītakins, a seventeenth priest named *Sadasya* was also required.[26]

The rites continued for five days; though the ceremonies, viz., selection of priests (*ṛtvikvaraṇam*), sacrificer's initiation (*dīkṣaṇīyeṣṭi*), initial sacrifice (*prāyaṇīyeṣṭi*), purchase of Soma (*Soma-krayaṇa*), reception of Soma (*ātithyeṣṭi*) etc., covering first four days served as a prelude to the actual *Soma* sacrifice, which was performed on the fifth day. On this fifth day called *sutyā* the ceremony of extraction of Soma (*Somābhiṣava*) took place. The preparations started long before the dawn. All the required utensils, viz., *droṇakalaśa, daśāpavitra, pūtabhṛt*, etc., were kept arranged. The Hotṛ priest recited the verses known as *prātaranuvāka* at the early dawn (i.e., before the chirping of birds). Just after it the pressing of Soma started, which was done in all the three *savanas*, called morning, midday and third *savana*. Soma was placed on a slab of stone and sprinkled with the water named *vasatīvarī*. The juice was extracted by pressing it with another piece of stone. After being percolated through a sieve named *daśāpavitra* the juice was kept in a pitcher, i.e., *droṇakalaśa*. In all the savanas *stotras* were chanted and *Śastras* were recited. The pressing was followed by the libations of Soma, also of cakes, a hot mixture of milk and sour milk, etc. Then the remnants of oblations were partaken of by the sacrificer and his priests. After the midday libation sacrificial

---

25. *yadyu na vindanti . . . dvayāni vai phālgunāni lohitapuṣpāṇi ca aruṇapuṣpāṇi ca sa yāny aruṇapuṣpāṇi phālgunāni tany abhiṣuṇuyāt . . . yady aruṇapuṣpāṇi na vindeyuḥ ı śyenahṛtam abhiṣuṇuyāt . . . yady śyenahṛtaṁ na vindeyuḥ ı ādārān abhiṣuṇuyāt . . . yadi ādārān na vindeyuḥ ı aruṇadūrvā abhiṣuṇuyāt . . . yady aruṇadūrvā na vindeyuḥ ı api yāneva kāṁśca haritakuśān abhiṣuṇuyāt . . .* — *ŚB* 4.5.10.1-6

26. *sadasyaṁ saptadaśaṁ kauṣitakinaḥ samāmananti ı* — *ĀpDS* 10.1.10

fees were distributed among the priests. The third and last libation of Soma was followed by the ablution ceremony (*avabhṛtha iṣṭi*). All the oblutions of this ceremony were offered in the water, where all the priests along with the sacrificer went to take a bath, and this rite marked the conclusion of Agniṣṭoma. (For further details see *ĀpDS* X-XIV; *BŚS* VI-X; *KŚS* VII-XI, *HDS*, vol. II, part 2, pp. 1133-1203).

OCCASIONAL

Now the occasional rites (*naimittika*) which people performed neither daily nor under any desire, but they had to perform it under certain circumstances (may be auspicious or not), e.g., in the pleasure of begetting a son people performed *Putreṣṭi* meant for Vaiśvānara Agni.[27] If there was any fire incident people sacrificed to Kṣāmavat Agni to get rid of it.[28] Similarly funeral rites, ancestral rites, viz., the *Pitṛmedha, Piṇḍapitṛ-Yajña*, etc., should come under this group.

Pitṛmedha was performed in respect of the death of an *agnihotrin*. In the *AV* there are at least four hymns (18.1-4) which are entirely devoted to *Pitṛmedha*. From the textual context it appears that some of these formulas were employed at the time of cremation. The rites of *Pitṛmedha* have been recorded in the *ŚB* (12.5.2.1-15). The sentence *athaitāṁ āhutiñjuhoti putro vā bhrātā vā yovā 'nyo brāhmaṇaḥ syāt* (*ŚB* 12.5.2.15) suggests that preferably these rites were performed by the son of the dead person. In the absence of son, his brother or some other brāhmaṇa could do it for him. The *ŚB* has remarked about this rite: *tāṁ vā etāṁ yajamānātmāhutim antato karoti* (*ŚB* 12.5.2.13). This is the offering of the sacrificer's body, which he performs at the end. Most probably as the sacrificer's

27. *vaiśvānaraṁ dvādaśa kapālaṁ nirvapet putre jāta iti* I
— *TS* 2.2.5.3; *BŚS* 13.8

28. *yasya gṛhān dahaty agnaye kṣāmavate puroḍāśam aṣṭākapālaṁ nirvapet bhāgadheyenaivainaṁ śamayati nāsyāparaṁ gṛhān dahati* I
— *TS* 2.2.2.5

body was used here as oblation, therefore, this rite has been named as *Pitṛmedha* in the later texts.

Another ancestral rite *Piṇḍapitṛyajña* has been described through a narrative in the *ŚB* (2.4.2.1-24). From this story we come to know that *Piṇḍapitṛyajña* was performed every month on the new moon day.[29] Afternoon was fixed as the proper time of offering this rite. According to the *TB*'s[30] instruction people performed this rite on the former day of new moon rite. In this rite three oblations (*piṇḍa*s) were offered to the father, grandfather and great grandfather of the sacrificer.[31] After having offered the oblations the sacrificer paid obeisance to them.[32] In the *TB*[33] this *Piṇḍapitṛyajña* has been declared as the only sacrifice for the Fathers, others being offered to the gods.

Another ancestral rite was performed as a part of Cāturmāsyayāga by offering (1) a cake (prepared on six potsherds) for Soma Pitṛmat, (2) parched barley grain for the Fathers, seated on *barhi*s, and (3) a porridge of parched grains cooked in milk for the Fathers, consumed by the Fire.[34] On

---

29. *athainaṁ pitaraḥ । prācīnāvītinaḥ savyaṁ jānvā cyopāsīdan । tān avravīt-māsi māsi vo 'śanam . . . tad vā etān māsi māsy eva pitṛbhyo dadato yadaivaiṣa na purastāt na paścāt dadṛśe ।* — *ŚB* 2.4.2.2, 2.4.2.7

30. *indro vṛtraṁ hatvā asurān parābhāvya so 'māvāsyāṁ pratyāgacchat te pitaraḥ pūrvedyur āgacchan । . . . asmabhyam eva pūrvedyuḥ kriyatā । tam ebhyaḥ punar adaduḥ । tasmāt pitṛbhyo pūrvedyuḥ kriyate ।* — *TB* 1.3.10.1-2

31. *sa dadāti asāvetat te–ityeva yajamānasya pitre । asāvetat ta iti pitāmahāya । asāvetat ta iti prapitāmahāya . . .* — *ŚB* 2.4.2.19

32. *namaskaroti । namaskāro hi pitṛṇāṁ ।* — *TB* 1.3.10.8

33. *eṣa vai manuṣyāṇāṁ yajñaḥ । devānāṁ vā itare yajñāḥ ।* — *TB* 1.3.10.9

34. *sa pitṛbhyaḥ somavadbhyaḥ ṣaṭkapālaṁ puroḍāśaṁ nirvapati somāya vā pitṛmate . . . ।*

    atha pitṛbhyo barhiṣadbhyaḥ । . . . te dhānā pitṛbhyo varhiṣadbhyaḥ । . . . atha pitṛbhyo 'gniṣvāttebhyaḥ । . . . — *TB* 2.6.1.4-6

account of its being distinguished from monthly *Pitṛyajña*, it was called *Mahāpitṛyajña*. Through the performance of these rites people's respectful attitude towards the dead ancestors has been hinted at.

OPTIONAL

To the third group belong prayers, worships and rites, which were performed optionally for the fulfilment of their desires. In spite of not being daily rites they had relevance to common people's life, because they were performed in order to obtain results pertaining to various aspects of everyday life.

As already mentioned, on the one hand people uttered prayers and invoked gods (seeking their favour) in order to propitiate them and at the same time to avoid disease,[35] misfortune[36] in their everyday life, to overcome enemies in strife and struggles. On the other hand, they were habituated to perform rites (*kāmyeṣṭis* — as recorded in the *YS*'s[37] texts) for the same purpose. From this their reliance on both the *dṛṣṭa* and *adṛṣṭa phala* can be presumed. It is interesting to observe that prayers and rites were employed even to perfect well-knit household relationship.[38] Attaining glory,[39] immortality[40] and heaven[41] also were other objects of their desire.

---

35. *MS* 2.2.7; *KS* 11.3; *TS* 2.2.10, 2.3.5, 2.4.14, etc.
36. *ṚV* 1.128.5, 1.129.10.11, 10.87.1; *AV* 19.55.1; *VS* 11.75; *TS* 1.2.14.6, etc.
37. *MS* 2.1.10, 2.2.2-4, 2.4.7-8; *TS* 2.2.1-5, etc.
38. *ṚV* 5.28.3; cf. *AV* 7.13.10; *VS* 33.12; *TB* 2.41.1, 2.5.2.8, etc.
39. *vācaspataye caruṁ nirvapet śrīkāmo* — *MS* 2.2.5.
40. *apāma somam amṛtā abhūmāganma jyotir avidāmadevān* । — *ṚV* 8.48.3
41. *ṚV* 1.31.7, 6.1.7; *TS* 2.3.4; *MS* 4.10.1, etc.

Gṛhya Rites

All these Śrauta rites were complicated by nature and too much expensive for the common people, therefore, it was not always possible for all of them to perform. But as a counterpart of these Śrauta rites there were some Gṛhya rites also, which people performed on every important occasion, e.g., at the advent of new season (*ŚB* 2.6.3.13), consecration of a newly built house (*AV* 3.12) partaking of new fruits of the season (*AB* 7.19), celebration of new year (*AV* 3.10.2-3), out of snake fear, etc. In spite of not being daily rites* they were closely concerned with the livelihood of common people. Therefore, performance of these rites had an important role in their livelihood, because they were simpler in form, less expensive, more popular and participated by all the family members. Not only that, the sacrifices enjoined by the Śrauta-Sūtras were meant for an *āhitāgni* only, while Gṛhya rites were obligatory upon all the householders.

In the Brāhmaṇa texts these Gṛhya rites have been called *pākayajña* the offering of cooked food. In the *TS*,[42] sacrificer's partaking of the remnant of oblation has been regarded as a form of *pākayajña*. Invocation of Iḍā also has been considered as representation of *pākayajña* in the *Br*[43] texts. But as regards their varieties or any further details only the Sūtra literature provide us information. However, Āgrayaṇeṣṭi has been discussed in the Brāhmaṇas[44] and Aṣṭakā[45] has been mentioned in several passages.

---

* Daily Gṛhya rites have been discussed in the previous chapter under the Daily Duties of a householder. See, Social Life, Ch. 7.

42. *prātar madhyandine sāyaṁ tan manorvratam āsīt* । *pākayajñasya rūpam iti* . . . — *TS* 6.2.5.4

43. *iḷām upāhvayate, iḷāvidhā vai pākayajñāḥ* . . . — *AB* 3.40; cf. *ŚB* 1.8.1.16, 1.8.1.18

44. *AB* 7.9; *ŚB* 2.4.3.1ff; *TB* 1.6.1.9.

45. *AV* 3.10.2-3, 3.10.8, 3.10.12; *TS* 4.3.11.8, etc.

Scholars are not unanimous regarding the number of *pāka-yajñas*. However, the *GDS*[46] has recorded names of seven types of *pākayajñas*, viz., (1) *Pārvaṇa*, (2) *Śrāvaṇī* or *Sarpabali*, (3) *Āśvayujī*, (4) *Āgrahāyaṇī* or *Pratyavarohaṇa*, (5) *Āgrayaṇeṣṭi*, (6) *Piṇḍa-pitṛyajña*, and (7) *Aṣṭakā*. There are disputes among scholars regarding the proper time of their celebration and ritual ceremonies also. Ram Gopal has discussed these Gṛhya rites with all their niceties (For details, see *IVKS*, Ram Gopal, Ch. XVIV-XVIII).

The ceremony of entering a newly built house (*Śālā-karman*) was another popular domestic rite. From the *AV* (3.12) it appears that people performed it to consecrate the newly built house, before they started to live there (so that their living in the new house would be safe and secured). Having taken two important necessities of daily life, i.e., fire and a well filled water pot the householder and his wife entered the new house.[47] The wife, clad in grass robe carried the water pot on her head.[48] Probably she did it under the intention that her household in the new house would be full of prosperity and abundance.

Thus, at every step of life by performing various rites, people tried to establish a friendly connection with gods.

Death as Viewed by People

As already mentioned people's attitude towards this world and worldly life was very much optimistic. Their attraction

---

46. *aṣṭakā pārvaṇśrāddhaṁ śrāvaṇyāgrahāyaṇī caitry āśvayujīti sapta pākayajña-saṁsthāḥ* । — *GDS* 1.8.19

47. *imā āpaḥ prabharāmy ayakṣmā yakṣmanāśanīḥ* ।
gṛhān upa prasīdāmy amṛtena sahāgninā ॥
— *AV* 3.12.9

48. *mānasya patni śaraṇā syonā devī devebhir nirmitāsy agre* ।
tṛṇaṁ vasānā sumanā asastvam athāsmabhyaṁ sahavīraṁ rayiṁ dāḥ ॥
pūrṇam nāri prabhara kumbham etaṁ ghṛtasya dhārām amṛtena saṁbhṛtām ।
imām pātṝn amṛtenā samaṅgdhīṣṭāpūrtam abhi rakṣāty enām ॥
— *AV* 3.12.5, 3.12.8

for this life has been prominently expressed in the utterance of prayers to the gods seeking long life and in the performance of sacrifices (with the same desire) as well. Quite normally as a lover of this life they tried to avoid the premature approach of death. The hymns, e.g. :

(1) *paraṁ mr̥tyo anu parehi panthām* (R̥V 10.18.1) a request to death to depart away,

(2) *mr̥tyoḥ padaṁ yopayanto yadai ta drāghīya āyuḥ prataraṁ dadhānāḥ* (10.18.2), people's effort to efface the step of death, or

(3) *imaṁ jīvebhyaḥ paridhiṁ dadhāmi maiṣaṁ nu gād aparo artham etam* (10.18.4), their effort to keep death beyond the limit of this world of living beings,

lend support to the fact.

The passages of Funeral Hymn (*R̥V* 10.18; *AV* 18.1-18.4) throw some light on pre-cremation and post-cremation rites prevalent at that time. From all this, it appears that death to the Vedic people was nothing but a natural termination of life. Of course, its first blow was always painful and overwhelming to the relatives (of the dead) especially to his near and dear ones (e.g., wife, sons, etc.).

> *iyaṁ nāri patilokaṁ vr̥ṇāna nipadyata upatvā martya pretam* ।
> *dharmaṁ purāṇam anupālayantī* ॥ — *AV* 18.3.1

The description of a widow lying beside her dead husband, and ready to follow him (even after death), makes us feel the pangs of separation with which the woman was stricken. The phrase *dharmaṁ purāṇam anupālayantī* (rendered as preserving the ancient custom) suggests that custom of following the husband in his death, was known to the people. But the passage *udīrṣva nāri abhijīvalokam* (*R̥V* 10.19.8; cf. *AV* 18.3.2), i.e., a request to the widow to return back to the normal life proves that this custom was not compulsory. The woman overwhelmed with grief was ready to sacrifice her life. But her relatives were there, they knew that the approach of death was invariable and quite natural also. But to embrace death just under the craze of grief/out of emotion, was not supportable. From the *ĀGS* (4.2.18) *tām utthāpayed devaraḥ patisthānīyaḥ* . . . we find that people did not allow the widow to die; rather they consoled her and brought her back home. The term *devaraḥ patisthānīyaḥ* (the brother-in-law as representative of husband) indicates that in some cases the said person married the widow. Because no people can live with grief only. Further, the passage *prāñco agāma nṛtaye hasāya* (*ṚV* 10.18.3) (we have gone forth for dancing and for laughter, to further times prolonging our existence) indicates that other relatives of the dead after having rendered proper duties to the deceased person, returned back to the normal course of life.

In the Brāhmaṇa texts[49] death has been described as the third birth. Three births of a man have been recorded in the *ŚB*,[50] the first one being his physical birth, second one his initiation in the sacrifice and third one being through the cremation rite. According to the *ŚB* people believed that after death the person would be born again in the next world. At the time of cremation if *gārhapatya* fire reached him first (people believed) that man would be established in Heaven permanently. If *āhavanīya* touched him first, that was considered as a sign of becoming (the person's) foremost to conquer the other world. If *anvāhārya pacana* reached him first

---

49. *ye vai tat karma kurvate mṛtvā punaḥ sambhavanti te sambhavanta evāmṛtatvam abhisambhavanti* । — *ŚB* 10.4.3.10

50. *trir ha vai puruṣo jāyate* । *etānneva mātuścādhi pituścāgre jāyate* । . . . *sa yad yajate taddvitīyaṁ jāyate* । *atha yatra mriyate yatraitam agnāvabhyādadhāti – sa yat tata sambhavanti – tat tṛtīyaṁ jāyate* ।
— *ŚB* 11.2.1.1

that was considered a sign of his getting ample food in the next world.[51]

But they believed that of course the world (of dead) was different from this one (where living people belonged to). That is why from the very beginning they tried to maintain a safe distance between these two worlds (of the dead ones' and living ones'). Therefore, after the completion of funeral rites when the mourners returned back they were given ointments of eyes and feet, with the intention that thereby they would keep the influence of death away from them.[52] With the same intention, they deposited a clod (brought from the boundary of cremation ground) in the midway which according to their belief served as a boundary between this world and the world of death.[53]

In the Darśapūrṇamāsa rite, a grass effigy of the sacrificer was burnt under the notion that through this rite the sacrificer would reach Heaven.[54] With reference to this context the *ŚB* has instructed the priest to burn the effigy in such a manner so that the sacrificer would reach Heaven after having lived a full span of this life,[55] which appears to indicate

51. *tam yadi gārhapatyaḥ pūrvaṁ prāpnuyāt, tad vidyāt, pratiṣṭhāḥ evam agniḥ pūrvaḥ prāpat, pratiṣṭhāsyati, . . . atha yady āhavanīyaḥ tad vidyāt, mukhya evam agniḥ pūrvaḥ prāpat, mukhato lokān ajaiṣī, . . . atha yad anvāhāryapacanaḥ tadvidyāt, annād evam agniḥ pūrvaḥ prāpat, annam atsyati,* — *ŚB* 12.5.2.9-11

52. *tebhya āgatebhya āñjanābhyañjane prayacchanti* । *eṣa ha mānuṣo 'laṅkāraḥ* । *tenaiva taṁ mṛtyum antardadhate* । — *ŚB* 13.8.4.7

53. *maryādāyā vā eva loṣṭram āhṛtyāntareṇa nidadhāti . . . jīvebhyaścaitāṁ pitṛbhyaśca maryādāṁ karoti* । . . . — *ŚB* 13.8.4.12

54. *atha prastaram ādatte* । *yajamāno vai prastaraḥ* । *tad yatrāsya yajño 'gan – tad evaitat yajamānaṁ svagākaroti* । *devalokaṁ vā asya yajño 'gan devalokam evaitad yajamānam api nayati* । — *ŚB* 1.8.3.11

55. *athaikaṁ tṛṇam apagṛhṇāti* । *yajamāno vai prastaraḥ* । *sa yat kṛtsnaṁ prastaram anupraharet – kṣipre ha yajamāno 'muṁ lokam iyāt; tatho ha yajamano jyog jīvati* । *yāvad u evāsyeha mānuṣam āyuḥ – tasmād evaitad apagṛhṇāti* । — *ŚB* 1.8.3.16

that people always tried to avoid the premature death; but its approach in the mature age of man was always welcome. This idea, i.e., the feeling of a dying person (on the eve of his death) has been recorded in the Āraṇyaka (*ŚĀ* 4.15) and Upaniṣads.[56] From these texts, it appears that people accepted death most calmly, as a natural termination of life tenure. When the person could feel the approach of death he called his son and transferred his powers and traditions in the prescribed way.

The account of a dying father's bequest of his powers and tradition to the son has been recorded in the Upaniṣads (*SĀ* 4.15; *Kauṣ* 2.15; *BU* 1.5.17-20). The preparation of this transformation has been described in detail in the *Kauṣītaki Upaniṣad*[57] (2.15). The father, when about to die having strewn the house with new grass, laid the fire, placed a full water pot and a jar of rice, clothed in a new garment, called his son, gave him last instructions and transferred his tradition (from himself) to him and the son accepted it accordingly. According to the *BU*[58] he did it with the desire, should anything be left undone by him through any slip, the son would exonerate him from all those things. He would live in this world through his son (*BU* 1.5.17).

---

56. *BU* 1.5.17; *Kauṣ* 2.15.

57. *athātaḥ pitāputrīyaṁ sampradānam iti cā 'cakṣate | pitā putraṁ preṣyann āhvayati | navais tṛṇair agāram samāstīryāgnim upasamādhāyodakumbhaṁ sapātraṁ upanidhāyāhatena vāsasā saṁpracchannaḥ svayaṁ śyeta etya putra upariṣṭād abhinipadyate | indriyair asyendriyāṇi saṁspṛśya apivā 'syābhimukhata evāsīta | athāsmai samprayacchati | . . .*

— *Kauṣ* 2.15

58. *tasmāt putram anuśiṣṭam lokyam āhustasmād enam anuśāsati . . . sa yadyanena kiñcid akṣṇayā 'kṛtaṁ bhavati tasmād enaṁ sarvasmāt putro muñcati tasmāt putro nāma | sa putreṇaivāsm̐lloke pratitiṣṭhati |*

— *BU* 1.5.17

Desire for Heaven

In the early stage people were more interested about this world and worldly life. They employed their every effort to procure success in these aspects, but performance of sacrifice and attainment of worldly success could not satisfy them totally. That people were conscious about the existence of a higher world (Heaven) beyond this material one, has been suggested in some passages (scattered in Vedic Saṁhitā and Brāhmaṇas).

Heaven has been mentioned as the dwelling place of divinities.[59] Three divisions of this heaven, viz., *uttama* the highest, *uttara* the middle and *pārya* or *avama* the lowest have been recorded in the *ṚV*.[60] The *AV*[61] has given us three other names for three heavens; those are *udanvatī*, *pīḷumatī* and *pradyaus* as the residence of the Fathers. In the *ŚB* heaven has been mentioned as a counterfeit of this world (8.3.3.5), somewhere as a place of safety (12.8.1.22), etc. That heaven was one of people's chief desired objects has been reflected in the prayers uttered to the deities.[62] In some cases people wanted to achieve the same region with the deity (*sālokya*), even sometimes identification with him (*sāyujya*/*sārūpya*).[63]

This yearning for heaven has become more prominent in the Brāhmaṇa texts. There are some passages, e.g.,

---

59. *ṛco 'kṣare parame vyoman yasmin viṣve adhi devā niṣeduḥ* ।
— *ṚV* 1.164.39

60. (i) *yad uttame madhyame vā yad vāvame subhagāso divi ṣṭha* ।
— *ṚV* 5.60.6

    (ii) *ṚV* 4.26.6.

    (iii) *pārya* — *ṚV* 6.40.5

61. *udanvatī dyaur avamā pīḷumatī madhyamā* । *tṛtīya ha pradyaur iti yasyām pitara āsate* ॥ — *AV* 18.2.48

62. *ṚV* 1.31.7, 6.1.7, 9.113.

63. *AB* 1.6, 2.24, 3.41; *ŚB* 11.4.4.2-7, 11.6.2.2-3, 12.1.3.1-21, 13.4.3.15.

atha prastaram ādatte । *yajamāno vai prastarastad yatrāsya yajño 'gaṁstad evaitad yajamānaṁ svagā karoti* । *devalokaṁ vā asya yajño 'gan* । *devalokam evaitad yajamānam api nayati* ॥

— *ŚB* 1.8.3.11

or

tad yadājiṁ dhāvanti imam evaitena lokam ujjayati । *yad brahmā rathacakre sāma gāyati . . . antarikṣalokam evaitenojjayati* । *atha yad yūpaṁ rohati devalokam evaitenojjayati* ॥

— *ŚB* 5.1.5.1

which indicate that people were worried about their life after death. Sacrifice has been considered as the means of attaining heaven. In the context of different sacrifices so many rituals have been mentioned which according to their belief resulted in heaven. As for example, in the *Darśapūrṇamāsa* rite, a grass effigy of the sacrificer was burnt with the idea that through this rite the soul of the sacrificer would reach heaven. A similar rite has been traced in the context of *Vājapeya* sacrifice where the sacrificer and his wife mounted a ladder (kept aside the sacrificial campus) which appears to be an acting of their ascending heaven.[64] From this it becomes evident that they believed perfection in the sacrifice would lead them to heaven. Hence, they tried to perform these rituals almost perfectly to confirm their position in the Heaven (*ŚB* 1.8.3.11-20). Even at the time of cremation, along with the dead body all the sacrificial implements were piled on the funeral pyre under the notion that the sacrificer thus supplied with sacrificial weapons would reach his desired spot in the heaven.[65]

In the *JB* (1.42, 1.44) a graphic description of the blissful atmosphere of heaven has been recorded in the episode of

64. *atha niśrayaṇīṁ niśrayati* । . . . *sa rokṣyañjāyām āmantrayate 'jāya ehi svo rohāva 'iti . . . sa rohati . . .* — *ŚB* 5.2.1.9-11

65. *sa eṣa yajñayudhī yajamānaḥ yatha bibhyad āmoṣam atīyat evam eva* । *yo 'sya svarge loko jito bhavati tam abhyatyeti . . .* — *ŚB* 12.5.2.8

Bhr̥gu and Varuṇa. Bhr̥gu the son of Varuṇa was inflated with pride and felt himself superior to his father. Varuṇa being aware of this fact wanted to teach him some lesson. He caused Bhr̥gu's soul to come out under the spell of a temporary trance and sent him to visit different quarters. Bhr̥gu visited four cardinal points and intermediary space and saw five visions. In the sixth region he visited a beautiful scene full of heavenly bliss and profound serenity. He found there five rivers where thousands of white and blue lotus are blooming merrily amidst sparkling waves of honey, where heavenly nymphs disport themselves and the whole atmosphere charged with sweet aroma, that constantly wafted from the lotuses and the sound of music and dance which regale the ears. The *Kaṭha*[66] has described heaven as a place beyond grief and fear. Dwellers of that place attain immortality. Here knowledge of fire has been mentioned as a means of attaining heaven. The *CU* has prescribed some *upāsanā*s for the same purpose (*CU* 3.13.6, 8.3.3, 8.3.5).

In course of time the sphere of their attention was broadened into refinement of things connected with their way of living. From the study of Āraṇyaka texts (esp. the *SĀ* X) it appears that people felt quite disinterested with the complicated performance of external sacrifices (which required a lot of things, time and processing); that is why those were replaced by the internal ones. This internal *Agnihotra* has been described in the tenth chapter of the *Sāṅkhyāyana Āraṇyaka*, performance of which (on account of being totally mental) had nothing to do with external ceremonies and ingredients.[67] Hence, it was called Mānasa Agnihotra. Further, the account

66. *svarge loke na bhayaṁ kiñcanāsti na tatra tvaṁ jarayā bibheti* ।
ubhe tīrtvā 'śanāyā-pipāse śokātigo modate svargaloke ॥

— *Kaṭha* 1.1.12

67. *athāta ādhyātmikam āntaram agnihotram ityācakṣate* । . . . *mano dhūmo* । *manyur arcayitā aṅgārāḥ śraddhā payo vāk samit satyam āhutiḥ prajñātmā sa rasaḥ* . . . — *SĀ* 10.8

of Prāṇāgnihotra has been recorded in the *CU* (5.19.1-5.23.2). Actually it was nothing but partaking of food by the enlightened aspirant. But it was not the ordinary intake of food, but eating, having taken it as the performance of *Agnihotra*.[68] By taking a mouthful of rice (or any food), the aspirant satisfied his vital airs one by one. Therefore, that much food only was (to be) taken as much it was enjoined for offering an oblation.[69] Not only eating but (the activities of) entire life has been considered as sacrifice (*CU* 3.17.1-4).

Quest for Supreme Knowledge

Thus, a gradual change has been noticed in their thought and practices. Their awareness of the mystery beyond this creation, query about its Creator (which was germinated only in the *R̥V*) increased more and more. Their desire of conquering the limitations of worldly and heavenly pleasures and thirst for higher and higher knowledge led them finally to the quest of Supreme Truth-cum-Bliss, nothing other than Liberation. Attainment of heaven was highly desirable, but it too was not imperishable and (on the completion of enjoying acquired merit) resulted in rebirth. People wanted to get released of this un-ending cycle.

In the Upaniṣads[70] two types of knowledge have been recorded which are to be acquired as an order of procedure

---

68. *tad yad bhaktaṁ prathamam āgacchet taddhomīyam* । *sa yām prathamām āhutiṁ juhuyāt tāṁ juhuyāt prāṇāya svāheti prāṇas tr̥pyati . . . atha yāṁ dvitīyāṁ juhuyāt tāṁ juhuyāt vyānāya svāheti vyānastr̥pyati* । *. . . atha yāṁ tr̥tīyāṁ juhuyāt tāṁ juhuyād apānāya svāhety apānastr̥pyati* । *. . . atha yāṁ caturthīṁ juhuyāt tāṁ juhuyāt samānāya svāheti samānastr̥pyati* । *. . . atha yām pañcamīṁ juhuyāt tāṁ juhuyād udānāya svāhety udānastr̥pyati* । *. . .* — *CU* 5.19.1-5.23.1

69. *āhutiśabdād avadānapramāṇam annam prakṣiped ityarthaḥ* । *. . .* — Ś on *CU* 5.19.1

70. *dve vidye veditavye iti . . . parā caivāparā ca* । *tatrāparā-r̥gvedo yajurvedaḥ sāmavedo 'tharvavedaḥ śikṣā-kalpo-vyākaraṇaṁ niruktaṁ chando jyotiṣam iti* । *atha parā–yayā tadakṣaram adhigamyate* । — *Muṇḍ* 1.1.4-5

to reach this Supreme Truth. One is lower (*aparā*) comprising of the Vedas and their supplementaries and related subjects (which have been discussed so far, under Education System — See Ch. 6); and the other is the Higher, i.e., *parā vidyā* by which that Imperishable Truth can be realized.

People's quest for this Supreme Knowledge has been reflected in many passages of Upaniṣads.[71] With a desire to attain this Supreme Truth, Maitreyī could neglect all the earthly treasures.[72] The *BU*[73] states that "people sought for this Supreme Knowledge through the study of Vedas, sacrifice, charity, austerity, etc. Knowing Him they became sage. Wishing for that Supreme Self the mendicants renounced their home. . . . Knowing this no more did they wish for any offspring. . . . Having forsaken all the desires they wandered about like mendicants." In the *CU* (7.1-7.26) we find that Nārada, an eminent scholar, even after having acquired proficiency in so many subjects felt deficiency in his knowledge and approached Sanatkumāra for further instruction (just to achieve this Supreme Truth).

Realization of this Supreme Knowledge required approaching the teacher (*gurūpasadana*) in a due manner and practice of celibacy (*brahmacarya*). The *Muṇḍaka* has instructed in a clear tone that the student with a desire to know Him should approach the teacher accordingly:

---

71. *Kaṭha* 1.1.20-29; *Praśna* 1.1; *Taitt* 3.1; *CU* 4.2.4, 4.5.1-4.9.3, 5.11.1-5.11.7, 7.1.3ff, 8.7.2ff.

72. *yannu ma imaṁ bhagoḥ sarvā pṛthivī vittena pūrṇā syāt katham tenāmṛtā syāmiti* । . . . *sā hovāca maitreyī yenāhaṁ nāmṛtā syāṁ kimahaṁ tena kuryām yad eva bhagavān veda tad eva me bruhīti* । — *BU* 2.4.2-3

73. *tam etaṁ vedānuvacanena brāhmaṇā vividiṣanti* । *yajñena dānena tapasā 'nāśakena* । *etam eva viditvā munir bhavati* । *etameva pravrājino lokam icchantaḥ pravrajanti* । *etaddha sma vai tat vidvāṁsaḥ prajāṁ na kāmayante* । . . . *te ha sma putraiṣaṇāyaśca vittaiṣaṇāyāśca lokaiṣaṇāyāśca vyutthāyātha bhikṣācaryaṁ caranti* । . . . — *BU* 4.4.22

tad vijñānārthaṁ sa gurum evābhigacchet
samitpāṇiḥ śrotriyaṁ brahmaniṣṭham
— *Muṇḍ* 1.2.12

In this connection, we may refer to the *BU*, which has mentioned an ancient custom — *vācā ha smaiva pūrva upayanti* (*BU* 6.2.7). The sentence indicates that if fellows of upper caste sought knowledge from the members of lower castes (as a matter of necessity), they approached by declaration only and not by approaching his feet or serving him.[74]

It is a remarkable point that even brāhmaṇas approached the kṣatriya teachers also in order to achieve a rare lesson. As a matter of fact the secret theory of Vaiśvānara Fire was totally in the grip of kṣatriyas (*kṣatrasyaiva praśāsanam abhūt* — *CU* 5.3.7), brāhmaṇas could not reach there henceforth. In the *ŚB* (11.6.2.1-10) we find the story where some famous brāhmaṇa erudites were overpowered by the kṣatriya king Janaka, a typical learned personality, whom (the brāhmaṇas) he asked about the rsecret doctrines of *Agnihotra*. Only Yājñavalkya could satisfy him to some extent, but not totally. The king complimented him but clearly mentioned the incompleteness of his knowledge regarding the uprising or progress of *Agnihotra*, its support, content, return or renascent world of these two. The king had a keen knowledge of all these points. When brāhmaṇas were about to challenge the king in a counter debate, Yājñavalkya pacified them just to avoid the humiliation of another defeat from a kṣatriya king. The most noticeable thing here is that Yājñavalkya in spite of being an eminent brāhmaṇa scholar did not hesitate to learn the said theory from the king, just for the fulfilment of his own knowledge.

---

74. *vācā ha smaiva kila pūrva brāhmaṇā kṣatriyan vidyārthinaḥ santo vaiśyān vā 'kṣatriyā vā vaiśyān āpady upayanti śiṣyavṛttyā hyupāgacchanti nopāyanaśuśruṣādibhiḥ* I — Ś on *BU* 6.2.7

In the *CU* (5.3.1-5.10.10) we find that king Pravāhaṇa silenced Śvetaketu (by some questions, answers of which were unknown not only to him but to his father also) and treated his father Āruṇi as a student, *ciraṁ vasety ājñāpayāñcakāra* (*CU* 5.3.7) and communicated to him the doctrine which has never heretofore dwelt in the brāhmaṇas.[75]

Another learned king was Aśvapati Kekaya to whom six learned brāhmaṇa scholars approached to know the doctrine of Vaiśvānara self. The *Kauṣ* (4.1) tells us the story of Dṛpta Bālāki, who went to Ajātaśatru, the King of Kāśī to instruct him but ultimately was embarassed and silenced by the display of the king's superior knowledge at every step of the same topic. Finally he approached the king like his student. The king instructed him but without any pupilage. The same story has been traced in the *ŚB* (5.3.7) and the *BU* (2.1.1ff) with a slight variation.

It is interesting to observe that sometimes with a view to attain knowledge (even about *Brahman*) pupils addressed superhuman beings like Bull, Fire, Swan, Diver bird,[76] etc., as their teacher *brabītu me bhagavān iti* (*CU* 4.5.2-4.8) and achieved knowledge from the same.

PUPILAGE

Normally practice of pupilage was considered an important prerequisite factor of education. But in some special cases (probably in cases of competent and worthy students) exceptions to this rule have been noticed, e.g., Yama in the *Kaṭhopaniṣad* (1.1.14-15, 1.2.16ff) finding Naciketā well-mature and devoted, had instructed him on the fire rite and Supreme

75. *yathāyaṁ nu prāk tvattaḥ purā vidyā brāhmaṇān gacchati tasmād u sarveṣu lokeṣu kṣatriyasyaiva praśāsanam abhūd iti tasmai hovāca* । — *CU* 5.3.7

76. *atha hainaṁ ṛṣabho 'bhyuvāda satyakāma . . . brahmaṇaśca te pādam brabāṇīti . . . agniṣṭe pādaṁ vakteti . . . haṁsaste pādaṁ vakteti . . . madguṣṭe pādaṁ vakteti . . .* — *CU* 4.5.1-4.8.1

Soul without any pupilage. In the *CU* (5.11.1) we find the story of Aśvapati who taught six brāhmaṇas without any initiation or pupilage. The example of Gārgya Bālāki (*BU* 1.2.5) also may be considered in this account. In this connection, we may mention the name of Maitreyī and King Janaka, who in spite of not being regular students were instructed by Yājñavalkya.

ITS TENURE

Though tenure for general education has been mentioned in the Upaniṣads[77] as twelve years, in case of *brahmavidyā* it was not always fixed within this limit. If it was necessary on part of the student (for the completion of his study or perfection of his knowledge) scope of *brahmacarya* could be widened. As for example, we may mention here the name of Upakosala Kāmalāyana who in spite of practising twelve years' studentship was not considered eligible for instruction by his teacher.[78] Another student Śvetaketu, who after having studied Vedas for twelve years thought himself well read[79] but actually was ignorant of the knowledge of *Brahman*.[80] Āruṇi finding his son's knowledge incomplete undertook him at his own guidance and taught him the doctrine of everything by the knowledge of only one (*ekavijñānena sarvavijñānam*). Sometimes, the length of this tenure depended on the profundity of the subject. In the narrative of Indra, Virocana and Prajāpati we find that Virocana after practising thirty-two years' studentship was satisfied with his knowledge of

77. *CU* 4.10.1, 6.2.1, etc.

78. *upakosalo ha vai kāmalāyanaḥ satyakāme jābāle brahmacaryam uvāsa* । *sa ha dvādaśavarṣāṇyagnīn paricacāra* । *sa ha smānyān antevāsinaḥ samāvartayaṁstam ha smaiva na samāvartayati* । — *CU* 4.10.1

79. *sa ha dvādaśavarṣa upetya caturviṁśativarṣaḥ sarvān* ।
vedān adhītya mahāmanā anūcānamānī stabdha eyāya ॥
— *CU* 6.1.2

80. *śvetaketo yannu somyedaṁ mahāmanā anūcānamānī stabdho 'si uta tamādeśam aprākṣyaḥ yenāśrutaṁ śrutaṁ bhavaty amataṁ matam abijñātaṁ vijñātam iti* । *kathaṁ nu bhagavaḥ sa ādeśo bhavatīti* । — *CU* 6.1.3

this body as Soul,[81] whereas Indra had to wait there as a celibate for hundred and one years in order to attain a perfect instruction about Supreme Self.[82] But there was no hard and fast rule on this point. Competent students could manage it within a short period also. The sages mentioned in the *Praśna*[83] were competent enough who could manage to achieve their desired knowledge only after practising one year's pupilage.

Imparting and receiving lessons on Supreme Knowledge were not confined within the limit of so-called studenthood (*brahmacarya*). Sometimes the elderly pupils or even householders went to the teachers, whenever they required knowledge of some special doctrine or truth. Thus, in the *CU*[84] we find five great householders and theologians, viz., Prācīnaśāla Aupamanyava, Sātyayajña Pauluṣi, Indradyumna Bhāllaveya, Jana Śārkarākṣya and Buḍila Āśvatarāśvi all of whom were advanced in age, in order to have knowledge on Vaiśvānara, at first went to Āruṇi — and then to king Aśvapati — who was the best teacher of the subject. Further, the case of Nārada may be taken in this account. Nārada, even after

---

81. *tau ha dvātriṁśataṁ varṣāṇi brahmacaryam uṣatuḥ* । *tau ha prajāpatir uvāca kim icchantāvavāstam iti* । *tau hocatur ya ātmā 'pahatapāpmā vijaro-vimṛtyur–viśoko . . . so 'nveṣṭavyaḥ* । *. . . tau ha prajāpatir uvāca–ya eṣo 'kṣiṇi puruṣe dṛśyata eṣa ātmeti hovāca* । *. . . sa ha śāntahṛdaya eva virocano 'surāñjagāma* । — *CU* 8.7.3-4, 8.8.4

82. *tad yad āhur ekaśataṁ ha vai varṣāṇi maghavān prajāpatau brahmacaryam uvāsa* । — *CU* 8.11.3

83. *tān ha sa ṛṣir uvāca–bhūya eva tapasā brahmacaryeṇa śraddhayā saṁvatsaraṁ saṁvatsyatha* । *yathākāmaṁ praśnān pṛcchata* । *yadi vijñāsyāmaḥ sarvām ha vo vakṣyāma iti* । —*Praśna* 1.2

84. *prācīnaśala aupamanyavaḥ satyayajñah pauluṣir indradyumno bhāllaveyo janaḥ śākarākṣyo buḍila āśvatarāśviste haite mahāśālā mahāśrotriyāḥ sametya mīmāṁsayāñcakruḥ ko na ātmā kiṁ brahmeti* । *. . .*

tān hovācāśvapatir vai bhagavanto 'yam kaikeyaḥ sampratīmam ātmānaṁ vaiśvānaram adhyeti taṁ hantābhyāgacchāmeti tam hābhyājagmuḥ ।

— *CU* 5.11.1, 5.11.4

having completed the normal schedule of general education (where he studied a lot, yet found his knowledge deficient) approached Sanatkumāra in order to achieve knowledge on Self.[85]

In the later ages we find Āpastamba,[86] quoting the view of Śvetaketu, has stated that a person even after the completion of his general education should spend two months every year with his teacher if he wished to extend his knowledge. On this point Āpastamba himself opined that it would be contrary to the injunction of *Śāstra*s because after the completion of education everybody was supposed to enter domestic life; and house-holders had their own duties (prescribed by Śāstras).[87] In that case they would violate the fixed order. At last Āpastamba[88] admitted that a graduate who wished to master any subject could return to his teacher for the completion of his unfinished knowledge.

ELIGIBILITY

Instruction of this Supreme Knowledge (i.e., Absolute *Brahman*) was very limited. Therefore, the student had to qualify themselves through the practice of celibacy, profound *tapas* and development of inner qualities, e.g., *śama, dama, uparati, titikṣā, śraddhā, samādhāna,* etc. Because without concentration, self-control and calmness of mind Supreme

---

85. *so 'haṁ bhagavo mantravid evāsmi nātmavicchrutaṁ hyeva me bhagavad dṛśebhyas tarati śokam ātmavid iti so 'haṁ bhagavaḥ śocāmi tam mā bhagavāñchokasya pāram tārayatviti* । — *CU* 7.1.3

86. *niveśe vṛtte saṁvatsare saṁvatsare dvau dvau māsau samāhita ācāryakule vased bhūyaḥ śrutim icchanniti śvetaketuḥ* । — *ĀpDS* 1.4.13.19

87. *tacchāstra vipratiṣiddham* । *niveśe hi vṛtte naiyāmikānit śrūyante* । — *ĀpDS* 1.4.13.21-22

88. *yayā vidyayā na viroceta punar ācāryam upetya niyamena sādhyet* । — *ĀpDS* 2.2.5.14

Truth could not be attained.[89] Most probably that is why the sage Paippalāda instructed the newcomers to practise celibacy and *tapas* with faith before imparting knowledge to them.[90]

From the *CU*[91] we find that only the eldest son or a worthy student could inherit lesson on the cosmic significance of sacred scriptures. It was not to be imparted to anybody else even if the teacher was provoked by the gift of sea-girt earth, full of treasure.

The *Śvet*,[92] also has given more or less the same pre-requisities. The highest mystery conveyed through Vedānta in the ancient age, was not to be given to one whose passions had not been subdued nor to one who was not a son, nor to him who was not a pupil. The *Maitrī*[93] has allowed to preach the knowledge of Self only to a devoted student endowed with all necessary qualifications.

RESULT: LIBERATION

The result of acquiring this knowledge is to attain the self, so to say in terms of monistic philosophers *jīvo brahmaiva nāparaḥ* — to realize the individual self *jīva* (i.e., the essence of man) as identical with the Supreme Self *Brahman* (the essence of

89. *nāvirato duścaritaḥ nāśānto nāsamāhitaḥ* ।
nāśānta mānaso vā 'pi prajñānenainam āpnuyāt ॥
— *Kaṭha* 1.2.24

90. *tān ha ṛṣir uvāca* । *bhūya eva tapasā brahmacaryeṇa śraddhayā samvatsaraṁ saṁvatsyatha* । *yathākāmaṁ praśnān pṛcchata* । *yadi vijñāsyāmaḥ sarvān ha vo vakṣyāma* । — *Praśna* 1.2

91. *tajjyeṣṭhāya putrāya pitā brahma brūyāt* । *praṇāyyāya vā 'ntevāsine* । *nānyasmai kadācana* । *yadyapyasmā imām adbhiḥ parigṛhītām dhanasya* । *pūrṇāṁ dadyād etad eva tato bhūya . . .* — *CU* 3.11.5-6

92. *vedānte paramaṁ guhyaṁ purākalpe pracoditam* ।
nā praśāntāya dātavyam na putrāyāśiṣyāyava punaḥ ॥
— *Śvet* 6.22

93. *etad guhyatamaṁ nāputrāya nāśiṣyāya nāśāntāya kīrtayed iti* । *anantabhaktāya sarvaguṇasampannāya dadyāt* । — *Maitrī* 6.29

Universe). This Indwelling Self has been described as *aṅguṣṭhamātra puruṣaḥ*, ever seated in the hearts of men.[94] It is like a smokeless light (*adhūmakaḥ jyotiḥ*), controller of past and future, and is always there.[95] It is immanent as well as transcendant. With the dawn of this knowledge (of *Brahman*), all the internal fetters are broken, all the doubts are resolved and the aspirant becomes free from all the bondages of cause and effect.[96] Then he (*mumukṣu*) sees all beings in himself and himself in all.[97] Thus, having realized everything in himself he feels neither grief nor any illusion.[98] The *Kenopaniṣad* (2.4) declares boldly: *Brahman* is known then only when it is known as the Self of each state of consciousness, because thereby one gets Immortality:

pratibodhaviditaṁ matam amṛtatvaṁ hi bindate

Yājñavalkya explained to Maitreyī that to attain Immortality means to realize the Self and that is to be realized through hearing, reflection and meditation:

ātmā vā 're draṣṭavyaḥ śrotavyo mantavyaḥ nididhyāsitavyaḥ maitreyi, ātmano vā are darśanena śravaṇena matyā vijñānena idaṁ sarvaṁ viditam — *BU* 2.4.5

In order to dispel Nārada's ignorance Sanatkumāra also expounded to him the theory of Infinite Self (*bhūman*) through

---

94. *anguṣṭha-mātraḥ puruṣo 'ntarātmā sadā janānāṁ hṛdaye sanniviṣṭaḥ* ॥
— *Kaṭha* 2.3.17

95. *anguṣṭhamātraḥ puruṣo jyotir ivādhūmakaḥ* ।
iśāno bhūta bhavyasya sa evādya sa u śvaḥ ॥
— *Kaṭha* 2.1.13

96. *bhidyate hṛdayagranthiśchidyante sarva-saṁśayāḥ* ।
kṣīyante cāsya karmāṇi tasmin dṛṣṭe parāvare ॥
— *Muṇḍ* 2.2.9

97. *yastu sarvāṇi bhūtānyātmanyevānupaśyati* ।
sarva-bhūteṣu cātmānaṁ tato na vijugupsate ॥ — *Īśa* 6

98. *yasmin sarvāṇi bhūtāny ātmaivābhūd vijānataḥ* ।
tatra ko mohaḥ kaḥ śoka ekatvamanupaśyataḥ ॥ — *Īśa* 7

graded instruction (*CU* 7.1.4, 7.26.2). As because Supreme Self is devoid of any limitation and attributes; hence, beyond any type of meditation (*upāsanā*); therefore, meditation of all the symbols (from *nāman* up to *prāṇa*[99]) of *Brahman* (of course, this is *Saguṇa Brahman*) has been prescribed as the steps to the realization of this Self.

According to the instruction of the *BS*,[100] the aspirant should meditate repeatedly till the attainment of Liberation. Śaṅkara,[101] while commenting on the same states that processing of hearing (*śravaṇa*), reflection (*manana*) and constant meditation (*nididhyāsana*) should be repeated up to its culmination into the intuitive realization of *Brahman* just as husking should be continued so long as the rice is not produced. Beside this, by the term *upāsanā* (constant remembrance) and *nididhyāsana* (profound meditation) activities involving repetition are implied.[102]

The *CU* sentence *raśmīṁstvaṁ paryāvartaya* (1.5.2) has prescribed repeated meditation to achieve a desired result (may be in a different context). Śaṅkara concludes that in case of knowledge of Supreme *Brahman* also, repetition of instructions leading to that knowledge is necessary.[103]

---

99. *nāmaivaitāḥ nāmopāssveti* । . . . *vācam upāssveti* । . . . *mana upāssveti* ।. . . *saṁkalpam upāssveti* । . . . *cittam upāssveti* । . . . *dhyānam upāssveti* । . . . *vijñānam upāssveti* । . . . *balam upāssveti* । . . . *annam upāssveti* . . . *āpa upāssveti* । . . . *tejo upāssveti* । . . . *ākāśam upāssveti* । . . . *smaram upāssveti* । . . . *āśām upāssveti* । *prāṇam upāssveti* । . . .

— *CU* 7.1.3-7.15.1

100. *āvṛttir asakṛd upadeśāt* — *BS* 4.1.1

101. *darśana-paryavasānāni hi śravaṇādīni āvartyamānāni dṛṣṭārthāni bhavanti, yathā avaghātādīni taṇḍulādiniṣpatti-paryavasānāni tadvat*

— Ś on *BS* 4.1.1

102. *api ca upāsanam-nididhyāsanam ca iti antarṇītavṛttiguṇā eva kriyā abhidhīyate* — Ś on *BS* 4.1.1

103. *tasmāt parabrahma-viṣaye api pratyaye tadupāyopadeśeṣu āvṛttisiddhiḥ*

— Ś on *BS* 4.1.2

Further, the indicatory sign also conveys the idea of repetition.[104] *Abhyāsa*, one of the six *tātparya nirṇāyaka liṅga*s (characteristic marks for ascertaining true connotation of Upaniṣadic texts) means to present the theory frequently. As for example, we may mention here the case of Śvetaketu, who was instructed by his father Āruṇi repeatedly *tat tvam asi* (That Thou art), at least for nine times.[105]

Hence, it is proved that achievement of supreme knowledge requires regular practice up to the Self-realization.

svasvarūpa caitanya sākṣātkāra paryantaṁ śravaṇa manana-nididhyāsana samādhy anuṣṭhānasyāpekṣitatvāt

— *Vedāntasāra*, 181

Thus, the eligible student, having been instructed properly by his teacher, meditated on his own and attained the Supreme Truth.[106] The *BU* states that the knower becomes (identical with) the Knowledge Itself.

brahmaiva san brahmāpyeti — (4.4.6)

People considered Liberation to be the *summum bonum* of human life, but it must be confessed that it is extremely difficult to attain and obviously it was not meant for all. Therefore, importance of practising *trivarga* has never been denied. Even in the Upaniṣads a correct code of conduct (to be followed by householders) has been supported, so that everyday life should be conducted accordingly. The *Taitt* has exhorted the departing students:

---

104. *liṅgācca* । — *BS* 4.1.2

105. *prakaraṇapratipādyasya vastunastanmadhye paunaḥ punyena pratipādanam abhyāsāḥ* । *yathā tatraivādvitīya–vastūni madhye tattvamasīti navakṛtvaḥ pratipādanam.* — *Vedāntasāra* 186

106. (i) *te tam arcayantaṁ tvaṁ hi naḥ pitā yo 'smākam avidyāyāḥ paraṁ pāraṁ tārayasīti,* — *Praśna* 6.8.

(ii) *tasmai mṛdita-kaṣāyāya tamasas-pāraṁ darśayati bhagavān sanatkumāraḥ* । — *CU* 7.26.2.

satyaṁ vada/dharmaṁ cara | svādhyān mā pramadaḥ |
ācāryāya priyaṁ dhanam āhṛtya prajātantuṁ mā vyavacchetsīḥ ||

satyān na pramaditavyam | dharmān na pramaditavyam |
kuśalān napramaditavyam | bhūtyai na pramaditavyam |
svādhyāyapravacanābhyāṁ na pramaditavyam ||

devapitṛkāryābhyāṁ na pramadityavyam | mātṛdevo bhava |
pitṛdevo bhava | ācāryadevo bhava | atithidevo bhava ||

yāny anavadyāni karmāṇi tāni sevitavyāni | no itarāṇi |
yāny asmākaṁ sucaritāni tāni tvayopāsyāni ||

no itarāṇi | ye ke cāsmāc chreyāṁso brāhmaṇāḥ teṣāṁ tvayā āsanena praśvastitavyam | śraddhayā deyam | aśraddhayā 'deyam | śriyā deyam | hriyā deyam | bhiyā deyam | atha yadi te karmavicikitsā vā vṛtta-vicikitsā vā syāt ||

ye tatra brāhmaṇāḥ sammarśinaḥ | yuktā āyuktāḥ | alūkṣā dharmakāmāḥ syuḥ | yathā te tatra varteran | tathā tatra vartethāḥ | athābhyākhyāteṣu ye tatra brāhmaṇāḥ sammarśinaḥ | yuktā āyuktāḥ | alūkṣā dharmakāmāḥ syuḥ | yathā te teṣu varteran | tathā teṣu vartethāḥ | eṣa ādeśaḥ | eṣa upadeśaḥ | eṣā vedopaniṣat | etad anuśāsanam | evam upāsitavyam ||

— *Taitt* 1.11.1-4

Speak the truth. Practise virtue. Let there be no neglect of your (daily) reading. Having brought to the teacher the wealth, that is pleasing (to him) do not cut-off the thread of the offspring. Let there be no neglect of truth. Let there be no neglect of virtue. Let there be no neglect of welfare. Let there be no neglect of prosperity. Let there be no neglect of study and teaching.

Let there be no neglect of the duties to the gods and the fathers. Be one, to whom the mother is a god. Be one, to whom the father is a god. Be one, to whom the teacher is a god. Be one, to whom the guest is a god. Whatever deeds are blameless, they are to be practised not others. Whatever good

> practices there are among us, they are to be adopted by you, not others.
>
> Whatever brāhmaṇas there are (who are) superior to us, they should be comforted by you with a seat. (What is to be given) is to be given with faith, should not be given without faith, should be given in plenty, should be given with modesty, should be given with fear, should be given with sympathy.
>
> Then if there is in you any doubt regarding any deeds, any doubt regarding conduct, you should behave yourself in such matters as the brāhmaṇas there, (who are) the competent to judge, devoted (to good deeds), not led by others, not harsh, lovers of virtue would behave in such cases. Then, as to the persons who are spoken against, you should behave yourself in such a way, as the brāhmaṇas there (who are) competent to judge, devoted (to good deeds), not led by others, not harsh, lovers of virtue, would behave in regard to such persons.
>
> This is the command. This is the teaching. This is the secret doctrine of the Veda. This is the instruction. Thus, should one worship. — S. Radhakrishnan

From this teaching of the Upaniṣad it is clear that departing students were not instructed by their teacher to give up this world but to lead virtuous lives as householders and promote the welfare of the community. That, a householder also could attain Liberation (even if he had not embraced the fourth stage *saṁnyāsa* and practised *tapas*), only by following this code of conduct properly throughout his life, has been clearly expressed in the *CU*.

> *ācāryakulād vedam adhītya yathāvidhānaṁ guroḥ karmātiśeṣeṇābhisamāvṛtya kuṭumbe । śucau deśe । svādhyāyam adhīyāno dhārmikān vidadhad ātmani sarvendriyāṇi sampratiṣṭhāpyāhiṁsān sarvabhūtāny anyatra tīrthebhyaḥ sa*

khalvevaṁ yāvad āyuṣaṁ brahmalokam abhisampadyate | *na ca punar āvartate* || — *CU* 8.15.1

Having studied the Vedas in the teacher's house, in accordance with the injunctions during leisure after performing the duties to the teacher, he returns home from the teacher's house, and takes up the duties of a householder. Then he studies the scriptures in a sacred place and makes his sons and disciples virtuous. Then withdrawing all the organs into the Self, not injuring any creature other than what is prescribed in the scriptures, living in this way to the end of his life, he attains the world of Brahma. He does not return again. — Swami Gambhirananda

Bibliography

Agrawal, V.S., *India as Known to Pāṇini*, Varanasi: Prithvi Prakashan, 1963, 2nd rev. edn.

Aitareya Āraṇyaka, tr. A.B. Keith, Anecdote Oxoniensia, Oxford: Oxford University, 1909.

Aitareya Brāhmaṇam, ed. with comm. of Sāyaṇācārya, Sudhakar Malaviya, Pracyabharatiya Granthamala, 14 vol. I-II, Varanasi: Tara Printing Works, 1986.

———, tr. A.B. Keith, *Rigveda Brāhmaṇas*, ed. C.R. Lanman, Harvard Oriental Series, vol. 25, 1920, rpt. Delhi: Motilal Banarsidass, 2nd edn., 1981.

———, tr. R.S. Trivedi, *Aitareya Brāhmaṇa*, ed. Buddhadeva Bhattacharya, Ramendra Sundar Racana Samagra, vol. II, Calcutta: Granthamela, 1976.

Āpastamba Dharma-Sūtram, ed. with Ujjvalā comm. of Haradatta, U.C. Pandey, Kashi Sanskrit Series No. 93, Varanasi: Chaukhambha Sanskrit Sansthan, 3rd edn. 1992.

———, tr. G. Bühler, *Āpastamba's Aphorisms on The Sacred Law of the Hindus*, Bombay Sanskrit Series No. 44, Poona: BORI, 3rd edn. 1932.

Āpastamba Gṛhya-Sūtram, ed. with Anākulā comm. of Haradatta, U.C. Pandey, Kashi Sanskrit Series No. 59, Varanasi: Chowkhambha Sanskrit Series Office, 1971.

Āśvalāyana Gṛhya-Sūtram, ed. with *Vṛtti* of Nārāyaṇa, Gṛhyapariśiṣṭa and Kārikā of Bhaṭṭakumārila, V.S.R.R.G.S. Gokhale, Anandashram Sanskrit Series No. 105, Poona: Anandashram, 1978.

Atharvaveda (*Śaunaka*), ed. with comm. of Sāyaṇa, Vishvabandhu, V.V.R.I. Series No. 13-16, Part I-IV, Hoshiarpur: VVRI, 1960-64.

———, tr. Maurice Bloomfield, *Hymns of the Atharvaveda*, ed. F. Max Müller, Sacred Book of the East, vol. 42, 1897, rpt. Delhi: Motilal Banarsidass, 1979.

———, tr. R.T.H. Griffith, *Hymns of the Atharvaveda*, vol. I-II, 1895-96, rpt. Delhi: Munshiram Manoharlal Publishers Pvt. Ltd., 1985.

———, tr. W.D. Whitney, *Atharvaveda Saṁhitā*, ed. C.R. Lanman, Harvard Oriental Series No. 7-8, vol. I-II, 1905, rpt. Delhi: Motilal Banarsidass, 1984.

Auboyer, Jeanine, *Daily Life in Ancient India*, tr. Simon Watson Taylor, London: Asia Publishing House, 1965.

Aurobindo, *The Foundations of Indian Culture*, 1918-21, Indian edn., Pondicherry: Aurobindo Ashram, 6th Imp., 1988.

Basham, A.L., *The Wonder That Was India*, 1954, Indian rpt., Calcutta: Rupa, 8th Imp., 1988.

Basu, Jogiraj, *India of the Age of the Brāhmaṇas*, Calcutta: Sanskrit Pustak Bhandar, 1969.

Baudhāyana Dharma-Sūtram, ed. with Vivaraṇa comm. of Sri Govinda Swami, U.C. Pandey, Kashi Sanskrit Series No. 104, Varanasi: Chaukhambha Sanskrit Sansthan, 4th edn., 1994.

Baudhāyana Śrauta-Sūtra, ed. W. Caland, vol. I-II, 1903-04, Delhi: Munshiram Manoharlal Publishers Pvt. Ltd., 2nd edn., 1982.

Bhāṣika Sūtra of Maharṣi Kātyāyana, ed. with comm. of Mahāsvāmin and Anantabhaṭṭa, B.B. Chaubey, Punjab University Indological Series No. 4, V.V.B.I.S. & IS, Hoshiarpur: Punjab University, 1975.

Bhatta, C. Panduranga, *Dice-Play in Sanskrit Literature*, Delhi: Amar Prakashan, 1985.

Brahma-Sūtra Śāṅkara Bhāṣyam, ed. with comm. of Bhāṣyaratnaprabhā of Govindānanda, Bhāmatī of Vācaspati Miśra and Nyāyanirṇaya of Ānandagiri, J.L. Shastri, rpt., Delhi: Motilal Banarsidass, 1996.

———, tr. Swami Gambhirananda, *Brahma-Sūtra Bhāṣya of Śaṅkarācārya*, Calcutta: Advaita Ashram, 5th Imp., 1993.

(*The*) *Bṛhadāraṇyaka Upaniṣad*, tr. with comm. of Śaṅkara, Swami Madhavananda, Calcutta: Advaita Ashram, 8th imp., 1993.

Chakrabarty Chhanda, *Common Life in Ṛgveda and Atharvaveda*, Calcutta: Punthi Pustak, 1977.

Chāndogya Upaniṣad, tr. with comm. of Śaṅkara, Swami Gambhirananda, Calcutta: Advaita Ashram, 2nd edn., 1992.

Dandekar, R.N. *Vedic Bibliography*, Government Oriental Series, 5 vols, Poona: BORI, 1946-93.

Deussen, Paul, *The System of the Vedānta*, tr. Charles Johnston, Indian rpt., Delhi: Karan Publications, 1987.

Edwards, Michael, *Everyday Life in Early India*, London: B.T. Batsford Ltd. and New York, G.P. Putnam's Sons, 1969.

Eight Upaniṣads, tr. with comm. of Śaṅkara, Swami Gambhirananda, vol. I, 1957, 2nd rev. edn., rpt., 1991, vol. II, 9th imp. 1992, Calcutta: Advaita Ashram.

Eighteen Principal Upaniṣads, edn. V.P. Limaye & R.D. Vadekar, Gandhi Memorial Edition, vol. I, Poona: Vaidika Samsodhana Mandala, 1958.

Gautama Dharma-Sūtram, ed. with Mitākṣarā Comm. of Haradatta, U.C. Pandey, Kashi Sanskrit Series, No. 172, Varanasi: Chaukhambha Sanskrit Sansthan, 3rd edn., 1993.

Gobhila Gṛhya-Sūtram, ed. with comm. of Bhaṭṭanārāyaṇa, Cintamani Bhattacarya, 1936, Delhi: Munshiram Manoharlal Publishers Pvt. Ltd., 2nd edn., 1982.

Gonda, Jan, *History of Indian Literature* (Saṁhitā and Brāhmaṇas), vol. I, Fase-I, Wiesbaden: Otto Harrasowitz, 1975.

Gopal, Ram, *India of Vedic Kalpasūtras*, Delhi: Motilal Banarsidass, 1959, 2nd edn., 1982.

Gopatha Brāhmaṇam, ed. Vijayapala Vidyavaridhi, Bahalgarh: Savitri Devi Bagedia Trust, 1980.

The Gṛhya-Sūtras, tr. H. Oldenberg, ed. F. Max Müller, Sacred Book of the East Series Nos. 29-30, Part I-II, 1982, rpt., Delhi: Motilal Banarsidas, 1989.

Jacob, Col. G.A., *A Concordance to the Principal Upaniṣads and Bhagavad-Gītā*, 1891, rpt., Delhi: Motilal Banarsidass, 1985.

Jaiminīya Brāhmaṇa of the Sāmaveda, ed. Raghuvira & Lokesh Chandra, 1955, Delhi: Motilal Banarsidass, 2nd Rev. edn., 1986.

Jain, S.C., *India as depicted in the Jain Canons*, Bombay: 1947.

Kāma-Sūtram, ed. with Jayamaṅgalā comm. G.D. Shastri, Kashi Sanskrit Series No. 29, Varanasi: Chowkhambha Sanskrit Sansthan, 1929.

Kane, P.V., *History of Dharma-Śāstra*, Government Oriental Series, Class B, No. 6, vol. II, Part I-II, Poona: BORI, 2nd edn., 1974.

Kapiṣṭhala Kaṭha-Saṁhitā, ed. Raghuvira, Meherchand Lacchmandas Sanskrit & Prakrit Series No. 1, Lahore: Meherchand Lacchmandas, 1932.

Kāṭhaka Saṁhitā, ed. Pt. Sripada Damodara Satvalekar, Paradi: Svadhyaya Mandala, 1943.

Kātyāyana Śrauta-Śutram, ed. with comm. of Karka Acarya Pattabhirama Shastri, Sanskrit Vidyapeetha Granthamala, No. 32, vol. I-II, Delhi: Lal Bahadur Shastri Kendriya Vidyapeetha, 1982-83.

The Kauśikasūtra of Atharvaveda, ed. M. Bloomfield, 1889, rpt., Delhi: Motilal Banarsidass, 1972.

Law, B.C., *India as Described in Early Texts of Buddhism and Jainism*, London, 1941.

Macdonell, A.A., *A History of Sanskrit Literature*, 1899, rpt., Delhi, Motilal Banarsidass, 1971.

Macdonell, A.A. and Keith, A.B., *Vedic Index of Names and Subjects*, 1912, rpt., Delhi: Motilal Banarsidass, 1982.

Maitrāyaṇī Saṁhitā, ed. Pt. Sripada Damodara Satvalekar, Paradi: Svadhyaya Mandala, 1942.

Majumdar, G.P., A series of essays on *Indian Culture* "Man's Indebtedness to Plants; Dress and other Personal Requisites in Ancient India," vol. I, Part 2, Oct. 1934, pp. 191-208.

———, "Toilet", vol I, part 4, April 1935, pp. 651-66.

———, "Furniture", vol. II, Part I, July 1935, pp. 67-76 and vol. II, Part 2, Oct., 1935, pp. 271-90.

———, "Health and Hygiene", vol. II, Part 4, April 1936, pp. 653-54.

———, "Hearth and Home", vol. III, Part I, July 1936, pp. 71-78, and vol. III, Part 3, Jan. 1937, pp. 431-54.

———, "Domestic Rites and Rituals", vol. III, Part 4, April 1937, pp. 605-12, rpt., Delhi: I.B. Corporation, 1984.

Majumdar, R.C. *Corporate Life in Ancient India*, Calcutta: Calcutta University, 2nd rev. edn., 1922.

Manu-Smṛti, ed. with comm. of Kullūka Bhaṭṭa, J.L. Shastri 1983, rpt., Delhi: Motilal Banarsidass, 1990.

———, tr. G. Bühler, *The Laws of Manu*, Sacred Book of the East, vol. 25, 1886, rpt. Delhi: Motilal Banarsidass, 9th imp., 1993.

Mehta, Rohit, *The Call of the Upanishads*, 1970, rpt. Delhi: Motilal Banarsidass, 1990.

Monier-Williams, Sir Monier, *A Sanskrit-English Dictionary*, Oxford 1899, 9th rpt., Delhi: Motilal Banarsidass, 1986.

Mookerji, R.K., *Ancient Indian Education*, 1947, Delhi: Motilal Banarsidass, 3rd edn., 1960.

Muir, J. *Original Sanskrit Texts*, Part I-V, 1870-74, 1st Indian rpt., New Delhi: Crown Publication, 1988.

Mukhopadhyay, Bandana, *Life in Ancient India* (Based on Dhammapada: Aṭṭhakathā) Calcutta: Sanskrit Pustak Bhandar, 1996.

Nāradīyā Śikṣā, ed. with comm. of Bhaṭṭaśobhākara, U.R. Bhise, BORI Research Unit Series No. 8, Poona: BORI, 1986.

The Nighaṇṭu and the Nirukta, ed. with tr. Lakshman Sarup, 1920, rpt., Delhi: Motilal Banarsidass, 1984.

Omprakash, *Economy and Food in Ancient India*, Part I-II, Delhi: Bharatiya Vidya Prakashan, 1987.

Paippalāda Saṁhitā of the Atharvaveda, ed. Durgamohan Bhattacharya, Calcutta Sanskrit College Research Series No. 23-24, Kāṇḍa I-II, 1964, rpt., Calcutta: Sanskrit College, 1980.

Pandey, R.B. *Hindu Saṁskāras*, Benaras, 1949, rpt., Delhi: Motilal Banarsidass, 1982.

Pāraskara Gṛhya-Sūtram, ed. with comm. of Karka, Jayarāma, Harihara, Gaṅgādhara and Vishvanātha, M.G. Bakre, 1917, Delhi: Munshiram Manoharlal Publishers Pvt. Ltd., 2nd edn., 1982.

Principal Upaniṣads, tr. S. Radhakrishnan, Centenary edn., Oxford, 1953, Delhi: Oxford University Press, 1989.

Puṣpasūtram, ed. Mayuram Shri M. Ramanatha Dikshitar, Madras: C.P. Ramaswami Iyer Foundation, 1989.

Ṛgveda Prātiśākhya of Śaunaka, ed. comm. of Uvaṭa Ramprasad Tripathi, Sarasvati Bhavan Granthamala 121, Varanasi: Sampurnanand Sanskrit University, 1986.

Ṛgveda Saṁhitā, ed. with comm. of Sāyaṇa, N.S. Sontakke, 5 vols: vol. I 1933, 2nd edn., 1972; vol. II, 1936, 3rd edn., 1984; vol. III, 1941, 3rd edn., 1984; vol. IV, 1946, 2nd edn., 1983; vol. V, 1951, Pune: Vaidika Samsodhana Mandala.

———, tr. R.T.H. Griffith, *Hymns of the Rigveda*, The Chowkhamba Sanskrit Series No. 35, vol. I-II, Varanasi: Chowkhamba Sanskrit Series Office, 5th edn., 1971.

———, tr. H.H. Wislon, *Rigveda Saṁhitā*, vol. I-VII, 1950-88, rpt., Delhi: Cosmo Publications, 1977.

———, tr. Ramesh Chandra Dutta, vol. I-II, Calcutta: Haraf Prakashan, 1976, 2nd edn., 1987.

(The) Sacred Law of the Āryas, tr. G. Bühler, ed. F. Max Müller, Sacred Books of the East Series No. 2 & 14, Part I-II, Oxford 1879-82, rpt. Delhi: Motilal Banarsidass, Part I-1975, II-1984.

Samashrami, Acarya Satyavrata, *Aitareyālocanam*, Bibliotheca Indica Series No. 1145-1147, Calcutta: The Asiatic Society of Bengal, 2nd edn., 1906.

Sāmaveda Saṁhitā, ed. with Sāyaṇa's comm. Acarya Satyavrata Samashrami, Bibliotheca Indica Series No. 218, 224, 235, 244, 251, 270, 280, 285-86, 293, vol. I-V, Calcutta: The Asiatic Society of Bengal, 1874-78.

Sāṅkhāyanāraṇyakam, ed. Shridhara Shastri Pathak, Anandashram Sanskrit Series No. 90, Poona: Anandashram, 1987.

———, tr. A.B. Keith, *The Sāṅkhāyana Āraṇyaka*, New Delhi: Oriental Books Reprint Corporation, 1975.

Śāṅkhāyana Brāhmaṇam, ed. R.R. Gulab Rao Vajeshankar Ojha, Anandashram Sanskrit Series No. 65, Poona: Anandashram, 1977.

———, tr. Hari Narayan Bhattacharya, Calcutta Sanskrit College Research Series No. 73, Calcutta: Sanskrit College, 1970.

Śāṅkhāyana Gṛhya-Sūtram, ed. S.R. Shegal, Garibdas Oriental Series No. 42, 1960, Delhi: Sri Satguru Publications, 2nd rev. edn., 1987.

Sarma, S.S. *Plants in Yajurveda*, Tirupati: K.S. Kendriya Vidyapeetha, 1989.

Śatapatha Brāhmaṇam, ed. with comm. of Sāyaṇa and Harisvāmin, 5 vols., Delhi: Gian Publishing House, 1987.

———, tr. J. Eggeling, *The Śatapatha Brāhmaṇa*, Sacred Book of the East Series Nos. 12, 26, 41, 43 & 44, Part I-V, 1882, rpt. Delhi: Motilal Banarsidass, 1988.

(*The*) *Śrauta-Sūtra of Āpastamba*, ed. with comm. of Rudradatta, Richard Garbe, vol. I-III, Delhi: Munshiram Manoharlal Publishers Pvt. Ltd., 2nd edn., 1983.

Śrauta-Sūtra of Lāṭyāyana, ed. with comm. of Agniswamin Ananda Chandra Vedantavagisha, 1872, Delhi: Munshiram Manoharlal Publishers Pvt. Ltd., 2nd edn., 1982.

Suśruta Saṁhitā, ed. with comm. of Ḍalhana J.T. Acharya and N.R. Acharya, Jaikrishnadas Ayurveda Series No. 34, Varanasi: Chaukhambha Orientalia, rpt., 5th edn., 1992.

Śvetāśvatara Upaniṣad, tr. with comm. of Śaṅkara, Swami Gambhirananda, Calcutta, Advaita Ashram, 1986.

(*The*) *Taittirīya Āraṇyaka*, ed. with comm. of Bhaṭṭabhāskara, A. Mahadeva Sastri & K. Rangacarya, rpt., Delhi: Motilal Banarsidass, 1985.

Taittirīya Brāhmaṇam, ed. with Sāyaṇa's comm., N.S. Godbole, Anandashram Sanskrit Series No. 37, vol. I-II, Poona: Anandashram, 3rd edn., 1979.

Taittirīya Saṁhitā, ed. Pt. Sripada Damodara Satvalekar, Paradi, Svadhyaya Mandala, 2nd edn., 1957.

———, tr. A.B. Keith, *The Veda of the Black Yajus School*, Harvard Oriental Series No. 18-19, Part I-II, 1914, rpt. Delhi: Motilal Banarsidass, 1967.

Tāṇḍya Mahā Brāhmaṇam, ed. with comm. of Sāyaṇa, Ananda Chandra Vedantavagisha, 2 vols., Delhi: Chowkhamba Sanskrit Pratisthan, 1989.

———, tr. W. Caland, *Pañcaviṁśa Brāhmaṇa*, Bibliotheca Indica Series, Calcutta: The Asiatic Society, 1931.

Tilak, B.G. *The Orion*, Poona, 4th edn., 1955.

Upaniṣads, ed. & tr. F. Max Müller, Sacred Books of the East, vol. 1 & 15, Part I-II, rpt. Delhi: Motilal Banarsidass, 1988-89.

Upaniṣad-Saṁgrahaḥ, ed. J.L. Shastri, 1970, rpt. Delhi: Motilal Banarsidass, 1984.

Vājasaneyi Mādhyandina Śuklayajurveda Saṁhitā, ed. Pt. Sripada Damodara Satvalekar, Paradi: Svadhyaya Mandala, 4th edn.

———, tr. R.T.H. Griffth, Chowkhambha Sanskrit Studies, vol. 25, Varanasi: Chowkhambha Sanskrit Series Office, 4th edn., 1976.

Vatsyayan, Kapila, *Classical Indian Dance in Literature and Arts*, Delhi: Sangeet Natak Akademi, 1968.

Vedānta-Darśana, ed. with Śaṅkara's comm., Vaiyāsika Nyāyamālā, and the gloss Bhāvadīpikā Swami Chidghananda Puri, tr. Swami Vishvarupananda, vol. I-IV, Calcutta: Udbodhana Karyalaya, 2nd edn., 1989.

Index